D0845087

TOMMY GUN

ALSO BY BILL YENNE

Aces High: The Heroic Saga of the Two Top-Scoring American Aces of World War II

Sitting Bull

Guinness: The 250-Year Quest for the Perfect Pint

Rising Sons: Japanese American GIs Who Fought for the United States in World War II

Indian Wars: The Campaign for the American West

On the Trail of Lewis and Clark, Yesterday and Today

The Story of the Boeing Company

Superfortress: The Boeing B-29 and American Air Power in World War II

TOMMY GUN

How General Thompson's Submachine Gun Wrote History

BILL YENNE

Thomas Dunne Books

St. Martin's Press ❦ New York

THOMAS DUNNE BOOKS.
An imprint of St. Martin's Press.

TOMMY GUN. Copyright © 2009 by Bill Yenne. All rights reserved. Printed in the United States of America. For information, address St. Martin's Press, 175 Fifth Avenue, New York, N.Y. 10010.

www.thomasdunnebooks.com
www.stmartins.com

Design by William Ruoto

Library of Congress Cataloging-in-Publication Data

Yenne, Bill, 1949–
    Tommy gun : how General Thompson's submachine gun wrote history / Bill Yenne.—1st ed.
        p. cm.
    Includes bibliographical references and index.
    ISBN 978-0-312-38326-8
    1. Thompson submachine gun—History. 2. Thompson, John Taliaferro, 1860–1940. I. Title.
UF620.T5Y46 2009
623.4'424—dc22

                                                    2009017591

First Edition: October 2009

10 9 8 7 6 5 4 3 2 1

CONTENTS

PART ONE: Men and Arms

PART TWO: Bandits and Criminals

PART THREE: Wheelers and Dealers

PART FOUR: Guns and Glory

PART FIVE: Living Legend

The Thompson, only a few ounces
heavier than a Springfield rifle, is an
amazingly potent weapon. . . . the
deadliest weapon, pound for pound, ever
devised by man.

—*Time*, June 26, 1939

An American Icon

This is the story of a gun. Not just any gun, but an American icon. It can be said with little fear of contradiction that the Thompson submachine gun is both the most famous, *and* the most infamous, American firearm of the twentieth century—and perhaps of all time.

No other American gun, with the possible exception of the Colt .45, is more instantly recognized by the general public than the tommy gun. You mention those two words, and people conjure up an image. If nothing else, nearly everyone has heard of its being used by Al Capone's gangsters in the infamous St. Valentine's Day Massacre in 1929. In the popular media of that era, and in the enduring folklore of American culture, this was the moment that sealed the tommy gun's iconic status.

This book is not *just* the story of a gun, an inanimate object of steel and walnut, but also it is the story of the image, indeed the myriad of images, that are conjured up by the mere mention of its name.

This book is not *just* the story of a gun, but of the times in which it was created, and the times in which it was used and misused. This is the story of the heros and the antiheroes whose deeds, exploits, and lasting mythology were made possible—and made enduring—by the tommy gun's uniqueness. It is the many stories of many men who earned their nation's highest decoration for valor, both Medals of Honor and Victoria Crosses, with (and often *because of*) tommy guns. It is also the story of the men who thought it up, the captains of industry who built it, and those people who have kept and are keeping the memory of the tommy gun alive.

Like the mythical Forrest Gump, the Thompson submachine gun and its inventor continually popped up in an uncanny number of important moments in the history and the popular culture of the first half of the twentieth century.

As the tommy gun achieved its mythic status, and as that status was celebrated and exploited in Hollywood, we find the gun in the hands of none other than the man who portrayed "Mr. Gump." Just four years after he portrayed the fictitious Forrest in the film of the same name, Tom Hanks played the role of Captain John H. Miller, who famously carried a Thompson submachine gun across Normandy in his search for Private Ryan. Then, four years later, the gun cropped up again in Tom's hands. Mr. Hanks was on the road, the Road to Perdition, and again he carried a tommy gun under his arm.

Before he invented the gun named for him, General John Taliaferro Thompson had a series of Forrest Gump moments. A U.S. Army ordnance officer, he was at the right place at a serendipitous string of right times. Had he not been on a certain Tampa pier on a certain day in 1898, automatic weapons never would have been on the ground to provide fire support for American troops when Teddy Roosevelt's Rough Riders took Kettle Hill.

Colonel Roosevelt went on to become president and to be carved into Mount Rushmore. Colonel Thompson went on to become the "father" of sorts to a whole progeny of famous guns and ammo—from the longest-serving automatic pistol in American military history, the Colt M1911, to the still ubiquitous "thirty-ought-six" cartridge.

The general's son and business protégé, Marcellus Thompson, had his own string of eerily coincidental Forrest Gump moments. He married young and gorgeous Dorothy Harvey, the daughter of millionaire industrialist George Brinton McClellan Harvey. Shortly after George was named United States ambassador to Great Britain, Marcellus suffered the embarrassment of being indicted for running guns to the Irish Republican Army for use in killing British soldiers. One can imagine the awkwardness around the dinner table at the next family get-together.

Not unexpectedly, Dorothy's daddy insisted that she ditch Marcellus, which she did. The bizarre twists continue, however. When Dorothy remarried, it was on *St. Valentine's Day in 1929*—almost at the exact moment that Al Capone's gangsters were giving her ex-husband's gun its place in history at the St. Valentine's Day Massacre.

The Thompson submachine gun was born of war, the Great War, and of John Thompson's desire to create something that would break the back of that most insidious of wartime conditions, the meat grinder of the stalemate. Too late for World War I, the Thompson found its way into the hands of guerrillas, soldiers, and thugs, from the Emerald Isle to the dusty, distant corners of China and the muggy jungles of Central America. At home, it was the weapon of choice of colorful outlaws from Capone to Dillinger.

Meanwhile, the Thompson *literally* gave its name to notorious bad guys with household names that still resonate in the pantheon of pop culture. Mention the names of Vincenzo Gibaldi or George Barnes, and you get a blank stare, but mention "Machine Gun Jack McGurn" and "Machine Gun Kelly"—the monikers by which these gentlemen lived and died—and there is more than a spark of recognition. Of course, everyone knows exactly *which* machine gun they're named for.

In the hands of criminals, the Thompson wrought mayhem. An enduring part of the American cultural memory is of the streets of Chicago running red with blood spilled by the terrible wrath of the deadly tommy gun. Indeed, as cultural icons go, the image of the Thompson is not benign. It was not like a pair of Levi's, a bottle of Coca-Cola, or a beloved cartoon character. In the hands of the malevolent, the tommy gun was, as *Time* magazine observed in 1939, the "deadliest weapon, pound for pound, ever devised by man."

Men used it to kill, and this assured its infamy. Outlaws killed both good guys and bad with their Thompsons. So, too, did good guys cut down bad guys in equally horrible hailstorms of lead from the Thompson muzzle.

In World War II, that most unquestionably glorious of wars, good guys—*our* guys—killed bad guys with their Thompsons, earning the gun a place in the pantheon of weapons that helped win the war. More important, perhaps, than those killed by the tommy gun in World War II, are the incalculable thousands of British, Canadian, Australian, and American troops who survived the war because of the firepower of the Thompson submachine gun.

Yet, even at this moment of the Thompson's redemption, the dark shadow of Chicago in the twenties was still cast across its reputation. George MacDonald Fraser, the acclaimed author, was at one time a lowly infantryman, serving in His Majesty's armed services during World War II. Of the tommy gun, he wrote in his memoir *Quartered Safe Out Here* that he eventually threw his away, because it made him feel like "Lance-corporal Capone."

His Majesty's armed services had for a long time resisted adoption of the Thompson submachine gun for precisely this reason. They did not wish to be seen embracing a "gangster gun." The reason was simple. It was the image of Capone that turned them off, rather than the fact that the IRA, the threat to British law and order, had used tommy guns. Until World War II. Faced by a true threat of invasion by Hitler's legions, the British relented, asking the Thompson's makers to *please* sell them as many gangster guns as possible.

Indeed, Prime Minister Winston Churchill himself is seen in a widely distributed photograph taken in the terrible summer of 1940, when Britain's future hung in the balance. He has a Cheshire cat grin on his face and a gangster gun in his arms.

There is the Thompson myth and the Thompson reality. As Doug Richardson, a design engineer who lives and breathes Thompsons, once told me, "The Thompson is like Jesse James. There are a million stories about Jesse James, probably none of them but one are true. That's the same with the Thompson. The Thompson is a legend and it continues to grow every day."

As with most icons of popular culture, there is a literature of stories and sound bites by which tommy guns are described in the annals of popular culture. These, of course, are an amalgam of fact and fiction, of myth and reality.

Webster defines a myth as a falsehood, a thing having only an imaginary or unverifiable existence. There are, as Richardson suggests with his analogy to Jesse James, a lot of such myths about the tommy gun. For instance, while McGurn *earned* his nickname, Kelly was reluctantly talked into carrying a tommy gun by his wife, Kathryn Thorne—the tireless promoter of his tough-guy image who also coined his notorious nickname. Contrary to legend, Kelly never actually killed anyone with his machine gun.

There is also that ever-present myth of gangsters carrying their tommy guns in violin cases. Everyone who has seen a gangster movie (or three or four) "knows" that they did. In fact, a fully assembled tommy gun wouldn't *fit* in a violin case. A viola case maybe, but not a violin case. It may have happened one or twice, but not often. What gangster goes to a gunfight planning to be fumbling with the latches of a viola case?

During World War II, Thompson submachine guns were in the hands of most sergeants in most rifle companies in the U.S. Army in every theater of operations, but the pop folklore—if not the history—is silent on the fact that the army acquired the Thompson without enthusiasm and soon tried to replace it with something cheaper and easier to manufacture. The fact that the GIs themselves generally embraced the gun is a testament to the Thompson rather than to the bureaucrats who only unwillingly bought them on Uncle Sam's behalf.

Among the biggest false images about the Thompson submachine gun are those perpetuated by people who should know better. While nearly every American has heard of the tommy gun, almost no one has actually fired one. Through the years, I've met many people with broad firearms experience who have related stories about the Thompson. They told of the unbearable recoil, the difficulty in controlling the muzzle climb, of the inaccuracy at longer range, and so on. And did I mention being told that it is uncomfortably heavy?

When asked whether they had experienced these things personally, most shrugged, admitting that they had, well, ummm, never actually fired a Thompson.

Some time before I began work on this book, I decided to find out for myself, so I tracked down a firing range that had a Thompson submachine gun. Like most boys in nonurban America, I grew up using bolt-action rifles, but like most civilians, I'd had no experience with automatic weapons.

When I picked up a Thompson for the first time, the myths shriveled or evaporated, one by one. First, I experienced the weight. Granted, a Thompson is heavier than a hunting rifle and I would not want to carry one on an all-day hike through the jungles of New Guinea with a fifty-pound pack on my back. However, it is not a difficult object to hold, even with one hand.

When I wrapped my finger around the trigger, other myths fell like the targets downrange. Arguably, the biggest myth that swirls around the Thompson is its controllability. Had I been accompanied by any of the numerous people who had warned me about muzzle climb in a Thompson, they would have each left the range red-faced that day. It is easy to keep on target, even when you first fire it and have had no prior experience with such weapons. A .45 caliber pistol does buck in the hand when fired, but a loaded Thompson weighs three of four times as much as a pistol. The weight actually contributes to its controllability.

As for recoil, I didn't notice it while I was shooting, and didn't actually think about it until I was leaving the range. I wondered why, if a Thompson kicked so hard, my shoulder didn't hurt—at all.

About a year later, when I began meeting more and more people who owned and routinely fired Thompsons, I began hearing stories of the opposite kind about the weapon's range and accuracy.

What to believe?

One way to find out.

Wanting to leave nothing to hearsay and hyperbole, I tried for myself. When an admitted amateur like myself can put half a magazine into a man-size target at half the length of a football field—in a few seconds on semiauto in his first competition shoot—you cannot denigrate the inherent accuracy of the Thompson.

Another important thing that comes from firsthand experience with a Thompson submachine gun is an appreciation of the craftsmanship and a sense of the tactile beauty of this deadly machine. All true Thompson submachine guns were manufactured before early 1944, and the most prized are from the initial batch that was made under license by Colt in 1921, many of which were modified en masse in 1928. This era was the golden age of American manufacturing, an age when precision workmanship and meticulous attention to detail were not high ideals, but minimum standards.

However, lest I perpetuate a laudatory myth of my own, I should point out that these same factors which contribute to the intrinsic greatness of the Thompson submachine gun *also* contributed to its weaknesses. The intricacy of its design was conceived by gunsmiths, not marketing professionals. The mechanical complexity that made it great, also made it very expensive. In the 1920s, a Thompson cost half as much as a new car. Al Capone could afford them, but police departments bought them sparingly and the U.S. Army acquired but a few demonstrators in the early days. Average shooters could not afford them.

By World War II, when the U.S. Army finally did have the budget, both production time and cost led the service to seek a cheap, stamped-metal replacement. Of course this was going on even as the army continued to buy 50,000 finely machined Thompsons every month.

In the army's ledger books, the Thompson could not compete during World War II with the cheaper M3 submachine gun, but how do they stack up in the history books, or in our memory of machines from times past?

Inexpensive, stamped-metal products may survive as monuments to industrial efficiency, but rarely are they remembered as objects of intrinsic beauty. A 1932 Ford Model 18 was a good, serviceable car *and* you could buy one for a nickel on the dollar of the cost of a 1932 Duesenberg Model J—but on which car would your eye rest longer? Behind which steering wheel would you rather sit?

As Doug Richardson has told us, and he could say the same of a Duesenberg, "The Thompson is a legend and the legend continues to grow every day."

There is the Thompson myth and the Thompson reality.

Ahead of their definition of a myth as falsehood, the folks at Webster define a myth as a story of ostensibly historical events that serves to unfold part of the worldview of a people or explain a practice or belief—a parable or an allegory. Allegories are not falsehoods, but symbols of inherent truths.

In the hands of Al Capone, who today is as much a metaphorical character as a real man, the Thompson submachine gun can be an allegory for brutal, calculating, heartless murder. In the hands of someone like Audie Murphy, who today is also as much a metaphor as he is real, a Thompson submachine gun can serve as a glorious symbol of the Allied triumph in World War II.

Still life with tommy gun: A shooter's collection of gear includes stick magazines,
a classic drum magazine, ear protection, and camera to record the action.
(Photo by Bill Yenne)

In your own hands, it can also be an object to be admired for what it is, an artifact from that golden age of American craftsmanship.

The Thompson submachine gun is a masterpiece of American industrial design, nicely proportioned and ergonomically easy to hold. The walnut stock may have added both unnecessary weight and unnecessary expense, but it also added something that is both tangible and priceless. Especially in the M1921 and M1928 examples, the tommy gun is a thing of beauty that links it to classic American guns like the Winchester '73 or Colt .45 of the Old West. To hold a Thompson and to fire one is to feel this and know this.

The Thompson submachine gun has style. It's a gun that everyone recognizes. With its classic lines and its distinctive profile, it can be described as the 1957 Chevy Bel Air of American guns. It's the gun that people want to touch, just as they want to sit behind the wheel of a Bel Air.

Like a Bel Air, or a Duesenberg, or a Harley-Davidson motorcycle, or any number of truly classic American machines, the Thompson is easy on the eye, familiar, and comfortable. Like these machines, it is part of our culture, part of our heritage, and an important part of our history.

The Thompson submachine gun is an American icon, and this book tells the story of how that came about.

PART ONE

Men and Arms

CHAPTER 1

Necessity

Necessity is the mother of invention.

The frequently used maxim is as true of weapons as of any aspect of industrial design. So it was with the Thompson submachine gun and for the man who thought it up.

First, there was the necessity.

In war, there is nothing, save death and mutilation, that a fighting man fears more than a deadlock. Stalemates tend to become meat grinders, in which neither side can advance and neither side dares to retreat. There is a reason that they call it a *dead*lock.

The worst stalemate—and the most terrible campaign in the history of warfare—was that on the Western Front in World War I.

This war, known as the Great War before a second world war necessitated numbering the first, had begun in the summer of 1914 with a series of ultimatums that issued from Europe's leading powers. Between the last week of July and the first week of August, declarations of war were exchanged, and soon the Central Powers of Germany, Austria-Hungary, and Turkey were officially at war with the Triple Entente of Britain, France, and tsarist Russia. There was a flurry of excitement, a flourish of angry banter and colorful banners, and troops rode off to war fully expecting to be home for Christmas. For those few weeks, the war seemed very abstract.

The opening gambit on the Western Front was a daring move by the Germans in mid-August that nearly brought the war on that front to a swift and decisive completion. Field Marshal Alfred Graf von Schlieffen, who had headed the German General Staff until his retirement in 1905, had drafted a bold strategy to defeat France in five weeks by sweeping through Belgium and the Netherlands, capturing Paris, and encircling the French army before it could fully mobilize. Military historians will argue forever about whether or not the Schlieffen Plan, as the field marshal wrote it, would have worked, but most indications are that it would have. If it had, there would not have been a stalemate.

But it was never implemented.

Schlieffen died in 1913, and Field Marshal Johann Ludwig von Moltke, who had succeeded him as chief of staff, decided to monkey with the plan by reducing the troop levels from those which Schlieffen had meticulously calculated. This was partly because of an unexpectedly effective Russian offensive on the Eastern Front, and partly because of a haughty underestimation of the armed forces of France by the German General Staff. The German armies had easily defeated France in a few months during the Franco-Prussian War of 1870–1871 and they were still feeling pretty cocky in 1914.

Despite the reduction of the size of their forces, the German offensive slashed quickly through Belgium and into France. It moved efficiently in its early stages, crushing the Belgians, mauling the French, and battering the British Expeditionary Force that had come in to help. However, as often happens in campaigns involving rapid movement, the German armies outran their supply lines and had to slow down. When they did, it gave the French and the Brits a chance to catch their breath and organize their defenses.

The Anglo-French forces managed to halt the German advance east of Paris in the First Battle of the Marne in September. Because their troop levels had been short-changed by Moltke's overconfidence, the Germans were unable to resume their offensive. Meanwhile, however, the French and British armies were insufficient to push the Germans *back*. Both sides dug in to fight the terrible war of attrition that would characterize the Western Front for nearly four years. In August nobody had expected that it would happen like this.

During these terrible years, some of the largest armies in world history built some of the longest and most elaborate networks of trenches and defensive positions that had ever been seen. Stretching from the Swiss border to the North Sea, many of these lines of "temporary" trenches are still visible nearly a century later.

The stalemate became the monster that consumed lives by the million. Numerous attempts—and several major campaigns—were launched in an effort to break out of the trenches. After seeing the German army advance hundreds of miles in a few weeks, it was disheartening to their military planners—and those of the Anglo-French Allies—that most of these campaigns measured their advances by less than ten miles, usually by fewer than five, sometimes by less than one.

One case in point was the bloody campaign on the Somme River, often called the "Meat Grinder of the Somme," during the latter half of 1916. The Allies initially committed twenty-four divisions in a massive effort to break the stalemate, eventually pouring seventy-six more into the meat grinder. On July 1, the initial assault by the British cost 57,470 casualties, including 19,240 killed in action, making it the bloodiest single day in the history of the British army. When this horrible battle ended half a year later, the British had taken 420,000 casualties, the French 204,000, and the Germans 435,000. The front lines had moved five miles.

In 1917, the Battle of Passchendaele, also known as the Third Battle of Ypres, lasted three months, cost more than 700,000 casualties, and resulted in an advance that was measured in mere yards. These minuscule gains, balanced against almost incomprehensible losses, had a crushing effect on morale both in the trenches and on the home fronts of the affected nations. Until the introduction of the American Expeditionary Force into combat in the summer of 1918, the deadly deadlock was never broken.

This gridlock existed because neither side had nor could achieve a decisive advantage. Artillery was deadly, and millions of rounds were fired, but you don't gain ground with artillery. You gain ground with infantry.

During the bloodiest years of World War I on the Western Front, both sides were far more adept at defending against the other side's infantry than they were in giving their infantrymen a means to crack the impasse.

Both sides desperately sought weapons that might provide that offensive edge. Poison gas was deployed, but it only served to drive up casualty figures. Large, lumbering vehicles that the British called tanks (as in water tank) to disguise the fact that they were armed and armored, were introduced, but the initial results were disappointing. You only gain ground with infantry.

The yards or miles could not be captured if not for the troops. Those men who survived artillery barrages and the poison gas attacks stood up, climbing from the relative safety of the trenches, and ran or crawled forward, through the mud, the tangled masses of barbed wire, and the withering fire of the heavy machine guns. They called this hellish world between the opposing trenches "no-man's-land" for a reason.

An infantryman who survived no-man's-land long enough to reach the enemy trenches faced the prospect of trying to capture those trenches with his rifle or his sidearm.

Year after year, as the nightmare on the Western Front was unfolding, a number of people had the idea that the stalemate might be broken by putting a machine gun into the hands of the infantryman. Having been used in the Boer War (1899–1902) and in the Russo-Japanese War (1904–1905), machine guns were first used on a mass scale as a standard weapon during World War I. Though they had proven their potent deadliness, they were heavy as hell, and awkward to boot. Putting a machine gun into the hands of the infantryman was much easier said than done. A single soldier could hardly, if at all, carry one alone. They were good for a fixed gun position, but not as an infantry weapon.

But *why* couldn't they be?

One of several men who decided to answer the question was General John Taliaferro Thompson, late of the Small Arms Division of the U.S. Army Ordnance Department.

CHAPTER 2

Inventors

John Thompson had grown up an army brat.

His father was Lieutenant Colonel James Thompson, a New Yorker whose family had been in the United States since a decade after the Pilgrims had landed at Plymouth Rock. His mother was Julia Maria Taliaferro of the Virginia Taliaferros, who had been on this side of the Atlantic almost as long. Originally known as Tagliaferro, which means "ironcutter," the family was one of the first to immigrate from Italy, and was to include such luminaries as Richard Taliaferro, the famous Williamsburg architect, and Colonel Lawrence Taliaferro II, a Revolutionary War patriot. Also in the family was General William Booth Taliaferro, a Confederate officer who commanded a brigade under General Thomas J. "Stonewall" Jackson.

During the Civil War, families were often divided, and so it was for Julia Maria, that daughter of the Confederacy. The man she married was an 1851 graduate of West Point, and later a Union Army artillery officer who served heroically at Chickamauga and elsewhere.

John Taliaferro Thompson was born on New Year's Eve in 1860, about two months after Abraham Lincoln was elected the sixteenth president of the United States and a month before Jefferson Davis was declared the first president of the Confederate States of America.

John and his older sister Frances grew up at the military posts at which their father served during a career that took them as far west as California after the war. When John was nine, James retired from active duty and took a job at Indiana University teaching history and military science. The father's influence apparently inspired the son, and young John decided on a military career for himself. At seventeen he applied and was accepted to the colonel's alma mater, the U.S. Military Academy at West Point.

Thompson graduated from West Point in eleventh place in the class of 1882. Like his father, he chose the artillery as his branch of service, and the newly minted second lieutenant Thompson was posted to the Second Artillery Regiment at Newport, Kentucky, the same outfit in which his father had been serving when John was born.

Shortly after leaving West Point, John married Juliet Estelle Hagans, the daughter of an Ohio judge. Her family, like that on John's paternal side, had long roots extending back into the American Republic's colonial origins. Their son and only child, Marcellus, was born in 1883.

John's early career was uneventful professionally. The Indian Wars, in which the U.S. Army was actively engaged, were winding down, and artillery units were now rarely deployed. His career in the mainly peacetime army took him up the ladder to a posting with Ordnance Department headquarters in 1890, and in 1896 he was detailed to West Point as a gunnery and ordnance instructor.

The first major turning point for his career came in February 1898, shortly after the battleship *Maine* blew up during a port call in the harbor at Havana, Cuba. Relations between the United States and Spain, who had owned Cuba for half a millennium, were already strained, and Spanish agents were quickly blamed for the sinking of the ship, as well as the deaths of 266 officers and seamen.

Subsequent investigations are split over whether the *Maine*'s forward magazine exploded because of the spontaneous combustion of coal dust that ignited the ammunition within the ship, or because a mine detonated outside the hull. However, this debate is academic. The best modern interpretation of the evidence supports the former, but as far as public opinion in 1898 was concerned, it was the latter, and "Remember the Maine" became the rallying cry for a war against Spain.

The sinking of the *Maine* was the catalyst that would take the United States to war, but a number of factors had been leading in that direction for some time. Not the least of these was the growing support in the United States for Cuban independence from Spain. In the eighteenth century, Spain owned half of the Western Hemisphere, but now possessed only a handful of islands in the Caribbean, of which Cuba was the crown jewel. The formal declaration of war on April 23 was preceded by a congressional resolution signed by President McKinley that called for Cuban independence while disavowing American intentions to annex Cuba.

The opening battle in the Spanish-American War was a naval contest. On May 1 in the Philippines, Commodore George Dewey, commanding the Asiatic Squadron, resoundingly defeated the Spanish navy in the Battle of

Manila Bay. Five weeks later, the U.S. Marines captured Guantánamo Bay in Cuba, which was used as a base of operations for a naval battle on July 3 in which the Spanish navy's Caribbean Squadron was destroyed.

The naval actions set the stage for the ground war in Cuba, which would initially involve capturing Santiago, Cuba's second-largest city. Leading the American V Corps in this operation would be Major General William "Pecos Bill" Shafter, who had earned a Medal of Honor while leading Union troops during the Civil War. As Shafter's ordnance officer, the War Department picked John Taliaferro Thompson.

Granted a leave from his duties at West Point, Thompson headed for Cuba. He made it as far as Tampa, Florida, where the docks were groaning under the immense weight of men, material, and horses that swirled about in a state of disorganization as they awaited transportation to the front. As ordnance officer, Thompson's immediate task was to sort out the mountains of crates of firearms and ammunition that were to be loaded on ships and to make sure that a reasonable proportion of both was matched with the numbers of troops preparing to disembark.

During the last week of June, as Thompson was fighting this Battle of Tampa, the first echelons of Shafter's V Corps were landing at Daiquiri and Siboney, east of Santiago, and establishing the American base for the Santiago operation.

On July 1, a force of about 15,000 American infantry and cavalry troops attacked El Caney and San Juan Hill on the approaches to the city. The latter fight is recalled as the most famous battle of the war, mainly because of the participation of the 1st Volunteer Cavalry Regiment, better known as the "Rough Riders," led into battle by Colonel Theodore Roosevelt. The Rough Riders actually captured Kettle Hill, a small hill adjacent to San Juan Hill, but Roosevelt's bold charge served to initiate the momentum that led the whole brigade to victory.

Though he was not at San Juan Hill, John Taliaferro Thompson played an important role, albeit inadvertent, in the American victory. As the ordnance officer in Tampa, Thompson was accosted on the docks by a young lieutenant, John Henry Parker. The young man told Thompson that in the stack of ordnance that was being prepared for shipment, there were more than a dozen Gatling guns, the precursor to the modern machine gun. Thompson checked the paperwork. There were no orders that these guns should go to Cuba.

Though Dr. Richard Gatling had introduced his gun in the early 1860s, and it had been used by the U.S. Army in the Civil War, the service had still not, by 1898, developed a tactical doctrine for integrating this fast-firing automatic weapon into operational units.

Parker argued that such weapons would be valuable to American troops in both offensive and defensive operations. They would give American troops a mobile source of high-volume fire to support an attack or defend against one. The guns ought to be going to Cuba.

Had he been a typical bureaucrat, of which all too many wore the army uniform in 1898, Thompson would have told Parker that those in authority had issued no paperwork and therefore the Gatling guns would remain in their crates, and their crates would remain on the pier in Tampa. But John Taliaferro Thompson was not a bureaucrat, and he knew that everything Parker was saying was true.

Thompson not only issued the documents that permitted loading the Gatling guns aboard the transport ship *Cherokee,* he issued orders that would allow Parker to report directly to Shafter when he reached Cuba. As it turned out, Shafter welcomed Parker's idea and allowed him to field a Gatling gun detachment in the San Juan Hill operation. In the field, Parker's men provided the covering fire that helped the Americans capture the hill. This accomplished, the Gatling gun detachment continued to fight on, later being called on to take out a Spanish artillery battery at a range of two thousand yards. The Gatling guns were not incidental bystanders at San Juan Hill and Santiago; they played an indispensable role in those victories.

After a two-week siege, Santiago surrendered on July 17, and on July 25 General Nelson Miles began the short campaign that captured Puerto Rico. Faced with the loss of Santiago and Puerto Rico, as well as of its Pacific and Caribbean fleets, Spain threw in the towel and agreed to a cease-fire on August 12. The formal peace treaty followed in December and America's shortest and easiest major war was over. Having defeated a large European empire, and with the Philippines, Guam, Puerto Rico, and various other smaller islands now in its possession, the United States would enter the twentieth century as a world power.

Well, at least the general public *perceived* the United States as having achieved an immense global prestige in a quick and effortless war. It was nearly not that way, however. Often things that look to have been easy were accomplished quickly only through luck. Such was the case in Cuba, and few people knew this better than John Taliaferro Thompson.

As he debriefed men who had seen action in Cuba, Thompson came to realize how dangerously outgunned the American troops had been. The

Spanish troops, armed with German-made Mauser Model 93 rifles firing ammunition with smokeless powder, were clearly better armed than the Americans.

In the 1890s, the U.S. Army still equipped most of its soldiers with the old .45 caliber "Trapdoor" Springfield single-shot rifles, whose basic design dated back to 1865, and which were carried by Custer's ill-fated troopers at the Little Bighorn. The definitive variant, the Model 1873, was the first breech-loading rifle that was standard-issue for the U.S. Army. The Trapdoor Springfield was so named because it was manufactured at the government-owned Springfield Armory in Massachusetts. The nickname came from its breech mechanism, which used a hinged breechblock that rotated up and forward, reminiscent of the movement of a trapdoor.

Apropos of the Springfield Armory, it should be noted that at this time, much of the ordnance used by the United States armed forces was manufac-tured in government-owned plants. In some cases, it was designed by outside firms and licensed to the government arsenals, and in some cases, it was de-signed in-house. For independent firms, having the weapons manufactured by their customer saved them a great deal of investment in plant and machin-ery. The practice continued well into the twentieth century. For example, the U.S. Navy operated its own aircraft factory from 1918 through World War II.

By the 1890s, the U.S. Army had begun to look at more advanced rifle designs, with an eye toward finally replacing the Trapdoor Springfield. The German Mauser was among those rifles studied, but the winner was a .30 caliber bolt-action, repeating rifle designed in Norway by ordnance officer Captain Ole Herman Johannes Krag and gunsmith Erik Jørgensen. Manufac-tured by the Springfield Armory as the Model 1892, the Krag Jørgenson was an improvement over the Model 1873, but production moved slowly. By 1898, there were too few in the inventory to equip all the troops who went to war.

In combat, the men who were assigned the new rifle found the Krag Jør-gensen to be inferior to the enemy's Mausers in both accuracy and hitting power. When Thompson queried the veterans of the Cuban battles, they told him so. The men complained that the process of loading the Model 1892 was too slow and that the gun could not always accommodate the high pressures in the chamber that came with high-velocity ammunition. In the defense of the Norwegians, however, high-velocity rounds of the type used in 1898 had not been anticipated earlier in the decade.

Captain Thompson's findings alarmed the Ordnance Department, and he was reassigned to the Springfield Armory to solve the problem. It was an unusual and amazing case of a peacetime military bureaucracy having the foresight to assign the right man to the right job. Thompson first looked into developing a high-velocity round that would work in a Krag Jørgensen, but the bolt-locking mechanism still couldn't be made to stand up to the chamber pressure.

With the shortcomings of the Krag Jørgensen made ever more obvious, Thompson turned to developing its successor. In this endeavor, he was supported by his boss, Brigadier General William Crozier, who had been promoted in 1901 by Theodore Roosevelt—now *President* Roosevelt—to succeed the aging General Adelbert Buffington as chief of ordnance. Crozier, like Thompson, understood that modernization and application of practical lessons learned was essential for the Ordnance Department.

Thompson used as his pattern the Model 1893 Mauser, the gun against which American troops had battled in Cuba's swamps and hillsides. The result of his work was the remarkable Springfield Model of 1903 (officially abbreviated as M1903), a .30 caliber magazine-fed, bolt-action rifle that was formally adopted as the standard U.S. Army rifle in June 1903.

It is a tribute to Thompson that the M1903 was also selected by the U.S. Navy and Marine Corps, who still relied on Trapdoor Springfields, although they also had newer Remington-Lee Model 1885s, and Lee Model 1895s. Also a tribute to Thompson is that the M1903 would remain the standard U.S. Army rifle until World War I, when it would be supplanted by yet another rifle fathered—or at least midwived—by Thompson, the M1917. Some M1903s remained in the U.S. Army inventory until the eve of World War II, and a number of them were used during the later conflict, often as sniper rifles. A few survived in service, albeit mainly as parade guns, until after the turn of the twenty-first century.

Thompson also worked to develop a smokeless-powder cartridge for the M1903. Introduced in 1906, it was designated the .30-'06, shorthand for the caliber and year. This cartridge type went on to become one of the most widely used in the twentieth century. Nobody who has used a hunting rifle in the past century is unaware of the ubiquitous phrase "thirty ought six." This same ammunition continued to be U.S. Army standard in both Thompson's later M1917, as well as in its successor, the famous M1 Garand of World War II.

Having transformed rifles and ammunition for the U.S. Army, John Taliaferro Thompson turned to the service pistol. For nearly two decades, from 1873 to 1892, the standard-issue service pistol had been the Colt Single Action Army (SAA). It was a .45 caliber, six-round revolver produced by the firm of Samuel Colt, who had developed and patented the practical, revolving-cylinder, repeating pistol in 1839. Colt's remarkable "six-shooter," known alternatively as the "Peacemaker" or the "Colt .45," became the signature weapon, not only of the U.S. Army, but of the cowboys, marshals, and bandits of the Wild West. The Colt SAA was, in short, the "gun that won the West."

By 1892, however, the West had been won, and the army turned to a smaller, lighter service revolver. This weapon, the Colt M1892, was also a revolver, but it fired .38 caliber ammunition. The army was armed with the M1892 when it went to war in Cuba, as well as during its long-running battles in the Philippines during the early part of the twentieth century. In what is seen by some as a precursor to the wars that would be fought a century later, the U.S. Army found itself battling Islamic insurgents in a distant corner of the world.

At the Ordnance Department, Crozier and Thompson had heard the complaints about the M1892 that had come out of Cuba, and they were now hearing them come back from the Philippines. Report after report filtered in telling of troops being attacked by insurgents who continued their assault even after being hit several times with .38 caliber rounds. At the same time, it was also reported that the older .45 caliber Colts *were* effective in close combat. Essentially, the larger, heavier, and lower-velocity .45 caliber round had more "stopping power."

As an interim solution, the army responded by reaching into the warehouses of supplanted weapons and supplying their troops, as well as the indigenous Philippine Constabulary, with .45 caliber pistols and ammunition. These guns included the old Colt SAA .45s, as well as updated M1902 .45 caliber single-action pistols.

General Crozier understood that this was an interim solution, and once again he turned to John Taliaferro Thompson for a long-term remedy in the form of a new service pistol. Crozier teamed Thompson with Major Louis LaGarde of the Medical Corps, a U.S. Army surgeon who had studied gunshot wounds and the grisly science of wound ballistics, the effects of ammunition of various calibers on the human body.

In 1904, Thompson and LaGarde traveled to Chicago. There they made arrangements with the Nelson Morris Company Union Stockyards to shoot about a dozen head of live cattle with assorted guns and several calibers of ammunition. Today, computer modeling would be used for such experiments, but in 1904 the only way was the direct field-test approach. Thompson and

LaGarde extrapolated in their report that a "military pistol or revolver should have a caliber not less than .45."

Though the live animal tests were not as decisive as might have been hoped, at least they pointed the Ordnance Department in the right direction. Crozier was apparently sufficiently impressed with Thompson that he promoted him to the rank of major, made Thompson his senior deputy, and gave him a free hand in organizing the Small Arms Division. When Crozier was out of town, Thompson, now a major, also filled in as acting chief of ordnance.

During this period, Major Thompson was ably assisted by Theodore Eickhoff, a young civilian employee of the Ordnance Department who would become an important part of Thompson's ventures in later years. A 1908 graduate of Purdue, Eickhoff had joined the Ordnance Department as an electrical and mechanical draftsman, originally in the Artillery Division. He had worked his way up to a position as Thompson's assistant at the Small Arms Division within a year. In this role, he became the major's right-hand man during the long development process of the U.S. Army's new pistol.

Over the next several years, as Thompson and Eickhoff were building their close professional relationship around the service pistol project, there were many experiments, followed by numerous official evaluations. Armed with the essential data of a "caliber not less than .45," and a magazine capacity of at least six rounds, various gunmakers submitted their ideas to the Small Arms Division to be evaluated by Thompson and Eickhoff. The proposals came from such familiar names as Colt, Knoble, Savage Arms, Webley, and White, Merril, as well as several German firms, including Deutsche Waffen- und Munitionsfabriken (DWM) in Berlin, where the principal designer of pistols was Georg Johann Luger, later the creator of the legendary Luger automatic pistol.

Another name among the Germans who sent proposals for this notional U.S. Army automatic pistol was that of Theodor Bergmann. Unlike Thompson, his is not today a household name, although the two men are linked by synchronicity. Several years later, during World War I, both men would independently have the same idea, and would become fathers to the same weapons concept, the submachine gun.

Thompson and Bergmann would never meet. Under Thompson's leadership, armed with Eickhoff's guidance and expertise, the Ordnance Department decided to buy American.

It was in the course of the service pistol project that Thompson did meet another famous gunsmith, and one whose name is indeed well known. And for good reason. The brilliant John Moses Browning was probably the most important individual American gunsmith since Samuel Colt. He designed pistols for Colt in the early twentieth century, but he had also designed highly regarded weapons for Remington and Winchester. As designer of the Colt M1902 that was serving as an interim U.S. Army .45 caliber pistol, Browning built upon this experience, working and reworking it into the answer to Thompson's search for a new service pistol.

Eventually, the competition between all of the gunmakers came down to just two, Colt and Savage. The ultimate test, a 6,000-round endurance test held in March 1911, tipped the balance. The Savage pistol suffered three dozen malfunctions, the Browning-designed Colt experienced zero. This winning gun was officially adopted as the U.S. Army service pistol on March 28 under the designation "Model of 1911" (M1911). This seven-round .45 would remain the standard U.S. Army pistol for more than seven decades—through both world wars—and is still being used in the twenty-first century.

In parallel with the long road leading to the M1911, the Small Arms Division was also overseeing the development of its ammunition. The result was the .45 caliber Automatic Colt Pistol (ACP) rimless cartridge, also developed by John Browning. Originally a 200 grain (13 gram) bullet with a muzzle velocity of 900 feet per second, it was later standardized at 230 grains (15 grams) with an 850 feet per second velocity.

The low velocity translates to greater hitting power because the higher the velocity, the more likely the round is to pass straight through a target on a narrow path, rather than tumbling, tearing, and doing extensive damage. It has been said that a target hit by a low-velocity slug tends to go down and stay down.

The ACP's lower velocity also minimized recoil, making the M1911 easier to use than other handguns. The ACP is worth mentioning because Thompson would later adopt it as the standard ammunition for his submachine gun.

Major John Taliaferro Thompson, promoted to colonel in 1913, had a lot in which he could take pride. Even if he had never gone forward with the weapon that would become his signature gun, the weapons over which he had overseen development through 1911 would extend his legacy through the remainder of the twentieth century and beyond.

In the October 30, 1913, issue of the trade journal *Arms & the Man,* it was appropriately stated, "No man of his grade in the Army of the United States has performed more distinguished and valuable service than Colonel

General John Taliaferro Thompson (1860–1940) served two decades with the U.S. Army Ordnance Department, developing many key weapons systems. Horrified by the carnage of the World War I trench stalemate, he created his Thompson submachine gun as a private venture. After the war, however, the U.S. Army lacked funds to buy it, so Thompson looked to other markets.
(Bill Yenne illustration)

Thompson. This is natural, because he is an officer of exceptional ability. He has the type of mind in which the constructive faculty is highly developed; that is, he has 'that power of intellect by which the soul groups knowledge into systems, scientific, artistic, and practical.' Moreover he has the practical imaginative quality by which he is able to project his thoughts into the future and resolve an occasion yet to arrive."

From the M1903, to .30-'06 ammunition, to the M1911, John Taliaferro Thompson's impact on revolutionizing small arms and ammunition for the U.S. Army is so far-reaching as to be legendary.

Yet the best was still to come.

CHAPTER 3

Invention

Colonel John Taliaferro Thompson retired in 1914 after thirty-two years in uniform, leaving the U.S. Army on the eve of its greatest challenge since the Civil War. He had, however, unquestionably left its Small Arms Division in a far better condition than it might have been had he not served.

He left the service in November, three months after the crowned heads of Europe tumbled into the Great War, and just as the world was starting to get an inkling that this was going to be a long and serious war, not a showing of flags and a few skirmishes and home for Christmas.

As Thompson departed, he did as many retiring officers have done and continue to do. He went into private industry. He joined Remington Arms, which was then, like Colt and Winchester, one of America's leading gunmakers. Incorporated in 1865, Remington had evolved from the small gunsmithing firm started by Eliphalet Remington II, and which had been mass-producing flintlock rifles in Ilion Gorge, New York, since the 1820s.

When the Great War began, the arms industries in the nations that were involved were running at full capacity. The United States was the largest major world industrial power that was not among the combatants, so the combatants naturally turned to American gunmakers as a supplementary source. Approached by the government of Tsar Nicholas II of Russia, Remington accepted an order for 1.5 million Mosin-Nagant 7.62 mm bolt-action rifles. Meanwhile, in England, the Royal Small Arms Factory at Enfield was swamped with orders for the Enfield .303 caliber rifle, and outsourced to Remington. To accommodate these huge orders, the company contracted with the Baldwin Locomotive Works to build a rifle factory at their huge 184-acre Eddystone complex near Chester, Pennsylvania, about twelve miles southwest of Philadelphia. The Eddystone Rifle Plant would later become the world's largest rifle factory, and John Thompson would come to Pennsylvania to be the chief engineer at the factory—with a hefty increase in his pay envelope over his army salary. Beginning on New Year's Eve 1915 and continuing until January 11, 1919, the thousand-foot Eddystone production line would build 1.96 million rifles for delivery to both the British and American governments.

Meanwhile, John and his wife, Juliet, who had been empty nesters for about a decade, moved into a nice home in Media, Pennsylvania, north of Chester. Their son, Marcellus, had followed in the footsteps of both his father and grandfather, first to West Point, and then by joining the artillery as his branch of service—albeit the coast artillery rather than the field artillery. Recalled as lacking his father's attention to detail, Marcellus Thompson graduated last in West Point's Class of 1906. Reportedly, he later bragged of this dubious distinction.

After a number of posts in Cuba and Florida, Marcellus wound up assigned to Washington, D.C., in 1911, where he became a fixture on the society party circuit, and where he courted a number of prominent young ladies. In 1914, Marcellus tied the knot with the beautiful Dorothy Harvey, the daughter of George Brinton McClellan Harvey, who had made a fortune building urban electric railroads before he turned to buying and managing newspapers. Among his holdings was the successful and prestigious *Harper's Weekly*.

In 1915, as the Great War dragged into its second calendar year, John Thompson watched the nature of modern warfare change dramatically. From his desk at Remington, he had watched in the headlines as the great, slashing German offensive bogged down, and he watched the developing horror of trench warfare. He also watched as machine guns came into their own as weapons of war. He thought back to that day in the summer of 1898, when young Lieutenant John Henry Parker had approached him on the Tampa docks with his idea that the crates of Gatling guns might actually be useful if sent to Cuba.

During his own time in the Ordnance Department, Thompson had been preoccupied with rifles and pistols; he had not explored the capabilities of machine guns and automatic rifles. Indeed, the prevailing school of thought within the U.S. Army before World War I was that a weapon with a high rate of fire was counterproductive because it would just tempt the user not to aim, but to fire indiscriminately, and therefore, to waste ammunition. Where was John Henry Parker when they needed him?

This was not to say that machine guns of a more advanced type than Gatling's gun did not exist in the first decades of the twentieth century, nor that the Ordnance Department had not acquired a few for the U.S. Army. Three decades earlier, in the 1880s, Hiram Maxim had invented the true precursor to the modern machine gun. Maxim, by the way, was the man who also invented the still-ubiquitous mousetrap, and who narrowly lost the race to invent a practical light bulb to Thomas Edison.

The U.S. Army acquired a handful of Maxim guns, but European armies, especially the British and Germans, stockpiled sizable numbers of Maxim-derived Vickers or Maschinengewehr machine guns before the Great War, and began mass-producing them by the thousands when the war began.

Maxim's gun differed mechanically from Gatling's. In the Gatling gun, a hand crank rotated multiple barrels and a geared mechanism loaded a cartridge in one barrel, fired the cartridge in the next barrel, and extracted a spent cartridge from the next. Maxim's had a single barrel, and used the force of the recoil from one shot to eject the spent cartridge and to set in motion the mechanism that inserted and fired the next.

John Browning, meanwhile, developed a "blowback" system wherein the gas pressure from a round being fired blew the spent cartridge back against the bolt, opening it. A coiled spring, compressed by the blowback, would push the bolt closed, pulling a new round into the chamber. However, blowback was potentially dangerous if the automatic bolt opened too quickly. For the time being, Maxim's recoil method was deemed the most practical, and it was used in the machine guns that were built before World War I.

If the world of military theory needed a graphic demonstration of the machine gun's immense and deadly potential on a battlefield, it needed only to wait for the Great War. The machine gun's rate of fire, which was from around seven to ten rounds per second, could stop an infantry charge almost before it started. So what if the gunner did not carefully aim his gun? If a stream of fire was poured into group of soldiers, the damage was potentially fatal to all.

However, as we have noted, machine guns were generally heavy, awkward, and hard to move. Most machine guns, such as the German Maschinengewehr 08 or British Vickers, weighed fifty to one hundred pounds or more. Even "light machine guns" such as the American-designed Lewis, that was widely used by the British, weighed nearly thirty pounds.

Among the lightest of the light machine guns in widespread use in the early years of the war were two French 8mm weapons, the Chauchat Fusil-Mitrailleur and the Hotchkiss Modèle 1909, which was designed by Lawrence Benet and Henri Merci. The former was equipped with a rifle-type stock and a pistol grip, but it weighed twenty pounds or more when fully loaded, so it could hardly be called a rifle. The French army used it to support infantry attacks by assigning one to a member of a rifle squad, but it was too cumbersome to be practical for an infantryman to carry during combat.

The heavier Modèle 1909 was developed by the American gunmaker Benjamin Hotchkiss, who had emigrated to France in 1867. It was used by the French Army firing the 8 mm round, and by the British, firing their standard .303. While Thompson had been at the Small Arms Division, the U.S. Army had also acquired seven hundred of these, which were equipped to fire the American .30-'06 round. These were manufactured at the Springfield Armory under the designation M1909.

While many designers were thinking in terms of scaling down machine guns to an easily portable size, Thompson's thoughts were of an automatic rifle that could somehow put the firepower of a machine gun into a weapon the size of a standard infantry rifle.

As he read reports of the carnage on the Western Front in 1915, Thompson began meshing the necessity for a deadlock buster with the potential of inventing a man-portable machine gun. He leaned back in his chair and closed his eyes. He imagined the lucky soldier who made it across the hail of bullets in no-man's-land to the German trench.

The soldier stood over the trench in a position to attack the enemy.

He raised his Lee-Enfield and fired.

One enemy went down.

He ejected a spent cartridge casing and squeezed the trigger again.

How long did it take to fire those two rounds. Was it two seconds or three?

It did not matter, because in those few seconds, in the seeming eternity that it took between shots, a dozen Mausers were trained on him and a dozen rounds converged on him.

The brave soldier, who was lucky enough to get across no-man's-land in one piece, was lucky no more. He was dead.

What if? John Taliaferro Thompson wondered.

What if that brave soldier, who was lucky enough to get across no-man's-land in one piece, could bring to bear the same rate of fire as a machine gun? What if he had such a capability in a weapon that was as easy to handle as an infantry rifle?

Instead of one shot, followed by the time taken to eject a cartridge, a stream of continuous fire would sweep the trench. It would be like a "trench broom," he thought.

Multiply a single soldier by a platoon, or a company, and the advance would go forward until the stalemate was swept away.

A trench broom.

Why not?

Thompson knew the answer to the why not. It was the complexity of the mechanisms that made a machine gun work. The moving parts—rods and pistons and gears—were many, and scaling the existing machinery down to the size of a rifle was going to be a serious challenge. It would involve not only miniaturization, but simplification. Parts could be reduced in size only so far. They had also to be simplified.

Each night, John Taliaferro Thompson went home from Eddystone and tinkered with his idea as tales of the carnage on the Western Front filled the headlines in the newspaper that lay on his dining room table.

Later that year, Thompson read somewhere, probably in the professional literature rather than in the daily paper, about an invention that promised to be his breakthrough.

Up in Massachusetts, a naval officer, Commodore John Bell Blish, had invented a simple metal lock that used static friction to prevent the bolt from opening prematurely.

As an officer on the gunboat *Vicksburg* during the Spanish-American War, Blish had the opportunity to observe large naval cannons in action. Because his ship was on blockade enforcement duty off Cuba and not engaged in combat, Blish had plenty of time to casually watch *Vicksburg*'s guns being fired in practice. What he observed as the guns were fired, and as great pressure was exerted on their breeches, was the phenomenon of static friction. This is the force that resists *potential* movement, as opposed to kinetic friction, which resists movement. A simple example of static friction is when an object comes to a stop as it slides down a sloped surface. He saw this as plausibly useful in slowing the blowback of a breech in an automatic weapon.

Formally patented on March 9, 1915, the "Breech-Closure for Firearms," better known as the Blish lock, consisted of a "new and improved explosion chamber closure," which the inventor explained in his patent documentation as "adaptable to breech-loading arms of all calibers, which may employ any variety of breech-loading ammunition."

The chief characteristic of his invention was, in the words of his patent description, "exemplified by the employment of pressure generated by the discharge of the breech-loading piece, as the sole factor for locking the breech closer, for actuating the breech closer to open the breech, and for ejecting the cartridge case, obturator [a device used to obstruct a hole], or other ammunition adjunct remaining in the piece after firing; and also, if

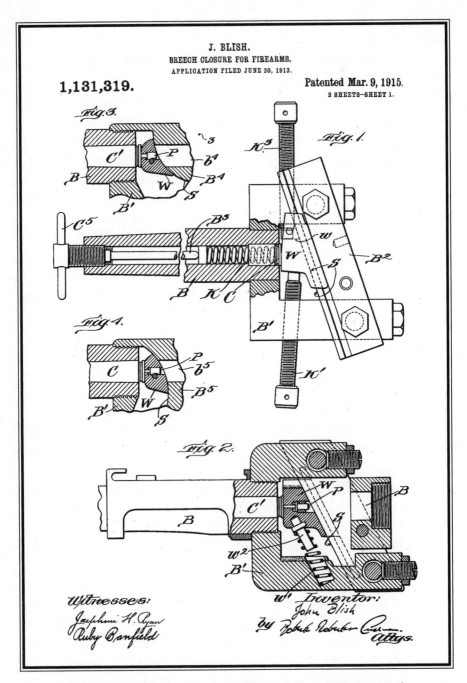

The original 1915 patent drawing for the Blish lock: Some said it was pointless, others said that it was the essence of Thompson submachine-gun engineering.
(Collection of the author)

desired, for reloading and refiring the piece, in case the firearm is of the automatic class."

The phrase "automatic class" certainly caught John Thompson's eye.

Blish went on to write that in his invention "the pressure generated by discharge operates directly and without requiring intermediate mechanical translators of force and motion, in the chief and elementary functions of locking the breech closer and opening the same at the proper predetermined time. Ejection of the cartridge case accompanies the opening movement of the breech closer, since the cartridge case or its analogue is the means through which the pressure generated by discharge of the explosive is communicated to the breech closer."

That which truly excited Thompson was the inherent *simplicity* of the Blish lock. Blish himself had pointed out that previous automatic breech closers operated "through the agency of friction, inertia of parts, or resistance of springs, or several of these factors which have been relied on to control the opening of the breech closure; or have been extracted by gas pressure working through mechanical trains."

As Blish proudly explained, in his invention "no resort is had to any of these agencies."

Many people—albeit not all—who have studied the technical nuances of Thompson's own invention have suggested that it would have been technically possible *without* the Blish lock. However, it can also be said that the Blish lock was the breakthrough that gave Thompson the confidence to move forward. In that sense, it was vital.

And move forward he did. Without quitting his day job, Thompson decided that he would start his own armament company to develop and build his automatic rifle. He contacted Blish and explained that he'd like to trade stock options in the new company for a license to build the patented Blish lock. Having had no other takers, Blish agreed.

In 1915, Americans were still fiercely opposed to becoming embroiled in "Europe's war," but Thompson imagined that there would be a huge market in both Britain and France for his "trench broom." The horrors of that standoff on the Western Front were only getting greater every day.

John Thompson now had two of the four things that he needed to join the ranks of America's great gunmakers. He had a vision. He foresaw an automatic rifle, and he would soon foresee a handheld machine gun that would be a milestone innovation both technologically and militarily. He now had the rights to the Blish lock, which he saw as the key technology to making his automatic weapon a practical reality.

Thompson still needed a good chief engineer, but he already had someone in mind. Theodore Eickhoff, his assistant at the Ordnance Department, had also left the government in 1914. He had gone back home to Indiana to work in the family cider business, but Thompson had a sense that he could be lured by another opportunity that was a bit more technologically challenging.

Thompson also still lacked investment capital. He did, however, know people who knew people.

Thompson was a likable man, who got on well with others. In their piece on his retirement from the U.S. Army in 1913, the journal *Arms & the Man* had praised "that admirable quality . . . of putting at ease everyone who comes in contact with him."

Among those with whom he formed a congenial relationship was his son's father-in-law, George Brinton McClellan Harvey, although they were a study in contrasts. Thompson was quiet and introspective, while Harvey was a blustering, outspoken media tycoon in the William Randolph Hearst mold, who unabashedly used his newspapers to advance his own strong opinions on the matters of the day.

When Thompson had made his decision to start an arms company, Harvey became one of his earliest confidants. It was still a secret project, Thompson explained. He did not want Remington to know. Nor did he want Colt and the other gunmakers to know. He wanted it kept close to the vest until he was ready to roll out his trench broom.

Thompson then went on to explain that he had three of the four parts that he needed to get the new project off the ground. Harvey thought for the moment, then told him that he knew just the right venture capitalist.

Harvey had met Thomas Fortune Ryan in the days when they were both making money in urban railroads. One of Wall Street's wealthiest financiers, Ryan was born near Charlottesville to an old Virginia family, though he later cultivated a rags-to-riches myth of a penniless orphan son of immigrants from Ireland. He became a Wall Street broker, taking a seat on the New York Stock Exchange in 1874, and went on to take his place as one of the movers and shakers in the Tammany Hall machine that essentially ran New York City politics. He got into the lucrative railroad business in 1883, when he started the New York Cable Railroad to run a line from Lower Manhattan to Midtown. By the turn of the century he dominated most of New York's surface rail transit. In his heyday, Ryan also controlled more than two dozen corporations from the American Tobacco Company to Equitable Life Assurance.

Would Ryan be interested in putting a little money into Colonel Thompson's gun project?

Definitely.

It was never clear *why* Thomas Fortune Ryan agreed to invest in an industry where the upside potential was more modest than railroads, tobacco, or insurance. Perhaps he thought it would be interesting. He had, after all, also invested in Royal Typewriter. He certainly didn't need the money. His net worth exceeded four billion in today's dollars.

Nor did he need or *want* the publicity. Ryan deliberately insisted that his financial involvement in an arms company not be disclosed. This suited Thompson, who was still keeping his plan quiet. Ryan did, however, want controlling interest in the new company. That, he explained, is how financiers do things. Thompson agreed. *He* needed the money.

The Auto Ordnance Corporation (later spelled Auto-Ordnance with a hyphen) was originally formed in August 1916, with Ryan taking a 45 percent stake and 25 percent going to Thompson and his extended family, including the Harveys. For his patent license, John Blish received 3.75 percent, and the balance of the stock would be sold on the market. The official headquarters of record was Ryan's office at 501 Fifth Avenue in New York City.

With Ryan aboard, Thompson now had three of the four things that he needed. The next call that he made was to Theodore Eickhoff, to make him an offer he could not refuse.

Just as John Thompson chanced to meet Theodore Eickhoff while working at the Ordnance Department, I, during the course of working on this book, chanced to come into contact with Mike Hensley by way of a Thompson Web forum. A Thompson submachine gun collector, Hensley is in possession of a very significant document relating to this point in the history of the gun. Consisting of more than a dozen typewritten pages dating to the 1940s, it is Eickhoff's own account of his career, especially with Thompson. Hensley had obtained this critical document by way of a friend who had come into possession of it back in the 1940s or 1950s while attending the same church as Eickhoff's niece.

"In the summer of 1916, Colonel Thompson sent me a telegram to come to Chester, Pennsylvania, and meet him at the railway station," Eickhoff writes. "At the appointed time, I made my appearance there, dressed in my best and wearing a stiff hat, which was popular in those days. To receive a request from an Army Colonel, to meet him for a interview, was an unusual and great experience and I put on my very best manners.

"Colonel Thompson was at the railway station when the train arrived;

and, after a cordial greeting of old time friends, we stepped into a Winston-six, which was the finest in that era, and a chauffeur drove us through the country-side to the Colonel's country home near Media, Pennsylvania."

Many accounts of the origin of the Thompson submachine gun concept maintain that Thompson got the idea for the gun before leaving the U.S. Army. This is logical, given that the stalemate of the Great War had not really manifested itself in the fall of 1914. However, Eickhoff writes that during the drive to Thompson's home on that first day, the colonel explained that the real reason for his retiring from the army was to attempt to get private capital interested in the development of an automatic rifle for the army.

Though Eickhoff insists that Thompson's acceptance of a position as an engineer for Remington Arms was "merely incidental" to his interest in his private venture, he recalls how enthusiastic Thompson seemed about his day job.

"He . . . was particularly elated about the production of barrels which had just been brought up to 200 per day," Eickhoff writes. " 'Barrels' seemed to be uppermost in his mind and his mind was saturated with 'barrel making.' I, on the other hand, had during the previous autumn helped my mother at home operate a customs [sic] cider mill where the neighboring farmers and orchardists bring their apples to have cider made. One of the headaches of this operation was to provide an empty supply of 'barrels' to contain the cider. My mind was still saturated with 'cider barrels.' Somehow my mind was slow in orienting itself from cider making to rifle making, and with the Colonel's frequent reference to 'barrels' I was just about to ask him as to where all those barrels were being used. But fortunately, before asking the question, a quiet voice within me said, 'why you dumb-bell, wake up; orient yourself and be quick about it; he is manufacturing rifles, and obviously he is talking about rifle barrels.' "

Soon, however, talk turned to the reason that Eickhoff had been summoned to Pennsylvania.

"In the quiet of his home, Colonel Thompson related that his great ambition was to develop an automatic shoulder rifle for the Army, within the prescribed limits of weight," Eickhoff recalls. "He had searched the existing patents and had found the Blish patent which, he was confident, could produce the satisfactory automatic breech action within the weight limit, and he felt confident of financial backing which he was presently negotiating, and was now ready to engage an engineer to undertake the development work.

He offered me the job of designing and engineering an automatic shoulder rifle."

Eickhoff willingly accepted, and after spending a few days "closing up" his work at the cider mill, Eickhoff went to work for Thompson.

At the time Eickhoff arrived in Chester to move into a spare room at the Thompson home, the company's operations consisted of a machine shop tucked into another room in the same house. Eickhoff was the only full-time employee. Thompson had kept his day job, while young George Goll, a talented mechanic, doubled as Thompson's driver and the company's first part-time employee.

Thompson gave his chief engineer a great deal of latitude in developing the weapon. Indeed, to underscore the clandestine nature of the enterprise, the cash infusions into the company that were made by Thomas Fortune Ryan came in the form of personal checks to Eickhoff.

"It was arranged that all my work was to be carried on in utmost secrecy," Eickhoff wrote. "I was not even to reveal the name of the [Auto-Ordnance] company, but to transact all business in my own name. My salary was paid monthly by Mr. H. H. Vreeland, Mr. Ryan's Office Manager at his New York office. I was to make frequent reports of progress to Col. Thompson and to make a monthly report of expenditures, with a request for funds for the coming month, to Mr. Vreeland."

This was admittedly not very businesslike, but it apparently worked. Such an arrangement also kept Thompson's name out of the loop, providing him with a level of confidentiality in case the intimation of a conflict of interest might arise.

Starting with a pistol-sized prototype handmade by John Blish, the three men test fired and tinkered, test fired and tinkered, then test fired and tinkered some more. In late 1916, Blish handmade a rifle with a Blish lock and let them try that.

When they had refined the mechanism to a place where they could go no farther with the equipment they had, Thompson contacted Ambrose Swasey and W. R. Warner, whom he had known since his days with the Ordnance Department. They ran a machine-tool factory in Cleveland, Ohio, that had done work for the U.S. Army, and had the means to build a prototype of Thompson's automatic gun.

Thompson's friends were apparently so comfortable with his project that they turned over a portion of the basement of their facility to Thompson's enterprise and gave Eickhoff free run of the place—and its wonderland of machine tools. By early 1917, Eickhoff was spending so much time over-seeing things in Cleveland that he moved there.

It was here, working in the basement of the Warner & Swasey Machine Works, that Theodore Eickhoff completed the first prototype of the weapon that would evolve into the Thompson submachine gun.

CHAPTER 4

War and Prototypes

It was the summer of 1917, and a great deal had happened in the year since John Taliaferro Thompson persuaded Thomas Fortune Ryan to finance his Auto-Ordnance Corporation. Since April, the machine tools at Warner & Swasey were working a great deal harder than they had been in the fall of 1916. So, too, were factories and machine shops all across the country, for the United States had now plunged into the Great War.

It was a turn of events that was not altogether unexpected, although nearly every American had hoped—and many had believed—that it would not come to this. Even as Thompson, Eickhoff, and George Goll were firing their Blish lock pistol in the woods behind Thompson's house in the fall of 1916, President Woodrow Wilson was running for reelection, in part on the back of the slogan "He kept us out of the war."

Wilson beat Charles Evans Hughes by a slim margin in November, but a month after he was inaugurated, Wilson turned his back on the campaign slogan. He formally asked Congress for a declaration of war on Germany and the Central Powers.

A majority of the electorate didn't mind. Domestic public opinion had been sliding toward this idea for some time. Germany's unrestricted submarine warfare against merchant ships—an attempt to strangle Britain by cutting off its supply lines—angered many in the United States. This was especially true after the sinking of the passenger liner RMS *Lusitania* in 1915, sending many Americans to watery graves. The line that made American intervention in the war inevitable was crossed in January 1917, when it was disclosed that German foreign minister Arthur Zimmermann was clandestinely trying to lure Mexico into attacking the United States.

The United States Congress finally declared war on April 6.

Soon after the declaration, John Taliaferro Thompson got a call from his old boss at the Ordnance Department, General William Crozier. Shortly after that, Thompson found himself back in uniform. As the U.S. Army began a rapid expansion of forces with an eye toward fielding an American Expeditionary Force, many retired officers were being recalled to active duty. Thompson was one of many, but in Crozier's mind he was a key man. Just as Thompson's experience in the army had made him desirable to Remington, his experience at the gunmaker now made him essential back at the Ordnance Department.

The first task that greeted Thompson in his new role as director of arsenals at the Ordnance Department was production. The U.S. Army faced the herculean task of mobilizing the largest force levels since the Civil War, and had nowhere nearly enough M1903 rifles to meet their needs. In April 1917, the U.S. Army was essentially a small, 127,000-man constabulary force with units stationed across the nation and in the Philippines. The French army, with more than eight million troops in service during the war, had suffered about that number of casualties during April 1917 alone.

Though it had performed reasonably well in the Spanish-American War of 1898, the U.S. Army had little experience of warfare in the industrial age. In the space of nineteen months, the number of personnel in the U.S. Army would rise to more than four million. They needed rifles.

The obvious answer was to simply gear up the arsenals and arrange with private contractors to build millions of M1903s. However, this was easier said than done. Remington had built, and Thompson had helped manage, what was touted as the world's largest rifle factory in Pennsylvania, but it was tooled to build British .303 Enfields. When Thompson sat down with Crozier and his staff, there were two options on the table. These were to convert the Remington Eddystone plant to M1903 production or to continue production and have the U.S. Army simply adopt the .303 Enfield rifle.

The new director of arsenals countered that neither choice was a good choice. The first alternative obviously involved expense and complexity, while the latter would present an enormous logistical headache if the army was using rifles with two different caliber cartridges, the standard .30-'06 and the British .303.

Thompson then argued for a third course. The Small Arms Division should develop a *new* rifle. He explained that both the Enfield and the M1903 were obsolescent. Who better to state honestly that the M1903 had seen its day than the man who had developed it? Thompson, who had been building Enfields at Remington for nearly three years, knew the British rifle's shortcomings and limitations and the features that made it obsolescent—just as he knew the same about his own M1903. Thompson's proposal was to create, in essence, a newer and better Enfield and design it for standard .30-'06 ammunition. Thompson further promised that the new weapon would be ready for production in four months.

Crozier accepted Thompson's recommendation, and the Model of 1917 U.S. Army rifle (M1917) was born. Over the course of the coming year, as manufacturing ramped up, more American rifles were made faster than ever before. A year after Thompson persuaded Crozier to endorse the M1917 plan, the rifles were rolling off the assembly lines at a rate of ten thousand a month. Thompson's own role in this vast project would earn him a Distinguished Service Medal and a promotion to brigadier general.

His new job may have allowed him to create a new weapon, but it rendered him as the absentee father of the one that was most dear to him. With Thompson working overtime at the Ordnance Department, work on his secret automatic rifle was in the hands of Theodore Eickhoff.

While Thompson's day job kept him busy, Theodore Eickhoff was 350 miles away in the basement of the Warner & Swasey plant in Cleveland. As American industry geared up for an unprecedented war effort, Eickhoff was struggling to build a single prototype of an all-new gun.

Eickhoff occupied a parallel universe, slowly tinkering with his "special project" while workers all around him were scrambling to fulfill orders for war matériel. He was plunging into the unknown.

One of his major technical issues, and one that took a lot of time to master, was the tendency of cartridge cases to expand when fired and to jam in the ejector. By late summer 1917, when he thought he'd resolved this problem, Eickhoff completed the full-scale prototype of the weapon that he and his boss called the Thompson Model 1 Autorifle.

Meanwhile, as John Taliaferro Thompson could see from the vantage point of his desk at the Ordnance Department, he was not the only American thinking seriously of the design of an automatic rifle that year. Another such man was the great gunsmith John Moses Browning, who had designed both the Colt M1911 automatic pistol and the .45 ACP ammunition to go with it.

Browning had, in fact, been working on an automatic rifle for some time, but not until after the United States entered the Great War did his project really get off the ground.

Thompson and Browning had taken entirely different approaches that were leading them to more or less the same place. Whereas the Auto-Ordnance Autorifle essentially involved making a rifle automatic, Browning's approach was to scale down an existing light machine gun. Browning looked at the French Chauchat Fusil-Mitrailleur, but focused on the Hotchkiss Modèle

1909, a small number of which had been acquired by the U.S. Army and were known as the M1909. While Thompson was starting from scratch, Browning stayed with the basic design of the M1909.

The result of his efforts would be the Browning automatic rifle, which is known universally by its initials sounded out B-A-R, though *not* by its obvious acronym, which would be pronounced "bar." Like the Thompson submachine gun, the BAR was a weapon with its roots in World War I that would play an important role as an infantry weapon in World War II.

Browning had managed to get the weight of his BAR down to below twenty pounds when empty, making it lighter than the Chauchat Fusil-Mitrailleur, but double the weight that Thompson and Eickhoff had in mind for the Autorifle. Both guns, in their early stages of development, were being designed to utilize the standard .30-'06 cartridge. This would soon change.

The development of the Autorifle moved at a snail's pace. The Model 1 prototype had exploded during test firing in August 1917. Fortunately, it blew up in Theodore Eickhoff's face only figuratively and not literally. Just as fortunate, though, Thompson did not see this failure as a setback. He saw it as an opportunity to start with a blank slate.

When Eickhoff's team in Cleveland became convinced that the .30 caliber rifle cartridge definitely would not function with the Blish automatic bolt action without lubrication, he penned a personal report to Thompson concerning what he called the "coefficient of ejection" for all the popular makes of cartridges.

"This coefficient was nothing more than the ratio of the effective thrust area of the chamber powder pressure against the bolt, versus the area of the cartridge case pressing against the chamber by the inflation of the cartridge case under the high chamber pressure," Eickhoff explained. "In simple words, it was the quotient obtained by dividing the area of the mouth of the cartridge case by the exterior surface area of the cartridge case contacting the chamber."

He added that the .30-'06 cartridges "functioned reliably and dependably in the test mechanisms" if they were waxed or lubricated, but concluded that this was impractical from a production standpoint.

When Eickhoff explained the "coefficient of ejection" to Thompson and pointed out that the .30 caliber cartridge had the poorest coefficient, he added that the .45 caliber ACP pistol cartridge had the highest coefficient. Why not, it was suggested, use the .45 ACP that had been developed for the M1911 automatic pistol while Thompson headed the Small Arms Division?

Meanwhile, John Browning, who had originally designed the .45 ACP cartridge, stayed with the .30-'06 for his BAR.

Around the time that Eickhoff came to Washington to deliver the bad news of the Model 1's failure, Thompson chanced to meet a young engineering prodigy named Oscar Payne. Employed by a firm of patent attorneys, Payne had been at the Ordnance Department for a presentation in connection with an ongoing case involving an alleged patent infringement that had arisen when the Ordnance Department had converted Benjamin Roberts muzzle-loaded rifles into breech loaders. During the session, John Thompson came to be greatly impressed with Payne's almost uncanny understanding of the intricacies of firearms.

Synchronicity brought Thompson, Eickhoff, and Payne together in the same room. It was only by chance that their respective jobs brought them together at the same place at the same time. During a break in the day's agenda, they got to talking, and talk turned to the project that Thompson and Eickhoff were working on. Out of their discussions came a whole new direction for the Auto-Ordnance weapon project. To date, they had been thinking of the Autorifle as a rifle-shaped weapon, firing rifle-caliber ammunition. Payne suggested that they abandon this presumption.

Why not think of the gun truly as a miniature machine gun, not as a modified rifle? Why not start the new design from that premise?

Thompson and Eickhoff embraced Payne's suggestions, and the Autorifle concept was set aside. It was not abandoned, but merely placed on a corner shelf so that Auto-Ordnance could follow the new trail on which Payne had now directed the company. Thompson was so impressed that he put Payne on the Auto-Ordnance payroll, and the new man accompanied Eickhoff back to Cleveland. Here they left the basement and moved into a nearby house that Warner & Swasey had used as an auxiliary wood shop. By October Auto-Ordnance had moved into a machine shop of its own thanks to Ryan's largesse and continued interest in this enterprise.

It is impossible to overvalue the decisions made by Thompson that came out of his brainstorming sessions with Eickhoff and Payne in early September 1917. They not only defined the changes that would ultimately make the gun possible, but the changes that would make it a unique weapon.

Oscar Payne began sketching his new weapon on the clean slate handed him by Thompson, and two weeks later he had it. On September 22 he completed the design for the weapon to which the Auto-Ordnance team gave the provocative name, "Persuader." In this design, Payne had redesigned the Blish lock in an effort to prevent the problems that had caused the Autorifle to fail.

Taking the "miniature machine gun" concept a bit far, Payne also designed the Persuader to be fed with a cartridge belt rather than a magazine.

By December, the initial tests with the belt proved the concept to be flawed, as the cartridges did not advance properly. In the meantime, Payne had improvised a metal magazine for testing the firing mechanism. It worked so much better than the belt that he and Eickhoff simply abandoned the belt altogether.

Early in 1918, a new prototype Auto-Ordnance gun with a box magazine emerged from the wood shop. Known as the "Annihilator," this gun moved a step closer, in terms of its overall design, to the eventual Thompson submachine gun.

The Annihilator was not without bugs, but one by one, Eickhoff and Payne worked through them. By the summer of 1918, a year after the disastrous failure of the Model 1 Autorifle, the two engineers were able to take Thompson into the woods near Cleveland for an afternoon of generally flawless shooting.

Thompson had by now shared the details of his submachine gun with General Crozier, who had taken something of an interest in the project. The Ordnance Department wished to evaluate the gun, and Thompson authorized Eickhoff and Payne to hire a crew of machinists to begin building a production series of Annihilators based on Payne's prototype.

Though the records are long lost, half a century after the fact William J. Helmer, author of *The Gun That Made the Twenties Roar,* interviewed men who were part of this operation. They confirmed that by the fall of 1918, the Annihilator was indeed in limited production. They were also sure that Thompson had arranged for the guns to be sent overseas to U.S. army units for provisional operational testing. Reportedly, the guns were in transit on November 11, 1918, the day the armistice came into effect.

It was around this time that someone on Thompson's team, probably either Eickhoff or Payne, coined the term "submachine gun." As Payne fine-tuned the weapon, it had become more of a machine gun than just another rapid-fire rifle. It had evolved beyond being an automatic rifle in the sense that the BAR was an automatic rifle. So, Thompson wondered rhetorically, if it was not a rifle, what was it? As Thompson had intended, it was smaller and lighter than a conventional machine gun. Therefore, the team reasoned, this made the Annihilator a *sub* machine gun. A new term entered the lexicon. Soon "submachine gun" would be written with Thompson's surname as its prefix.

Theodore Eickhoff recalled that Thompson himself had initially resisted the idea of calling the weapon a machine gun.

"All Machine Guns at the time fired rifle cartridges and he argued that this gun was not in the category with that class of machine gun," Eickhoff wrote. "We considered the term 'sub-machine gun' to indicate that it was of a lower category than a rifle cartridge machine gun, but considered the possibility of the term 'sub-machine' creating confusion with the designation 'sub-caliber.' I contended that the term 'sub-caliber' was known only in military parlance where in target practice small ammunition is fired in adapters from big guns merely for training purposes, and that the term 'sub-caliber' is not known to the general public. The General finally conceded to the use of the term 'sub-machine'; but now the question remained whose name should it take. He proposed to call it 'The Ryan Submachine Gun.' When this matter was brought to the attention of Mr. Ryan for his consent he said very brusquely, 'I'm no military man and what is more I know nothing about guns; General Thompson is a military man, knows guns, and is well known; we will call it '"The Thompson Submachine Gun."'"

Though the Annihilator never made it into action in the Great War, Browning's BAR had been accepted by the Ordnance Department in early 1918, and had become the Model of 1918 (M1918) automatic rifle. It entered mass production while Eickhoff was still tinkering and paying the price of delayed production for thinking outside the box with his gun. About 85,000 were produced during the Great War, but, ironically, the U.S. Army was so pleased and awed with the potential of the BAR that they balked at deploying it to frontline troops. A few were sent to the front two months before the armistice, but for the most part the army held it back because they were afraid the enemy would capture one and copy the design!

How might history had been different if the Annihilator had, like the BAR, been on the Western Front in September 1918?

The answer to the question is that *both* sides would have had them. John Taliaferro Thompson was not alone. Theodor Bergmann, who had been designing automatic pistols in Germany before the war, had also been dreaming the same dream at around the same time.

Like John Taliaferro Thompson, Bergmann recoiled in disgust at the grisly headlines coming back from the Western Front and thought that there had to be another way.

Like Thompson, Bergmann was an idea man. As with inventors from Thomas Edison to Hiram Maxim, his ideas were both sound and eclectic, but unlike Edison and Maxim, he needed someone with some technical expertise to help him realize his ideas. While Maxim designed the mousetrap before turning to automatic guns, Bergmann was an earlier tinkerer with automobiles. He sold this business to Karl Benz, whose surname is far from unfamiliar in the world of motoring, but that, as they say, is another story.

Like Thompson, Bergmann was not an engineer, but he employed them. The two men who were to Theodor Bergmann what Eickhoff and Payne had been to John Taliaferro Thompson was the father and son team of Louis and Hugo Schmeisser. They were gifted gunsmiths who were capable of innovation. The Schmeissers were at the core of the team at Bergmann Waffenfabrik that created the Bergmann Maschinenpistole 18 (MP18) for the German army. If Bergmann's name is not well known, that of the Schmeissers certainly *is*. (To get a little ahead of our story, it should be pointed out that ever since World War II the term "Schmeisser" has become synonymous with "German World War II submachine gun." However, the gun usually referred to by this appellation is the MP40, one of a few German submachine-gun types of the era *not* designed by a Schmeisser.)

The MP18 was the first practical, widely used submachine gun, though several other prototypical submachine guns, such as Beretta's Model of 1918, were built around this time. Like John Browning's BAR, it operated on the simple blowback principal. No Blish lock here.

The MP18 weighed just over ten pounds and fired 9 mm rounds from a twenty-round box magazine, or a thirty-two-round drum magazine. Originally designed for use with Luger automatic pistols, the latter magazine was called a "snail" because of its shape. Equipped with a wooden stock, the gun resembled a rifle, but had a wide, perforated barrel jacket.

This submachine gun first saw action early in 1918, some months before Thompson's Annihilator could have been ready for prime time, and was used to equip the *Stosstruppen*, shock troops, that led the infantry assaults in the German spring offensive. The weapon performed well tactically, just as John Thompson had imagined for his gun, and it must have come as a disappointment when he heard the details of the Germans having beaten him to the punch.

Disappointed was the feeling, however, of the German General Staff as the German strike force ran out of steam—mainly by outrunning their own supply apparatus—and sputtered to a halt. This was one of many setbacks—characterized by historians as beginning of the end—that the Germans would experience over the next several months as the Yanks arrived in droves to support the exhausted British and French.

CHAPTER 5

Marketers

On the eleventh hour of the eleventh day of the eleventh month, the guns fell silent on the Western Front.

Nobody who was alive at the time, nor anyone who grew up during the twentieth century with people who remembered November 11, 1918, would forget this phrase. World War I was over.

Millions of American troops were demobilized and mustered out of service. Among them was Brigadier General John Taliaferro Thompson. He left the service in December, and was awarded his Distinguished Service Medal in March 1919. He did not go back to Remington in Pennsylvania, but bought a home in Connecticut and spent his days at the newly established Auto-Ordnance corporate headquarters at 302 Broadway in New York. Here he was joined by his son Marcellus, who left the U.S. Army in December 1919 to join his father's business.

Marcellus Thompson had gone overseas during the war as a brevet lieutenant colonel, commanding a battalion in the 65th Artillery Regiment, one of six coast artillery units reorganized as field artillery regiments for service on the Western Front. When he came home, he resumed his permanent rank of captain, but saw no future for himself in the rapidly downsizing postwar army.

With the demobilization came an abrupt end to opportunities for a military market for the Annihilator. Nevertheless, Thomas Fortune Ryan continued to support Auto-Ordnance, and the team of Eickhoff and Payne continued to refine its design. They all saw the Thompson submachine gun as revolutionary. Never mind that the vast armies that might have hungered for it in 1917 had evaporated by 1919, Ryan still felt it worthy of his investment.

This enthusiasm did not mean that this invention was without its shortcomings. When new technology is being pioneered, and the only point of reference is in the familiar past, missteps are to be expected. Eickhoff and

Payne worked carefully, but they were building something that had never existed.

Through 1919 and into 1920 the Thompson submachine gun went through more than two dozen iterations while the growing Auto-Ordnance staff tinkered with various technical issues such as internal lubrication to prevent jamming. These weapon prototypes are generally lumped together under the omnibus "Model of 1919," or M1919, designation, despite their many differences.

No documentation survives to show exactly how many prototypes were completed in or about 1919 that would have come under the M1919 umbrella. As Thompson scholar Gordon Herigstad has told me, "There are only about six prototypes that have surfaced." Among these are two that are located at West Point, and Serial Number 6, which is at the Rock Island Arsenal Museum in Illinois.

Thompson collector Tracie Hill, author of *Thompson: The American Legend*, who has more M1919s than any other private party, told me that among his four such guns are number 17, which he believes to be the highest known serial number, as well as one gun that has no factory number.

Some number of these guns, including perhaps number 6, were evaluated by the military at the time. The official evaluations that had not occurred during World War I finally happened in the second quarter of 1920. The U.S. Army audition took place in Massachusetts at the Springfield Armory in April. During these tests, one instance of the gun jamming occurred in the firing of 2,000 rounds. A few months later, the U.S. Marine Corps tested the Thompson gun at Quantico, Virginia, firing 3,000 rounds with no jamming. In both cases, Thompson submachine guns were found to be more accurate than the evaluators had expected, and accurate at ranges beyond three hundred yards. The gun was later demonstrated at the national civilian gun match in Ohio in August 1920.

As pleased as the armed forces evaluators were with the performance of the gun, their enthusiasm was not backed by production orders. Nevertheless, Thompson and Ryan were sufficiently encouraged to make the decision to ramp up for production of the gun. Auto-Ordnance did not have any production capacity beyond the manufacture of hand-built prototypes, so John Thompson decided to contract out production. He approached Colt—officially Colt's Manufacturing Company (formerly Samuel Colt's Patent Firearms Manufacturing Company)—manufacturers of the M1911 automatic pistol, with which the Thompson submachine gun had .45 caliber ammunition in common.

The reaction from Colt was cagey.

Their opening gambit was to tell Thompson that they were not interested in licensed production of his gun; however, they *would* offer to buy the rights for a million dollars. This would be worth more than ten times that in today's dollars, and about double what Thomas Fortune Ryan had invested over the preceding four years.

When Thompson reported this offer to Ryan, the venture capitalist had a good laugh. He could read between the lines of Colt's transparent counterproposal. If Colt was willing to offer one million dollars for the Thompson submachine gun, it was only because the experienced arms manufacturer could see that it was worth *two* million.

No, Ryan and Thompson would not be selling out for a million dollars.

With their counteroffer rebuffed, Colt accepted Thompson's original offer and Auto-Ordnance contracted with Colt for $681,000 worth of machine-gun mechanisms and with other firms for ancillary parts, such as wooden stocks.

Among the parts ordered from other firms were the gunsights, which came from the Lyman Gun Sight Corporation. Now known as Lyman Products, the Connecticut firm is still in business and still making gunsights. Many people would later claim that Thompson was going overboard, and that the intricacy of these components was wasted on the Thompson gun. As Bill Helmer points out, they "provided for both range and windage adjustments more appropriate to a long-range rifle than a submachine gun." Precision aiming is less important when one is pouring the contents of a magazine into a target at several hundred rounds per minute. Designed for rifles, the Lyman gunsights gave the Thompson a degree of accuracy that was unnecessary in a fully automatic weapon. Further, they increased the time and expense of manufacturing the guns, which drove up the unit cost.

Rolling out of Colt's factory complex in Hartford, Connecticut, in March 1921, the first production series Thompson submachine guns were officially known as the Model of 1921, or M1921. They were generally similar to the last of the handmade Model of 1919 prototypes, and it is a testament to the basic design that they were also recognizably similar in appearance to all subsequent Thompson submachine guns.

In my conversations with Thompson aficionado Doug Richardson, he has gone so far as to call the M1921 the greatest submachine gun ever made, while noting the irony of the fact that it was almost *not* made because of the ambivalence of the postwar U.S. Army toward such a nontraditional weapon.

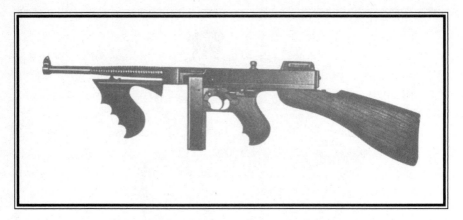

The classic Model of 1921 (M1921) Thompson submachine gun: Colt
manufactured all 15,000 under license from John Taliaferro Thompson's
Auto-Ordnance Corporation. *(Collection of the author)*

"The M1921 Thompson is an absolute classic of perfection," Richardson
told me with genuine excitement. "It should never have existed, but it does. I
have been unable to improve the M1921 Colt Thompson design [after more
than six decades of building Thompson parts for collectors] except in a couple
of areas where they didn't have the materials that we have today, such as the
buffer, the ejector threads, and the way the grip mount goes on the gun."

At Ryan's insistence, Auto-Ordnance ordered a total of 15,000 guns, with
serial numbers running from 41 through 15,040. Gordon Herigstad, who has
compiled the definitive documentation on M1921 production, points out that
the first forty serial numbers were set aside for the uncertain number of
M1919s. No one is certain how many there actually were. The highest number
among known guns is in the teens, and collector Tracie Hill has one with no
number, so this item of Thompson minutiae will probably never be known.

The M1921s had an attractive blued metal finish and lovely walnut wood-
work that would please the most discriminating collectors of fine hunting
rifles. They were relatively lightweight, and were designed to accommodate
both 20-round box magazines or 50-round cylindrical drum magazines,
known by the Roman numeral for 50 as L drums, that somewhat resembled
the "snail" magazines of the Bergmann MP18. A 100-round drum magazine,
known as a C drum (again, for the Roman numeral for 100) was also offered,
but it weighed more than eight pounds, thereby increasing the overall weight
of the Thompson to nearly twenty pounds.

In this widely reproduced Auto-Ordnance advertising illustration, a policeman fires an M1921 Thompson submachine gun from a motorcycle sidecar. In the late 1930s, the U.S. Army briefly equipped motorcycles with scabbard-mounted Thompsons.
(Collection of the author)

The M1921s had it all—except customers.

Auto-Ordnance had gone ahead with a first batch of components for the 15,000 units on the strength of the glowing initial reviews from the army and marines, but without advance orders from the services. The gun was now out of the hands of the engineers and in the hands of the Auto-Ordnance sales force whom Thompson and Ryan had hired to market their new product.

They had their work cut out for them. The Auto-Ordnance salesmen approached police departments in New York and other municipalities, and staged photo ops in which police officers were seen lovingly cradling the new weapons. The New York Police Department did buy a few for its riot squad, and so, too, did the police departments in San Francisco and Boston, as well as state police forces in six states, including the Texas Rangers.

Auto-Ordnance undertook a media blitz, and newspapers duly reported news of these interesting and potentially very potent submachine guns. Auto-Ordnance also courted police and military services in the United Kingdom and Latin America.

As early as December 1920 Thompson was in discussions with Birmingham Small Arms (BSA) in England about a licensed production deal similar
to the one that Auto-Ordnance had inked with Colt in the United States. The
gun that was developed was like the M1921, but configured with different
barrels and designed to fire ammunition in such standard European calibers
as 7.65 mm and 9 mm parabellum. Several governments, including France,
tested the gun, but no production orders were forthcoming.

According to Seth Nadel, who spent three decades as special agent with
the United States Customs Service, BSA only made nine of the guns, but,
curiously, two of them carried the serial number "8." One of these was in the
hands of a collector whom he met a half century later.

"All the 9 mm parts were taken out and it was rebarreled for .45," Nadel
told me. "I've shot the gun. When he registered it, ATF called him up to say
that he put the wrong number on the paperwork when he registered it. They
asked if he wasn't sure it wasn't 800 or 8000 something. No, it was serial
number 8."

Only a few countries were off limits to the Auto-Ordnance salesmen for
possible export deals. Recently defeated Germany had been forced by the
Treaty of Versailles to disarm, and was not a prospect. Neither was Russia,
where the Bolsheviks were winning the Russian Revolution, nor Mexico,
where the ongoing epidemic of unrest and violence was a bit close to home.

Meanwhile, the Bergmann MP18, the German submachine gun that had
preceded the Thompson, was being used by the police in Germany. The
Treaty of Versailles forbade Germany from maintaining an army, but nothing prohibited use of the MP18 with the original twenty-round magazine. Of
course, the MP18 was officially a "machine pistol" and not a "submachine
gun." Against the backdrop of growing social unrest in postwar Germany,
there was increased urban violence between extremist gangs, and plenty of
use for machine pistols on the defeated nation's chaotic streets.

John Thompson was also quick to take the new M1921s on another show-
and-tell for the American armed forces. In early April 1921, one year after the
services had their first kick-the-tires session with the M1919 prototypes, marines and soldiers had a chance to get their hands on production series
Thompson submachine guns.

At Quantico, the marines tried firing the gun from an airplane, but aiming was a problem. In defense of the gun, however, it had never been intended as an airplane weapon. The U.S. Army Infantry Board tested the gun
on the ground at Camp Benning (later Fort Benning) in Georgia, and gave it
a thumbs-up. They even found that it compared favorably to the Browning

automatic rifle—especially among soldiers who had to lug the BAR in maneuvers. The April 16 issue of *Army and Navy Journal* called the Thompson submachine gun "as near mechanical perfection as it is possible to make an arm of its type."

And?

Auto-Ordnance waited for the other shoe to drop. They waited for the phrase "we'll take ten thousand units," but it was not forthcoming from either service.

The silence was explained by the armed services' uncertainty as to how to classify a weapon that was neither a pistol nor a rifle, while not being large enough to fit the "official" definition of a machine gun.

In its attempts to apply an existing yardstick to the evaluation of the Thompson, the army tried to shoehorn it into the parameters of a rifle, examining its accuracy over long range. At distances beyond two hundred yards, the Thompson could not compare to a standard-issue Springfield, or even a BAR.

What about comparing the rate of fire of the Thompson against that of a Springfield?

What about comparing the weight of the Thompson against the much heavier BAR?

The evaluators didn't.

At this point, one recalls the U.S. Army half a century earlier when soldiers equipped with Trapdoor Springfields got into close combat with Cheyenne or Lakota or Apache warriors armed with lever-action Winchester repeaters. The Trapdoor Springfield certainly had long range accuracy, but in close combat, there was absolutely no question that the Winchester's rate of fire carried the day. Certainly this was fatally true on one particular day—June 25, 1876, at the Little Bighorn in Montana.

Dithering acquisition policy within the armed services is nothing new. Nor was a tight budget for new and innovative weapons in peacetime. Nevertheless, the Marine Corps at least incorporated a *picture* of a Thompson-armed Marine in a 1921 recruiting poster.

President Woodrow Wilson had called World War I the "war to end all wars," and many Americans believed him. When it came to military budgets, Congress certainly believed that the victory in 1918 would make future wars improbable, and they reduced U.S. Army spending accordingly.

Though a few Thompsons were acquired for testing purposes and the National Guard in several states bought small numbers, the peacetime army saw no need for the large orders that Auto-Ordnance sought.

This 1921 Auto-Ordnance advertising illustration shows a soldier firing an M1921 Thompson submachine gun fitted with a drum magazine. *(Collection of the author)*

At Auto-Ordnance the engineering staff went to work developing potential new products that were variations on a theme. In an effort to compete with the Browning automatic rifle, which *was* adopted by the army, Auto-Ordnance is said to have developed and proposed its Model of 1923 (M1923). Configured with a fourteen-inch barrel, complete with a BAR-style bipod, it was designed to fire .45 Remington-Thompson cartridges and offered greater range than the M1921. The U.S. Army showed less interest in the M1923 than it had in the M1921.

With the company essentially moribund after the failure to land a large military order, Auto-Ordnance began losing some of its key people. Oscar Payne departed in 1922 for Reed & Prince, an industrial products company that still operates in Massachusetts in the twenty-first century.

"The future of the gun business did not look bright," Theodore Eickhoff wrote later. "I entertained a desire to get into Industrial Work, so in the summer of 1924 I resigned my position with the Auto-Ordnance Corporation and joined the Trundle Engineering Company of Cleveland, Ohio, as a staff engineer."

The only significant United States military order for most of the 1920s

Going postal, this guard protects the U.S. Mail with his M1921 Thompson submachine gun. *(Collection of the author)*

came from the U.S. Coast Guard, which deployed the guns aboard their patrol boats. The next United States government order came from, of all agencies, the Post Office Department. They were used to equip guards after a well-publicized mail truck hijacking in 1926.

The following year, against the backdrop of the warlord-era unrest in China, the United States was asked to "send in the marines" to protect American property in Shanghai and elsewhere. When the marines did go in, they were armed, according to the *Marine Corps Gazette*, with 182 Thompson submachine guns—borrowed from the post office!

PART TWO

Bandits and Criminals

CHAPTER 6

In the Shadows

When Auto-Ordnance was formed in 1916, John Taliaferro Thompson had hoped to watch as the company set sail as a successful enterprise, then retire to his home in suburban Connecticut to tinker in his workshop. Instead, he found himself knocking on doors across Europe trying to sell his guns.

Having received no significant American military orders for the Thompson submachine gun after the demonstrations in 1921, Thompson took his show on the road, traveling with longtime Auto-Ordnance employee George Goll to England and to the Continent.

In Belgium, the nation that was overrun by Germany in 1914 and pulverized by both sides for the next four years, military planners could see the value of the gun. In a letter that Goll later shared with firearms historian Bill Helmer, the Belgian army's infantry chief, General Louis Bernheim, wrote emphatically that if his army had had Thompson submachine guns in 1914, the Germans never would have gotten through Belgium.

That sounded like an endorsement, a recommendation that Belgium ought to buy Thompson submachine guns. But as much as the Belgian army liked the gun, their purse strings, like those of the U.S. Army, were tied.

In 1921, official military planners in most nations, including the United States, had bought into the notion that the Great War really had been the "war to end all wars." Accepting this as fact, they had decided that buying new-fangled weapons was unnecessary.

Others, especially poor Belgium, which had been on the front lines in Europe, recalled the dictum of Publius Flavius Vegetius Renatus, who wrote in the fifth century, "Let him who desires peace prepare for war"—but they could not *afford* to buy Thompson submachine guns that cost half as much as a new car. All they could do was to *hope* that the Great War had been the last.

Of course, the Great War had not been the "war to end all wars." More than thirty wars broke out around the world in the three years following the armistice of 1918. There would be another dozen before 1930. For the most part—except perhaps for the last convulsions of the Russian Revolution—these were not great wars with the great armies of the powers. They were, like so many conflicts today and all through history, smaller-scale wars warranting little more attention than the occasional news item. They were civil wars, wars of liberation, border wars, and the like, and they were generally distant from American shores and American lives.

If Britain, France, Belgium, and the United States chose not to upgrade their armed forces with new weapons, the antagonists in these smaller wars, like the antagonists in the smaller wars of today and tomorrow, saw small arms as a vital necessity.

The market had changed. No longer was it the world of governments and organized armies with flags, heraldry, and long traditions. Auto-Ordnance and its staff now entered the shadowy world of warlords, strong men, and those individuals of whom it is said that they are one man's freedom fighters and another man's terrorists.

It was against this backdrop that Auto-Ordnance finally began to find the unexpected first major markets for its Thompson submachine gun.

In Belgium, General Thompson and George Goll had approached King Albert I. He could not or would not buy their gun for his Belgian army, but he whispered that he had another idea. Albert still ran the Belgian Congo in Africa as though it was his own private ranch (which it had *literally* been for his uncle, Leopold II, until 1908, when it became a Belgian colony), and he placed an order for a hundred Thompson submachine guns.

In China, the collapse of the Manchu Dynasty in 1912 brought an end to two millennia of imperial rule. Though a Republic of China was declared, it was such in name only. In reality, the country disintegrated into a myriad of fiefdoms run by various and competing warlords.

According to Justice Department documents that were uncovered by Bill Helmer in the 1960s, Auto-Ordnance was approached by an enigmatic intermediary about a substantial "Far Eastern deal" with an individual identified only as "the Ruler." This arrangement would have involved 50,000 Thompson submachine guns, extra magazines, and 50 million rounds of ammunition changing hands for $14.6 million.

Apparently nothing came of the deal, certainly not involving such numbers. However, it is reported that Yen Hsi-Shan, the warlord who ran the mountainous province of Shanxi, had his own gunsmiths manufacture knockoff replicas of the M1921. These he found especially useful in defending his railroad from bandits and from soldiers loyal to rival warlords.

Meanwhile, another war would bring other deals that fell into that shadowy world of terrorists or freedom fighters. The Irish War of Independence took place between the beginning of 1919 and a general cease-fire in the summer of 1921. With roots in many previous conflicts, the war began as a guerrilla campaign by the paramilitary Irish Republican Army (IRA) against the British government, which had ruled Ireland for centuries. The war eventually resulted in Britain's recognizing an Irish Free State in twenty-six of Ireland's thirty-two counties in 1922, but in the years immediately after World War I, the country was in a period of open warfare.

Irish public opinion, which for decades had favored home rule but still within the United Kingdom, now increasingly favored a fully independent Irish Republic. The British, who were once seen as a benign ruling class, were now regarded more and more as an oppressive occupying force. Sinn Féin, the political party spearheading the movement toward independence, won nearly three quarters of the votes in the Irish general election of 1918.

Open warfare then ensued, with the British army and British paramilitary "Black and Tan" thugs on one side, and the IRA on the other. There were a number of full-scale battles, and more than a thousand troops and paramilitary personnel from both sides were killed in action.

During this time, public opinion among Irish Americans in the United States supported the concept of Irish independence, although no more than a few die-hards actively supported the IRA's guerrilla campaign. Meanwhile, Anglophile Americans—particularly those who had fought alongside the British in World War I—supported His Majesty's government, although they generally distanced themselves from the extremism of the Black and Tans.

It takes no stretch of the imagination to see that the IRA and their American sympathizers could understand the value to their cause of a weapon such as the Thompson submachine gun. Nor does it take a stretch of the imagination to understand that the IRA could not openly come shopping for such a gun. American neutrality laws specifically forbade arming a faction that was in open rebellion against a nation, such as Britain, with which the United States was on good terms. This was a problem for the IRA, but problems are surmounted by ingenuity.

Conspiracy theories still persist—sometimes whispered, sometimes shouted—that Thomas Fortune Ryan himself was among those Irish Americans who actively supported the IRA, and who somehow had played a pivotal role in arranging for the sale of Thompson submachine guns to the rebel faction. Just four months after the Easter Rising of 1916, still regarded as the signature event on the road to Irish independence, Ryan wrote his first check to underwrite Auto-Ordnance. Was it a coincidence?

Some say that Ryan invested in Auto-Ordnance for the specific purpose of arming the IRA, but there is no real evidence that he did. It would be hard to prove. Certainly, he had little if any interaction with the day-to-day operations of Auto-Ordnance, so if this *had* been his intention, his hands would have been kept clean. Of course, being among the top ten richest men in America carries a certain degree of insulation.

Like many Irish Americans, Ryan had an outspoken empathy for the Irish Republican cause and he was a friend of Sinn Féin leader Eamon de Valera. But those who might have known personally of his involvement in an "Irish deal" are no longer with us.

As with the "Far Eastern deal," the paper trail for the "Irish deal" has largely disappeared, although certain facts are known through *New York Times* coverage and Justice Department documents that were tracked down by Bill Helmer half a century ago.

The "Irish deal" was actually a series of at least three somewhat intertwined deals involving various parties, mainly Irish Americans. These individuals acquired the weapons on their own behalf without officially disclosing to Auto-Ordnance that they were actually middlemen, and that the final destination for the weapons was war-torn Ireland. Whether Ryan, Marcellus Thompson, or anyone else within Auto-Ordnance management was informed of the ultimate purpose of the guns—or figured it out intuitively—is still an open question.

In February 1921, three men from New York, John Gallagher, John Murphy, and John O'Brien, placed an order with Auto-Ordnance for fifty Thompson submachine guns. They told salesman Owen Fisher that they were for shipment to "miners and sportsmen" in Alaska. Meanwhile, Frank Ochsenreiter and George Gordon Rorke placed orders for a total of five hundred submachine guns in January and April on behalf of a third party.

As he was the facilitator of this sizable sale, Rorke even managed to get himself hired as a commissioned sales rep of Auto-Ordnance. One is left to imagine the scene as the smooth-talking Rorke convinced Marcellus Thompson to take him aboard. Rorke was a Protestant Irish American from Virginia who had once worked as a manager for the L. C. Smith Typewriter Company in Richmond. Once a president of the Protestant Friends of Irish Freedom, he was well known as a supporter of the cause. Apparently, Marcellus was not troubled by this connection.

The third party, Rorke's "customer" for the guns, was a man by the name of Frank Williams, who had once been known as Laurence "Larry" De Lacy (or Delacey). Under the latter name, "Williams" was wanted by British authorities in Ireland on explosives charges. But as far as Marcellus knew, Mr. Williams was just another "sportsman."

Business with "sportsmen" was brisk that spring. Also in April, Auto-Ordnance salesman Owen Fisher met with a pair of former U.S. Army officers from Chicago, Patrick Cronin and James Dineen, who wanted to take a pair of guns on behalf of "friends," who might want to order considerably more.

The fifty guns ordered in February were delivered in care of P. J. Gentry's Irish pub in New York, while Cronin and Dineen picked up their pair from the company directly. Fisher even tutored them in the weapon's operation at the National Guard Armory at East 33rd Street and Park Avenue in New York. Pleased with their purchase, Cronin and Dineen took the guns back to Chicago to show off to their friends, who included Frank Williams and Irishman Sean Nunan, who was to be Ireland's ambassador to the United States in the late 1940s.

Dineen hand-delivered the two Thompson submachine guns to Ireland, where he demonstrated them personally to Michael Collins and Dick Mulcahy, the two principal leaders of the IRA military campaign against the British. The director of intelligence for the IRA, Collins later served as a member of the negotiating committee for the Anglo-Irish Treaty and as chairman of the Irish Provisional Government. Mulcahy was then the IRA's chief of staff.

Also present at the Thompson demonstration was Tom Barry, commander of the IRA's infamous West Cork Brigade, who recalled it in his memoir *Guerrilla Days in Ireland: A Personal Account of the Anglo-Irish War*. Barry wrote that they all enjoyed shooting the Thompson gun, and that "before we left the building Collins and Mulcahy had decided to purchase 500."

The Irish revolutionaries were so taken with the "Irish Sword," as they called it, that mention of it was made in folk songs from the 1920s. "The Merry Ploughboy" colorfully describes the "echo of a Thompson gun."

It is not known exactly how many Thompson submachine guns reached Ireland, but the number would have been much larger were it not for George Rorke's bad luck on the New Jersey docks on June 15, 1921. As *The New York Times* reported the following morning, "Six hundred machine guns, believed by Federal authorities to have been destined for Ireland, were discovered by customs agents yesterday on board the steamship *East Side* at Hoboken and later were seized on a search warrant by the Hoboken police. According to one report the ship was bound for Belfast, but this later was denied."

The *Times* went on to identify the weapons as Thompson submachine guns, calling them the "latest type of quick-firers," and said that they were in thirteen sacks hidden in the vessel's coal bunkers. The crew, who had noticed the burlap bags being loaded aboard the ship, tipped off the feds, who were actively watching the New York and New Jersey docks for illegal arms shipments to Ireland.

The federal agents had also placed Rorke under surveillance after he had closed the earlier deal with Auto-Ordnance for the large consignment of submachine guns. He was arrested, although not until later in the summer.

In a further thickening of the plot, none other than Frank Williams—using the name Frank Kernan—showed up on the dock as the federal agents were removing the guns. With him were Hoboken police officers, and he carried an affidavit stating that the guns were his property and had been stolen from his warehouse in Hoboken four days earlier. By claiming them as stolen property, he prevented the federal seizure of the guns. They would have to remain in New Jersey as evidence in a property theft case, and therefore were out of federal hands.

George Gordon Rorke finally had his day in court on September 27, where he denied all charges.

"It is absolutely ridiculous," Rorke's attorney, Guy Mason, told the *Times*. "Mr. Rorke was a bona fide employee of Auto-Ordnance Company of New York, and while he makes no denial that he sold the arms, he knew no more about their destination than I do. He was working on a commission for the company, and it was his business to sell its product. . . . The Department of Justice had been working on the case for several months. They knew Rorke was the salesman who closed the deal with the unknown men who purchased the arms, and have had him under surveillance for quite a time."

Investigated by the federal grand jury in Trenton, Rorke was finally released in November 1921 for lack of evidence. As the *Times* put it, "Nothing came of this inquiry to link Rorke with the alleged effort to disturb the peace of Great Britain."

Despite the grand jury's ruling, however, the feds continued to believe that where there was smoke, there should be fire, and they kept an eye, not only on Rorke, but on Auto-Ordnance as well.

In June 1922, a few days more than a year after the guns were seized aboard the *East Side*, the feds struck again, this time indicting not only Rorke but seven other men—among them Marcellus Thompson, the vice president of Auto-Ordnance!

This obviously implied that the feds had pretty good reason to believe that Marcellus knew where the guns were going. Proving it would be another matter, but for the time being the highly publicized arrest put Marcellus in an extremely awkward position. Not only was he being indicted on criminal charges involving armed insurrection against Great Britain, he was in perhaps even greater difficulty with respect to his family. A year earlier, his father-in-law, George Brinton McClellan Harvey, had been named the United States ambassador to Great Britain!

There are few things more touchy at a family dinner than having been caught by the feds running guns to people who are at war with the country to which your father-in-law is the ambassador. Meanwhile, there is hardly a worse faux pas at a diplomatic reception than having your son-in-law indicted for running guns to people trying to overthrow your host country.

This imbroglio was especially embarrassing for Ambassador Harvey because he *owned stock* in Auto-Ordnance. Beyond all the red faces, the affair tended to dampen any prospects that Auto-Ordnance might have had to interest the British government in making official purchases of their products.

As the *Times* reported on June 20, "Marcellus H. Thompson, son-in-law of Ambassador Harvey and Vice President of the Auto Ordnance Company of New York, appeared yesterday in the Federal Court in Newark to plead not guilty to a Federal indictment charging him with conspiracy to ship arms to Ireland in violation of the neutrality laws."

Also indicted for gunrunning in the case were the familiar Frank Williams and his brother Fred Williams, Frank Ochsenreiter, and Frank Merkling, the Auto-Ordnance corporate secretary who was the former secretary to Thomas Fortune Ryan.

"We do not know how guns got aboard the ship," Thompson told the *Times* as he headed into the federal courthouse in Newark. "Of course, we would not think of selling guns to persons we might suspect of reselling them into the hands of enemies of constituted governments."

According to the Associated Press, datelined London, Ambassador Harvey issued a response by way of his secretary, stating only that he had "nothing to say."

In the same news item, an unnamed "high Ulster Special Constabulary official in Belfast" insisted that the Ulster Constabulary had not used Thompson submachine guns, but that the weapons had been used *against* them "on several occasions." He added that the "Thompson gun had played a big part in the Clones Station fight last February, when four special constables were killed."

The case against Marcellus Thompson languished for a year. By that time, Britain's recognition of the Irish Free State, an arrangement supported by most people in Ireland, had marginalized the IRA military faction and the minority who still held out for total unification with the six Protestant counties in Northern Ireland. The conflict segued into an Irish Civil War, which lasted until the middle of 1923, though sporadic violence would continue in Northern Ireland through the end of the century.

Eventually, the case against Marcellus Thompson and the others just went away. Again, as with Rorke's first run-in, a lack of evidence caused the Justice Department to decide in 1923 not to prosecute. It was also for want of a star prosecution witness. Owen Fisher, who had promised to testify, suffered a nervous breakdown and died of pneumonia.

Though Marcellus walked on the gunrunning charge, it cost him his marriage. Dorothy was summoned to England to visit her angry and embarrassed parents in April 1923. Ambassador Harvey had asked her to England to attend the wedding of Albert, Duke of York—later King George VI—and she was even his dance partner at one of the balls that occurred as part of the festivities. Though they would not divorce for six years, and Dorothy soon returned to New York, she and Marcellus were clearly through.

Through also was George Harvey's diplomatic career. He was replaced by Frank Billings Kellogg, a favorite of the man who became president upon the death of Warren G. Harding in August 1923, Calvin Coolidge.

As for the guns, they were released to Frank Kernan, a.k.a. Frank Williams, as his "stolen property" and taken to Ireland.

For all the brouhaha, the Thompson submachine gun had played but a small part in the Irish War of Independence. Though its actual role was minor, it is still remembered. The folk songs mention it, and the Thompson gun retains a place in the mystique of that era of turmoil in Ireland.

CHAPTER 7

In the Headlines

If the role of the Thompson submachine gun in Ireland's turbulent years is a mere footnote in the lore of the weapon, the part it played in war closer to home helped to make the tommy gun a household name. This war, fought in America's cities, was the result of American lawmakers' ignoring one of nature's most treacherous dictums—the law of unintended consequences.

Near the end of the "war to end all wars," President Woodrow Wilson proposed the League of Nations, a world forum in which war could be replaced by debate. Most of the great nations of the world bought into his concept, but not his own. If World War I was really the "war to end all wars," most Americans reasoned, then why bother with entangling the United States any further in squabbles with the rest of the world? The United States had saved the day for Britain and France, and was ready to let them pick up the postwar pieces on their own.

The United States Congress ratified neither the Treaty of Versailles that ended World War I, nor membership for the United States in Wilson's League of Nations. What they *did* do was to turn inward and to ratify laws that would change the lives of American citizens. After having amended the Constitution only four times in the entire nineteenth century, Americans had already amended it four times since 1913, and two of those took effect in 1920. One of the amendments, the Eighteenth (passed in 1919 but implemented in 1920), banned the sale of alcohol, the other, the Nineteenth, gave women the right to vote.

The Nineteenth Amendment was a long-awaited step forward. The Eighteenth was a step backward into legislated morality. Prohibition was an earthquake that decimated labor-intensive industries, especially the brewing industry, as well as cultural traditions. Now regarded as one of the worst legislative disasters in United States history, Prohibition was undertaken with respectable, albeit naive, intentions and was even described at the time as the "Noble Experiment."

While forcing many family businesses—from the breweries of Wisconsin to the wineries of California—out of business, the Eighteenth Amendment and the Volstead Act that enforced it served to unleash a wave of organized crime, the likes of which has never been seen again in America, except for the war on drugs.

Prohibition did not eliminate the American taste for alcohol, of course. It just drove the source of supply into the greedy, welcoming hands of bootleggers and crime kings. There was big money in this illicit commerce, and the bootleggers were willing to invest in this new industry. They were also willing to use whatever force they deemed necessary to protect their investments and their enormous, untaxed incomes. Rival gangs bought politicians and city officials and ruled their turf with an iron fist. The term "gangster" entered the world lexicon.

To control their fiefdoms, the crime bosses needed armies, and the armies needed weapons. Again, as with Ireland, an unexpected market emerged for the Thompson submachine gun.

If Marcellus Thompson was inclined, as he may well have been, to let Auto-Ordnance guns slip into the shadowy hands of international gunrunners, his father remained a staunch law-and-order man. John Taliaferro Thompson had handed off the day-to-day management to Marcellus and was a figurehead, but he was still around. One can imagine that after his son's run-in with the law in 1922, he kept a much closer eye on things. On every occasion possible, he touted his submachine gun as being, to quote his corporate motto, "On the Side of Law and Order," and he was a strict enforcer of this image.

The elder Thompson had actively marketed the gun to law enforcement agencies, imagining it as the weapon that would give them a decisive edge against bandits and bank robbers, but gradually the guns trickled across to the dark side.

Sales figures of the Auto-Ordnance products in the 1920s had been a big disappointment for Marcellus and his father. Several hundred were sold to law enforcement agencies, and still others to railroad police and private security firms, but far fewer than the thousands Auto-Ordnance had hoped to sell. It was much to the chagrin of the Thompsons that their submachine gun would become known as the gun of choice for the armies of American criminals.

Though gangsters were active in nearly every major city in the United

States, it is Chicago that is popularly recalled as having been the central front in the Prohibition wars. Here the turf was initially divided between the essentially Irish North Side Gang, headed by the associates of Charles Dean "Dion" O'Banion, and Johnny "the Fox" Torrio's Italian families on the South Side. O'Banion's second in command was a Polish immigrant, Earl "Hymie" Weiss, who had grown up with O'Banion. The rising star in the Torrio organization was Alphonse "Al" Capone, also known as "Scarface" for the scars he had received earlier in life when he insulted New York hoodlum Frank Galluccio's sister. Galluccio slashed Capone's face three times; Al was lucky, Galluccio was aiming for his throat. Both Torrio and Capone had been active in the New York underworld before moving to Chicago. Also operating on the South Side, and allied with Torrio and Capone, was Frank McErlane, an unforgiving, ex-con crime boss known as an especially ferocious killer.

Between the rival gangs, there were mutual transgressions, involving members of both sides moving booze into the other's territory. These were met with retaliatory hijackings of shipments, interspersed with occasional peace overtures. When O'Banion set Torrio up for a police raid, the response escalated with a hit on the North Side boss in November 1924. One of the men involved in killing O'Banion was Francesco Ioele—a.k.a. Frankie Uale or Frankie Yale—a Brooklyn gangster who was a former associate of Torrio, and for whom Capone had once worked as an enforcer. Yale and two colleagues were detained by Chicago police shortly after the hit, but released because they had credible alibis.

With O'Banion dead, Weiss took over the North Side Gang, with George Clarence "Bugs" Moran as his lieutenant. In January 1925, they hit Torrio, severely wounding him. Moran reportedly ran out of ammunition just before he attempted to deliver the coup de grâce. Though Torrio survived, he turned control of the South Side operation over to Capone. This, in turn, set the stage for open warfare in which Capone and Moran would be the central figures. Though neither man succeeded in his numerous attempts to kill the other, many other Chicago gangsters would pay the highest price. Among the weapons hurling the lead was the Thompson submachine gun.

The debut of the Thompson in the Chicago Bootleg Wars had come in 1925, with the finger on the trigger being that of Frank McErlane. Though the conflict between the O'Banion and Torrio armies held central stage in Chicago, McErlane and his partner, Joseph "Polack Joe" Saltis, had an ongoing South Side dispute with the O'Donnell Brothers gang.

On September 25, 1925, as reported in the *Chicago Herald and Examiner*, Edward "Spike" O'Donnell was passing a drugstore at Western Avenue and 63rd Street when he heard someone call to him from a passing car. Moments later, McErlane was speeding away from the scene after having shattered the storefront windows of the drugstore with what is thought to have been the contents of an entire M1921 drum magazine. O'Donnell survived the messy assault, but McErlane was undeterred in his war against the O'Donnell clan.

Police reports of the September hit attempt asserted that "repeating rifles" had been involved, but soon the word spread that the gangsters had machine guns. In the wake of a subsequent attack that McErlane staged at Buff Costello's tavern on South Halstead Street on February 9, 1926, the headline in the *Chicago Tribune* correctly described the assailants as a "Machine Gun Gang."

Reported as wounded in this attack were John Foley and William Wilson. It is interesting that in the most publicized early attacks using Thompson submachine guns, none of the targets was killed outright. This could be written off to poor marksmanship, lack of proper familiarity with the characteristics of the gun, or the commonly seen tendency of gunners to simply spray the target area with lead instead of taking time to aim.

Another technical issue that made aiming the M1921 Thompson submachine gun difficult was the phenomenon of "muzzle climb." This is the tendency for recoil to push the muzzle of a weapon up slightly with every shot. With a rifle, the shooter aims before each shot, but with a stream of automatic weapons fire, it is neither possible nor intuitive to re-aim after each round. Therefore, with every round fired, the stream of fire climbs up and away from the target. The shooter must consciously hold the muzzle of the M1921 on the target as he squeezes the trigger.

It was not the lack of fatalities, however, that got the attention of the media and police in the initial machine-gun shootings, but rather a rate of fire in excess of eight hundred rounds per minute and the potential for sheer carnage that this represented. The *Tribune* reported that as he surveyed the scene, Police Captain John Stege made the observation that the men of his department also needed to be armed with Thompson submachine guns.

Though Stege wanted to see the boys in blue armed, the man most moved to action by the February 9 shooting was Al Capone. If Stege had to await formal authorization from the city bureaucracy, Capone was able to simply go to the gun store.

In the 1920s, various jurisdictions had gun licensing laws on the books, but these applied mainly to pistols. Because the Thompson submachine gun was relatively new, and public awareness of it was limited, nobody in government had yet thought to restrict its availability.

On April 27, three North Side gangsters died in a hail of .45 caliber ACP rounds in front of a tavern on West Roosevelt Road. The *Tribune* insisted that Scarface himself was the man wielding the gun inside the black limousine.

Chicago police found the gun, naturally with the serial numbers having been filed off. The media and the public now had a firsthand look at the mysterious handheld machine gun that was beginning to wreak havoc on the streets of the Windy City.

At his office in New York, Marcellus was still trying to forget the embarrassment of the "Irish deal" when the news reached him about the Capone gang having embraced his company's product. To head off the potential public relations fiasco, Marcellus raced to Chicago to offer his services to the Chicago police in nabbing the suspects. There was, he told them, a second, hidden serial number stamped on each gun, and concealed beneath the foregrip.

Thompson found the Chicago police less than enthusiastic with the information that he was able to provide. They let him examine the recovered submachine gun, but showed no interest in tracing its ownership. This Thompson did himself. He found the serial number and checked company records. Here he found that the gun was one of three that had been sold to a shop owned by a man named Alex Korecek. Thompson went to see Korecek, who admitted to having resold the gun, but he "forgot" to whom.

With this, Thompson went back to the police, who swooped in and took Korecek into custody. Being given the third degree by the cops didn't help Korecek regain his memory. Eventually, the shopkeeper was released, but against his will. He preferred jail to being on the same streets as the man whose name he had "forgotten." Amazingly, Capone returned the favor, forgetting about Korecek, who was allowed to survive and fade back into obscurity.

If Capone remained out of reach of the law, he was not beyond the potential grasp of Hymie Weiss and Bugs Moran. Noting the additions to Capone's arsenal, the North Side boss played the next hand in the Chicago arms race and acquired Thompson submachine guns of his own.

On September 20, had the North Side Gang not been a gang who couldn't shoot straight, the Capone story would have had its final episode. The attack on Capone's stronghold at the Hawthorne Hotel in the Chicago suburb of

Cicero involved a long line of cars filled with men firing weapons of every caliber—including the North Siders' new Thompsons. This drive-by attack was a scene that has been repeated, modified, and adapted by Hollywood countless times.

The scene even had a grand, theatrical finale when mobster Pete Gusenberg calmly stepped out of a car with his Thompson and pumped one hundred rounds of .45 caliber ACP ammunition into the Hawthorne's coffee shop, where Capone had been eating breakfast. The result of the shootout was an ankle-deep sea of broken glass and a devastated hotel lobby, but *nobody* was killed and the South Side's boss of bosses was untouched. Weiss's plan, like Gusenberg's bullets, had missed the mark.

On October 11, 1926, three weeks after the bungled attack, Weiss stepped out of his State Street offices for the last time. From a nearby car, tommy guns spoke, and his body was perforated by nearly a dozen rounds. Weiss's three-man bodyguard detail was also hit multiple times, but unlike their boss, they all survived.

With Weiss dead, Bugs Moran became the North Side boss. Over the next couple of years, an uneasy and often interrupted truce settled over Chicago's gangland.

Capone had trouble elsewhere. His cordial relations with Frankie Yale in New York were beginning to sour. Capone was disconcerted by Yale's failure to support his associate, Antonio "the Scourge" Lombardo, to head the Unione Siciliane in Chicago, but infuriated when some of his truckloads of illicit booze were hijacked coming out of New York. The two men had a gentlemen's agreement that Yale would help protect Capone's shipments, but the South Side boss smelled a rat. The rat turned out to be Frankie Yale.

On July 1, 1928, Yale was called home from his Brooklyn speakeasy. En route in his coffee-colored Lincoln, he was overtaken by another car, in which at least one of the three armed passengers was brandishing a Thompson submachine gun. Frankie Yale was probably dead before his bullet-riddled Lincoln crashed into a house on 44th Street where a bar mitzvah was in progress.

In Chicago the tension between Capone and Bugs Moran was also increasing. Like Yale, Moran was hijacking Capone booze. He was also hitting other Capone interests and killing Capone allies—including the submachine-gun slaughter of "Scourge" Lombardo.

Meanwhile, Capone bought a 25 percent stake in the Green Mill Cocktail Lounge on the North Side in the name of one of his enforcers. A thug in the same malevolent mold as Frank McErlane, this man was Vincenzo Gibaldi, a

A young lady receives a tutorial on the operation of the M1928 Thompson submachine
gun at FBI headquarters. *(Courtesy of the National Archives)*

mobster who was involved in some of the most infamous hits that were ordered by Capone. Having immigrated from Sicily with his family, he became a boxer under the Irish name "Jack McGurn," and had worked as a hitman for Frankie Yale in New York before moving to Chicago to work with Capone. In the context of his involvement in the Green Mill, Gibaldi/McGurn became notorious for cutting out part of the tongue of lounge singer Joe E. Lewis to dissuade him from moving his act to a rival club.

Though the Lewis mutilation found him wielding a knife, McGurn earned his lasting nickname with a Thompson submachine gun. It was a sign of the times that the private ownership of machine guns was so intertwined with gangster culture that an underworld enforcer would proudly embrace the nom de guerre "Machine Gun Jack" McGurn.

The gun itself soon earned a dictionary's worth of nicknames. The sensationalism that swirled around the Thompson submachine gun soon bred a morbid fascination with the new weapon and the arms race that suddenly seemed to be gripping Chicago. The media coined the term "tommy gun," an easy and obvious step from "Thompson Gun," the nickname that had

Captain John Stege of the Chicago Police Department is holding an open violin
(or viola) case displaying a disassembled Thompson submachine gun for reporters
in 1927. Gangsters probably did not actually use violin cases to take their
weapons into action. *(Courtesy of the Library of Congress)*

long been in use by Auto-Ordnance itself. Others simply called it the "Chopper." As witnesses described the detached staccato "rat-tat-tat" sound that it
made when fired, the phrase "Chicago typewriter" was added to the Thompson's roster of nicknames.

Today, the typewriter analogy seems merely a quaint and abstract metaphor, as this once ubiquitous office machine has slipped into the same tech-
nological oblivion as the butter churn and the rotary dial telephone.

Most people no longer hear the sound of a typewriter. I hadn't for years
until the day that I sat in my office reviewing tapes of an interview that I had
done at a Thompson submachine gun shoot. In the background was the un-
mistakable sound of a typewriter, a Chicago typewriter.

Another folkloric tale that began to circulate within American popular
culture as the tommy gun's legendary status evolved in the 1920s was that of
the Chicago hit men carrying their weapons in violin cases. As noted in the

introduction, the notion that gangsters routinely carried their guns in violin cases is probably just an urban legend. In fact, a ready-to-use Thompson submachine gun would not fit in a violin case. None of the Thompson scholars and aficionados with whom I have spoken seem to know exactly how this myth came about. A photograph of Police Captain John Stege holding a viola case containing a disassembled Thompson appeared in the *Chicago Daily News* in 1927, and may be the source of this popular image.

As Gordon Herigstad points out, most people who carried their Thompson to a hit, or to rob a bank, would not want to deal with a clumsy and awkward case. "The Thompson was not used on an everyday basis as though it was an everyday tool," he said. It was used on rare occasions when the job demanded the sort of firepower that the gun could bring to bear.

It was that firepower that fueled the rising notoriety of the tommy gun in the late 1920s. The legend had taken on a life of its own—a very colorful and frightening life of its own. Yet, the notorious image of the Chicago typewriter's role in society was only just beginning to evolve.

CHAPTER 8

Valentine's Day

The Bootleg Wars in Chicago, with the feud between Al Capone and Bugs Moran as their centerpiece, reached a crescendo on St. Valentine's Day 1929. It was to be a pivotal moment in the history of the Prohibition-era crime wave that has ever after been linked in popular culture with the Thompson submachine gun. If the tommy gun was famous—or infamous—before, it achieved iconic status on that bloody day.

For many months the war had gone on, punctuated occasionally by deadly violence and often by intrigue. At last, Capone decided to resolve the situation with Moran in that singular way that disputes found resolution in the Chicago underworld.

Five members of Moran's North Side gang had arrived at the SMC Cartage Company on North Clark Street in Chicago's Lincoln Park neighborhood just before 10:30 on the cold morning of February 14. Not coincidentally, Capone was out of town, vacationing in Florida.

There are various theories as to exactly why they came to North Clark Street, but one way or the other, they came. As the popular story goes, Capone had arranged for Moran to be invited to a warehouse on the North Side to inspect a recently arrived consignment of whiskey—and then he left Chicago. It has recently been suggested that they would not have arrived in their best suits and ties to receive a routine load of whiskey, but well dressed they were.

The five included Albert "James Clark" Kachellek, Moran's senior lieutenant; Adam Heyer, Moran's accountant; and "Gorilla Al" Weinshank, the manager of a number of Moran's "front" businesses; as well as Pete Gusenberg and his brother Frank. The Gusenbergs were Moran enforcers who had both taken part in the Hawthorne Hotel shoot-out in 1926, and who had been involved in the tommy gun death of Lombardo. With the gangsters were Reinhart Schwimmer, an optician and petty gambler who was a sort of North Side gang groupie, and John May, who worked part-time as a mechanic in the Moran motor pool.

It is supposed that Moran himself planned to be there as well, but he was running late. As one story goes, he arrived just as two men in police uniforms and two in street clothes entered the warehouse. Thinking that the rest of his gang was about to be busted, Moran and his bodyguards turned tail and left the area.

Moran could be forgiven for thinking that the two men in uniform were the police, although they were not. Unforgivable was the Capone lookout who mistook Moran's employee Al Weinshank for the boss himself.

The whole rendezvous had probably been an ambush engineered by Capone. The men who looked like the police were actually Capone hitmen who had been alerted to enter the building when the lookout told them that Moran was present. The fact that the man who looked like Moran was *not* Moran would be a critical mistake.

Inside, the faux cops lined the seven Moran gangsters—including the faux Moran—up against a brick wall. Two of the men in blue were carrying shotguns. The others carried M1921 Thompson submachine guns, serial numbers 2347 and 7580. Fingers wrapped around the cold steel of the triggers, and the ripping, thudding sound of exploding gunpowder echoed within the building.

When the real police arrived, the floor of SMC Cartage was a sea of red. Only John May's dog and Frank Gusenberg survived, although Gusenberg was dead within hours. When asked who shot him, he famously replied, "Nobody shot me." The only person more hated than the man who shot you was a rat—any rat. Frank Gusenberg was not going to die a rat.

The spectacular slaying garnered national media attention. Almost immediately, the papers dubbed it the "St. Valentine's Day Massacre," and indeed it was. It was the signature slaughter of the decade, and it remains as such in the folklore to this day.

"It's a war to the finish!" cried Chicago's police commissioner, William F. Russell, quoted in the February 25 issue of *Time* magazine. "I've never known a challenge like this. We're going to make this the knell of gangdom in Chicago."

It wasn't. They never even solved the case. Gusenberg was not a rat.

The CSI team who combed the room later calculated that at least seventy .45 ACP rounds had been fired.

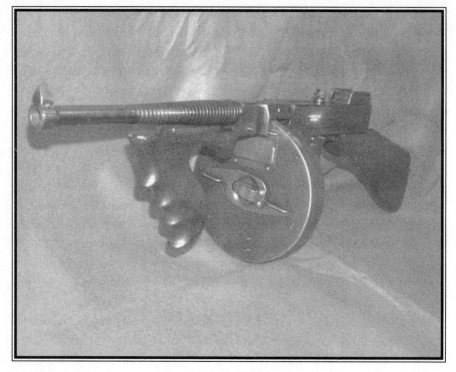

This M1921, serial number 2347, is one of two Thompson submachine guns
that are confirmed to have been used in the St. Valentine's Day Massacre. Both
are now in the possession of the Berrien County, Michigan, Sheriff's Office.
(Photo by and courtesy of Chuck Schauer)

Never determined, however, was "whodunit."

There was no shortage of suspects, but these did not include the conveniently vacationing Al Capone.

In the beginning, the police worked under the theory that the hit men had been members of Detroit's "Purple Gang," Capone allies who ran booze into the States from Ontario.

A late-model Cadillac was located a week later in a garage owned by Claude Maddox, a Capone associate late of the Egan's Rats Gang in St. Louis. Having determined the car to have been used by the shooters in the St. Valentine's Day Massacre, the police began looking for various St. Louis gangsters. These included Fred "Killer" Burke, a Detroit hit man thought to have been one of the first—if not *the* first—to have introduced the Thompson submachine gun into Detroit's underworld. The police had now decided that Burke had been one of the faux cops at SMC Cartage.

As they searched for Burke, the police also arrested and charged Capone enforcers John Scalise and Machine Gun Jack McGurn. However, Scalise was killed before the trial, and McGurn never went to trial. He claimed to have been with his underage girlfriend, Louise Rolfe, and she corroborated his story, earning her a tabloid nickname "Blonde Alibi."

To prevent her from testifying at the trial, McGurn married Louise, because a wife cannot be forced to testify against her husband. The murder charges were then dropped, but the authorities countered McGurn's legal maneuver with one of their own. They charged him with "white slavery" under the Mann Act, which mandates criminal penalties for conspiring to transport an underage female across state lines for "immoral purposes." He was convicted, but never did time. The conviction was overturned on appeal because Louise was determined to have been a willing participant.

McGurn was found murdered on February 15, 1936, seven years and a day after the Massacre. Nobody was ever convicted for that crime either.

Killer Burke remained on the lam until March 1931, and might have eluded capture indefinitely had he not gotten drunk and murdered a policeman during a routine traffic stop in St. Joseph, Michigan, in December 1929. When police raided his house there, he was not at home. Though he had managed to stay one short step ahead of the law that time, Burke had left behind a mountain of incriminating evidence from guns and ammunition to the spoils from bank robberies.

Among the guns were the two Thompson submachine guns that ballistics expert Calvin Goddard—and others through the years—have confirmed were the ones used in the St. Valentine's Day Massacre. One of them was also identified as the gun that had been used to kill Frankie Yale in New York in July 1928. Through Auto-Ordnance records, it was determined that at least one of the two submachine guns had once been sold by Peter Von Frantzius Sporting Goods on Diversey Parkway in Chicago, and had been in the possession of a man going by the name of Frank Victor Thompson (no relation to Marcellus).

Both guns remain in the possession of the Berrien County, Michigan, Sheriff's Office to this day. Lieutenant Mike Kline, the department's quartermaster, told me that the guns are still on display, and a popular stop when school tours come to visit.

He explained that they are both fully functional, and that they work as well as ever. They are even fired occasionally. Back in the 1940s, when the department ran a week-long kid's camp, the finale was a demonstration of the guns. It was always a crowd-pleaser.

Kline told me a story about how one of the two St. Valentine's Thompsons was borrowed by the FBI back in the 1960s for a display at Quantico. In the late 1970s, a Berrien County sheriff was at Quantico attending a training session, and he saw the gun. He mentioned to the FBI men that Berrien County actually owned the gun, and a disagreement ensued.

"No, it's ours," the FBI man insisted. "You guys gave it to us."

"Don't think so," said the sheriff. "I don't think we gave that away."

Fortunately the squabble did not end in a shoot-out, but as in the Old West, the sheriff triumphed. The "borrowed" Thompson has been back in Berrien County ever since.

Lieutenant Kline told me that the department has been a little leery about letting them go out, although he welcomes visitors who wish to view them. Various documentary film crews from the History Channel, the Discovery Channel, and others have come to film the guns through the years, often with Lieutenant Kline firing them for the cameras.

Burke himself would eventually die in jail while doing time as a cop killer, but no one was ever convicted in the St. Valentine's Day Massacre. The evidence of the tommy guns suggests that Burke was involved, although it has not been proven conclusively. He may have been there, or he might just have been the "cool-down guy," holding the guns for another triggerman. Numerous other individuals have been implicated. These range from McGurn to the noted Capone enforcer Antonio "Big Tuna" Accardo. Nobody really knows. Frank Gusenberg was not a rat.

The crime will probably *never* be solved.

The topic of speculation and conspiracy theories for decades, the historic significance of the massacre is that it served to reinforce the public distaste for the bootleg gangsters and the failed experiment of Prohibition that had made their reign of terror possible.

The St. Valentine's Day Massacre also underscored the potent capabilities of the Thompson submachine gun. Much to the chagrin of Marcellus Thompson and his father, the massacre forever made it, not the "law and order" gun, but the "gangster gun."

CHAPTER 9

Send In the Marines

Even as the bootleggers were battling one another with Thompson submachine guns on the streets of Chicago and other major American cities, U.S. Marines were embroiled in another gang war 2,050 miles to the south, in Nicaragua—and carrying their Post Office Thompsons.

When the United States sent the marines to China in 1927, they went into Shanghai's troubled streets packing the Thompsons borrowed from the Post Office Department. These men, in turn, came home praising the weapon that the Corps had not officially acquired when given the chance in 1921. Even if the acquisition bureaucrats remained cool to the Thompson, the soldiers and marines who had actually fired the Thompson were consistent in their praise. They generally loved it.

Meanwhile, the United States also dispatched marines to Central America, where the analogs of Chicago's North Side and South Side gangsters were also delineated by directions, in this case "right" and "left."

Of course, it would be an oversimplification to say that there were no rivalries within the gangs in either war zone. As in Chicago, rival Nicaraguan factions from the same end of the political spectrum would often be in conflict.

Nicaraguan politics in the 1920s were characterized by a revolving door of presidents, some elected and some put into power by a coup. These included members of the established Chamorro family, especially Emiliano Chamorro Vargas, who ruled from 1917 to 1923 and again in 1926, as well as Adolfo Díaz, who preceded him from 1911 to 1917 and followed him from 1926 to 1929. The lack of stability created an atmosphere of lawlessness in which factional shootings, hijackings, and kidnappings were common—just as in Chicago.

Official United States support for the various factions ebbed and flowed. To describe it could, and has, filled entire books, with the political perspectives differing widely. Suffice it to say, American investment—from mining to banana production—was an important pillar of the Nicaraguan economy, whether you wish to believe that the United States interests exploited the country or kept it afloat by providing a market for its resources. Against this backdrop, the Marine Corps was often sent to intervene when the unrest got out of control.

In 1926, a coup by Emiliano Chamorro, from the right, failed, bringing another rightist, Adolfo Díaz, to power. After Díaz was reelected as president, however, leftist forces led by José María Moncada Tapia set out to overthrow him. It was part of Moncada's previous playbook, as he had been involved in the 1910 revolution that overthrew the right-wing government of President José Santos Zelaya López.

In the spring of 1927, President Calvin Coolidge sent future Secretary of State Henry L. Stimson as a special envoy to negotiate a cease-fire. Under the settlement Stimson made, a power-sharing agreement was reached, and in 1928 elections were supervised by the marines, and Moncada, the left-winger, was elected president, a post he held until 1933.

A thorn in the side of both Díaz and Moncada—as well as of the marines—was a man named Augusto Nicolás Calderón Sandino. Calling himself "Generalissimo," he was described as a bandit by some and a revolutionary by others. The son of a wealthy coffee grower and a woman employed by him, Sandino left Nicaragua in 1921 on the run from attempted murder charges. He settled in Tampico, Mexico, where he worked for Standard Oil and spent his spare time dabbling in various peripheral religious and philosophical beliefs from the Seventh-Day Adventists to a group calling itself the "Magnetic-Spiritualist School of the Universal Commune."

Like many rootless young men in the 1920s, Sandino also became enamored of Soviet-style communism and the Comintern (Communist International), the Moscow-directed organization dedicated to overthrowing the establishment around the world "by all available means, including armed force."

Back in Nicaragua in 1926 after the statute of limitations on the attempted homicide charge had run out, Sandino became involved in Moncada's efforts to overthrow Díaz. During this time, he put together a ragtag band of gunmen who operated under a skull and crossbones flag and practiced the Comintern's "armed force" edict in opposition to the elected president.

After Moncada beat Díaz and became president, Sandino and his "Sandinistas" turned their armed force against *Moncada*. In 1931, Sandino issued what he called his "Manifesto of Light and Truth." In it, the former Magnetic-

Spiritualist waxed philosophical about how his gunmen were somehow the instrument of divine justice.

You don't argue with a man who thinks he's on a mission from God—especially when he has a tommy gun in his hand.

This conflict during the late 1920s was characterized by all the customary shootings, hijackings, and kidnappings, as well as deadly ambushes and gunrunning. The latter included importing Thompson submachine guns that had been sold to parties in Mexico by parties in the United States. The question of whether Auto-Ordnance itself knowingly supplied weapons to Latin American gangs or to third parties doing business with them will never be answered, just as the company's possible connection with the IRA will never be known for certain. If they ever existed, most of the company's receipts, invoices, and purchase orders for these transactions were lost long ago along with most of the Auto-Ordnance records.

The first large-scale use of the Thompson in Nicaragua was probably an attack by Moncada supporters in December 1926 that proved brutally effective, not to mention disheartening for the Díaz sympathizers.

In January 1927, the Marine Corps sent in its 5th Regiment, veterans of the Battle of Saint-Mihiel and the Meuse-Argonne Offensive in World War I. With them, they brought more than five dozen of the Thompson submachine guns that the Corps had acquired from the mailmen the year before.

Combat operations in the jungles of Nicaragua were a precursor to what the marines would experience in the South Pacific during World War II. Indeed, not a few individual marines would have firsthand experience with both. Such terrain, with its steep hillsides and thick vegetation, favors the defender. Ambush is made easy not only because concealment is easily possible, but the steep trails force troops to walk in single file rather than allowing them to spread out.

As Roger Peard later wrote in the *Marine Corps Gazette* in June 1930, the men quickly developed tactics to use their tommy guns to their full potential, saving many American lives. The marines could recognize possible ambush sites, but had no way to know whether the enemy might in fact be hiding there. However, they soon figured out that a short burst from a Thompson always got the skittish Sandinistas to return fire, thus, to paraphrase Peard, "depriving them of the advantage of surprise in their carefully prepared ambushes." Once revealed, the enemy were very vulnerable to the Thompson's withering rate of fire.

Lieutenant General Lewis Burwell "Chesty" Puller, the most decorated marine in history, who served with distinction during World War II and in

Korea, had his baptism of fire as a young officer in Nicaragua, where he earned two Navy Crosses. He was one of the first to adopt the Thompson submachine gun as part to the organizational equipment for a marine tactical unit.

In an interview for the Marine Corps Oral History Branch after his retirement, Puller recalled that the weapon was "a very good gun for Nicaragua because just like a shotgun with buckshot it is a very good gun in the tropics."

The implication is that often the Thompson was used at close range against targets concealed in dense foliage. Both buckshot and automatic weapons fire could be used in situations where precise aiming was not possible.

Against the backdrop of apparent stability that finally came with the inauguration of Juan Bautista Sacasa as Nicaragua's president, the marines finally pulled out in January 1933. Augusto Sandino died thirteen months later, gunned down, like Dean O'Banion or Frankie Yale, by a rival boss. In this case, the rival boss was Anastasio Somoza García, who ran the supposedly nonpartisan National Guard. Two years later, Somoza García toppled Sacasa, his wife's uncle, in a bloodless coup.

During their half dozen years in Nicaragua, the marines had become the first American troops to use John Taliaferro Thompson's trench broom in action. They found it, to quote a later Marine Corps manual, "one of the necessary infantry weapons."

CHAPTER 10

Send Them In with the M1928

Like Chesty Puller, the men in the field found the Thompson submachine gun necessary and indispensable, even if the bureaucrats in Washington had trouble deciding whether it was a rifle or a light machine gun.

Nicaragua had made believers out of the marines, and in 1928, the Navy Department, the parent organization of the Marine Corps, officially adopted the Thompson submachine gun—not only for marines, but for use aboard naval vessels. Apparently, the navy had been a bit embarrassed by having to borrow "necessary" weapons from the Post Office Department.

Augusto Nicolás Calderón Sandino's "Manifesto of Light and Truth" holy war against his old friends who now ran Nicaragua, and against the marines, would eventually provide the renaissance that revived the Thompson submachine gun.

World War I had inspired John Taliaferro Thompson's invention, and changing needs now required the reinvention and rebirth of a "new" Thompson submachine gun, the Model of 1928 (M1928). Those delivered under the U.S. Navy contract would be known as the M1928 Navy.

The Model of 1928 was not a new gun as the M1921 had been. As Auto-Ordnance launched the M1928 as a product line, it did not start a new M1928 submachine gun *production* line to manufacture all-new weapons, but assembled them from existing stocks of unsold M1921s and M1921 parts, adding and replacing certain parts and design features.

The M1928 incorporated several important changes that would remain a part of the basic Thompson submachine gun design in later models as well. The easiest change requested by the navy was to replace the pistol-style foregrip with a simpler grip that was parallel to the barrel.

Meanwhile, the navy had decided that the rate of fire in the M1921 had been unnecessarily high. Emptying a fifty-round magazine in four seconds on full-auto was considered to be a bit much. So, too, was the need to frequently change out the magazines in combat.

To address the rate of fire issue, General Thompson personally phoned Oscar Payne, who was now working for Reed & Prince. Thompson explained that there was, at last, the potential for the long-awaited serious military order for Thompson submachine guns. Could Payne help?

The former Auto-Ordnance man agreed to spend his spare time on the issue, and he did, although it took him most of 1927 to come up with what turned out to be a very straightforward solution. Payne eventually discovered that by increasing the weight of the weapon's actuator, the rate of fire could be slowed down to around six hundred rounds per minute, around two-thirds that of the stock M1921.

Design engineer Doug Richardson is quite outspoken in his assertion that the changes embodied in slowing down the rate of fire were unnecessary compromises that led to an inferior weapon.

"There is no engineering justification for the M1928," he told me emphatically. "Auto-Ordnance had a lot of trouble trying to make it work; it had more troubles than it was worth. It was less reliable than an M1921. It was less accurate than an M1921. . . . but the army wanted something that was *slower*! It was always '*slower*' [with military ordnance acquisition bureaucrats] until they ran into the German Schmeissers during World War II. All of a sudden, [they started saying] 'maybe *slow* is not that great.'"

Another engineering alteration incorporated into the M1928 was a simple device designed to eliminate muzzle climb. As with the Blish lock of 1915, this apparatus was invented by an active-duty military officer in his spare time. Actually, it was the brainchild of two men, father and son Marine Corps officers, both named Richard Cutts. Essentially, their invention was a slotted tube that attached to the tip of the barrel. The slots permitted part of the energy of the muzzle blast to be expended upward, counteracting the recoil effect.

The Cutts compensator, as it was called, was first proposed by Colonel Cutts and his son for use on the Browning Automatic Rifle. However, it proved impractical with the high-velocity .30-'06 rounds used in the BAR, and the invention was put on the shelf for several years. Rediscovered by Auto-Ordnance as the M1928 was under development, the Cutts compensator was incorporated into the M1928.

As with the Blish lock, there are those who will tell you that the Cutts compensator was a useful component and detractors who will insist that it was an unnecessary frill. Indeed, it was later abandoned for World War II

The top-slotted Cutts compensator was added to the muzzle of the M1928
Thompson submachine gun to reduce muzzle climb by expelling gas upward each
time a round was fired. *(Collection of the author)*

production guns. In any case, the Cutts compensator gives the M1928 a distinctive appearance that has often been described as "cool."

Meanwhile, as the weapon that became the M1928 was under development, Auto-Ordnance was working on a parallel development of a gun that would be designated as the Model of 1927 (M1927). To address the befuddled bureaucrats in the U.S. Army who remained confused about whether the Thompson submachine gun was a rifle or a light machine gun, Auto-Ordnance proposed what was officially described as the "Thompson Semi-Automatic Carbine."

Like the M1928, the M1927 was not a new production gun, but a retrofit of the stock M1921 in which specific parts were changed out, making it semiautomatic, and therefore redefining it as a carbine. Again, as with the M1921 six years earlier, the M1927 failed to win the hearts or minds of General Thompson's successors at the Ordnance Department, although a few M1927s were sold to police departments that were leery of the idea of unleashing fully automatic weapons on city streets.

The M1927 carbine is not to be confused with the distinctly different Thompson Autorifle. Though it was temporarily shoved aside as Auto-Ordnance focused its attention on the Persuader and Annihilator, the Autorifle was not abandoned. During the 1920s, later versions of the Autorifle received a positive reaction from both the U.S. Army and, with a .303 caliber barrel, from the British army as well.

As reported in the May 14, 1928, issue of *Time,* "the self-loading infantry rifle perfected by General Thompson was last week awarded the British War Office prize of $15,000 and will now be tried generally throughout the British Army. A rifle for each soldier to carry, to fire aimed shots from the shoulder without pausing to reload, the Thompson self-loader differs from a machine gun in that the trigger is pulled for each shot instead of held down for a continuous stream of lead. Rid of the necessity for bolting a new cartridge into the firing chamber between shots, as in hand-loading rifles, a soldier can aim 25 or 30 shots per minute with the Thompson self-loader."

After all that, however, neither the British War Office nor America's War Department adopted the Thompson Semi-Automatic Carbine and it went back on the shelf. Later, when the British acquired the M1928 during the early days of World War II, their field manual for the submachine gun referred to it as a carbine.

At least two semiautomatic M1927s were later converted to full auto by Auto-Ordnance itself. The New Mexico State Prison acquired a number of M1927s, of which two were returned to the factory to be reconfigured to full automatic as "M1921/M1927/M1928" guns. Chuck Olsen, a collector in Arizona, owns both and has shown me one of them. The gun came to Chuck by way of a dealer who got it from the estate of actor Steve McQueen. A videotape of McQueen firing the gun is said to exist.

During the early days of World War II, as Auto-Ordnance ran through stocks of M1921 parts from which to make M1928s, the Thompson submachine-gun assembly line finally would reopen. Initially, the newly manufactured submachine guns would be the same as the retrofitted M1921s that became M1928s. With minor modifications they would be designated M1928A1, with the suffix standing for "Alteration One."

Like the M1921, the M1928 Navy had been designed to accept the fifty- or hundred-round drum magazine, but the marines found the larger magazines cumbersome to carry and prone to jamming. The smaller, narrower twenty-round box magazines would become standard equipment for the M1928A1, although this weapon could also accommodate a drum magazine.

Aside from the U.S. Navy and Marine Corps contract, sales of the M1928 were sluggish. As firearms advisor Idan Greenberg points out, "This was a gun that sold in the early 1920s for $175. By the 1930s with a Cutts compensator added and a little heavier bolt and actuator, the M1928 was $225. You could buy a brand-new Ford for $440, so Thompsons didn't sell very well."

Meanwhile, Auto-Ordnance was also developing the little known M1929. Marcellus and the general reapproached their old friends in Belgium, this time with more apparent success than in 1921. They negotiated a license agreement whereby Belgium would manufacture thousands of tommy guns at their government-owned arms factory, Fabrique Nationale d'Armes de Guerre. The actual engineering for these guns was done by George Norman at Birmingham Small Arms (BSA) in England, which prototyped them in several calibers, including .45 ACP, 7.65mm, and 9mm. Designated as M1929, the gun had no Cutts compensator, but had a longer barrel and an overall length several inches greater than an M1928.

The Great Depression, however, crippled the global economy after 1929, and the order from the Belgians was canceled after just a handful of prototypes was made. Thus the tommy guns that the Belgian general staff felt might have saved their country from the Germans in 1914 were also *not* on hand when the Germans came knocking again in 1940.

CHAPTER 11

Public Enemies

In the United States, even before Prohibition was repealed by the Twenty-first Amendment in 1933, the power and influence of the Chicago mobsters had begun to wane. With bootlegging no longer profitable, the gangsters turned to vying for control of less ubiquitous vices, such as gambling and prostitution.

Al Capone went to jail in 1931 for income tax evasion, and the great boss of bosses spent the next eight years in prison, most of it at the federal pen at Alcatraz. He left jail a broken man, crippled by the effects of syphilis and dementia. In Chicago, Capone's operation was taken over by men such as Tony "Big Tuna" Accardo and Francesco Nitto, a.k.a. Frank Nitti. They in turn muscled into Bugs Moran's turf as his influence faded on the North Side.

It is an often-cited irony that of all the crimes committed by Al Capone—from bootlegging to kidnapping to extortion to murder, murder, murder, and more murder—the transgression that became his undoing was income tax evasion. After befriending and befuddling state and local law enforcement, Capone went down on federal charges. Organized crime and its bosses did not meet their match until *federal* law enforcement agencies began to get involved. Such agencies included the Bureau of Prohibition within the Treasury Department and the Bureau of Investigation within the Justice Department. If the gangsters ruled the Roaring Twenties, the following decade would be marked by the ascendancy of the G-men, the federal government crime busters.

One cannot look at the colorful criminals of the era without a nod to the corresponding lawmen. Of these, the best remembered within the annals of popular culture was a Treasury Department agent named Eliot Ness. A fan of Sherlock Holmes stories, Ness became a private security agent but joined the Bureau of Prohibition in 1927, where he was assigned to Chicago with the mandate to make a dent in the illicit booze trade. Corruption in law enforcement during Prohibition was widespread, and Ness was determined to form a squad that would not be lured by the sweet promise of bribery and payoffs. He put together a team of agents whom he felt were immune to criminal temptation.

Known as the "Untouchables" because they could not be bribed, Ness's team eventually assembled the evidence that was the ultimate undoing of Capone and many others.

If the end of Capone's career was an end of an era, a new era was beginning.

At least so far as the tabloid pop culture image was concerned, the suave, expensively dressed Chicago gangsters of the 1920s gave way in the 1930s to the desperate, often sociopathic criminals who emerged against the backdrop of the Great Depression. This economic downturn, the worst to strike the world in the twentieth century, began with the crash of the New York Stock Market in October 1929, only eight months after the St. Valentine's Day Massacre.

Bootlegging was replaced by bank robbery as the signature crime of the day. Among the facets of the Depression found especially abhorrent by the people of the United States were bank foreclosures. Many people, especially in poorer parts of the country, saw their neighbors losing their homes to what were perceived as greedy bankers. In turn, this led to a view in popular culture of bank robbers being almost like Robin Hood characters—never mind that they were stealing the depositors' money, not necessarily the bank's. Also omitted when casting these characters as heroes were the kidnappings and murders that punctuated their bank-robbing sprees.

From a sensationalist media perspective, though, the outlaws of the 1930s were just as colorful as the outlaws of the 1920s, although they were decidedly different sorts of people. The crime bosses of the 1920s had elaborate organizations, they dressed impeccably, and they lived a lavish lifestyle. Their crimes were generally well planned and well executed, and most, like Capone, covered their tracks so well that they were able to live their lives in plain sight. Like Ness's own squad, they were seemingly untouchable.

On the other hand, the iconic outlaws of the 1930s had more in common with their counterparts of the Old West. In nineteenth-century America, the dime-novel-buying public thrilled and swooned to tales of outlaws such as Jesse James and Billy the Kid. Like the romantic heros of the Old West, the criminals favored by the media of the 1930s traveled light and traveled widely. They lived from robbery to robbery and spent their time running from one hiding place to another.

Two things that the outlaws of the 1930s did have in common with their Roaring Twenties counterparts were that they excited the morbid fascination of the tabloid media and its readers, and they had a fascination of their own with the Thompson submachine gun.

As with men such as Al Capone and Bugs Moran, the names of the 1930s bad guys became and remain notorious. Names such as John Dillinger and Charles Arthur "Pretty Boy" Floyd are well known. While nobody may remember Lester Gillis, many of us recognize his nom de crime, "Baby Face Nelson."

Arizona Donnie Clark had four sons with petty criminal George Barker, and became "Ma" Barker. She is best remembered as the mother who turned her boys—and her "adopted" son Alvin "Creepy" Karpis—into thugs. Their 1931–1935 spree of armed robberies and cop killings is an ugly but indelible part of the history of the times, and of many decades of Hollywood treatments.

Though all of these criminals from this period will live on in the corners of pop mythology, the names of Bonnie Parker and Clyde Barrow are immortal, thanks to Hollywood director Arthur Penn. His 1967 film starring Faye Dunaway and Warren Beatty in the title roles still resides at number 27 on the American Film Institute's ranking of the top 100 movies of all time.

If the media could be held responsible for molding and perpetuating the myths of the tommy gun–toting thugs of the 1930s, it was certainly aided and abetted in this caper by the Bureau of Investigation. This agency, which became the Federal Bureau of Investigation (FBI) in 1935, provided not only an energetic foil for the criminals, but a classification system that gave the malefactors an official acknowledgment that added to their mystique. What self-respecting malcontent did not thrill to the notion of being labeled a "public enemy" by the federal government?

The term "public enemy" probably originated with Frank Loesch of the Chicago Crime Commission, who used it in 1930 to condemn crime bosses such as Moran and Capone, as well as enforcers such as Jack McGurn. As Laurence Bergreen quotes Loesch in his book *Capone: The Man and the Era*, the list of public enemies included "the outstanding hoodlums, known murderers, murderers which you and I know but can't prove. . . . I put Al Capone at the head and his brother next. . . . The purpose is to keep the publicity light shining on Chicago's most prominent, well known and notorious gangsters to the end that they may be under constant observation by the law enforcing authorities and law abiding citizens."

Placing Capone at the head of the list gave him the distinction of being

FBI special agents open fire at their targets using tracers in this dramatic nighttime demonstration at the bureau's range near Quantico, Virginia, circa 1935.
(Courtesy of the National Archives)

Public Enemy Number One, a term which itself became part of the pop culture lexicon.

The idea of a public enemy list was so appealing that it was "borrowed" by J. Edgar Hoover, the Bureau of Investigation's hard-boiled director, who, like Eliot Ness, was cultivating his self-image as that of a single-minded crimestopper.

The appellation of Public Enemy served both sides. It gave the criminals an irrefutable cachet, and it also gave the FBI—and Hoover personally—a public relations nudge when these criminals were finally apprehended. Unlike the perpetrators of the well-planned St. Valentine's Day Massacre, the Public Enemies on the FBI's list usually *were* apprehended—either dead or alive.

The men brandishing the Thompson submachine guns in the St. Valentine's Day Massacre were not then, nor will they ever be, identified with certainty. Four years later, the perps responsible for what has come to be known as the Kansas City Massacre were known immediately. That was part of the difference between the calculating gangsters of the 1920s and the brazen bandits of the post-Prohibition era.

Though faded from the popular memory of a bygone age, the events in Kansas City on the morning of June 17, 1933, caught the attention of the public—and curdled their blood.

Frank Nash was going back to prison. That was how it all started.

Nash had been on the lam since October 1930, having broken out of the federal penitentiary at Leavenworth, Kansas, where he had done six years of a twenty-five-year sentence for assault. The Bureau of Investigation had ended his nearly three years of freedom in Hot Springs, Arkansas, and they were transporting him back to Leavenworth via Kansas City.

The agents saw nothing amiss when they took him off the train in Kansas City—then they saw the not-so-pretty face of Pretty Boy Floyd.

Floyd's career as a criminal began when he was barely out of his teens, and when he was twenty-one, he went away for four years in the Missouri State Penitentiary for highway robbery. In May 1930, just over a year after he got out of prison in Missouri, he was in trouble again, this time sentenced to twelve to fifteen years in the Ohio State Penitentiary for robbing a bank in Toledo. However, he escaped in November 1930 and joined with Adam Richetti, then wanted for jumping bail on a robbery charge.

In June 1933, Missouri mobsters Richard Tallman Galatas, Herbert Farmer, Frank Mulloy, and Louis "Doc" Stacci asked Vernon Miller to free fellow gangster Frank Nash from the feds in Kansas City. Miller decided to import Floyd and Richetti to help him. They agreed, but they almost never made it to Kansas City.

On June 16, as Floyd and Richetti were passing through Bolivar, Missouri, they had car trouble. As they were getting their car fixed, Sheriff Jack Killingsworth passed by. Richetti recognized him from an earlier run-in and decided that the best thing to do was to kidnap the lawman at gunpoint. Brandishing one of the Thompson submachine guns they planned to use in the Kansas City caper the next day, they loaded the sheriff into a stolen car and drove off. Two stolen cars later, Killingsworth was abandoned, amazingly unharmed, in the middle of nowhere.

The two thugs were in Kansas City before midnight, listening to Miller outline his scheme.

The next day, seven armed men, police and federal agents, escorted Frank Nash off the train and through Union Station to a waiting Chevrolet. Nash and three officers were in the car when Floyd and Richetti appeared from behind a green Plymouth and opened fire with their Thompson submachine guns from a distance of about fifteen feet.

Four of the lawmen died, and two were badly wounded.

Frank Nash, the object of the escape attempt, was hit in the hail of .45 ACP rounds and died at the scene.

The bullet holes are still there, visible at eye level to the left of the eastern main entrance to Union Station—if you know where to look. If you don't, just ask at the information desk inside. As I discovered on my own visit, the volunteers there will be glad to show you.

Floyd, Richetti, and Miller escaped, but when the Bureau of Investigation began gathering fingerprints, their anonymity was lost.

The feds never got Miller. Sometime earlier, he had crossed Longie Zwillman, the boss of the New Jersey mob. As Miller was running from the Bureau, he should have been watching his back for Zwillman. Miller's dismembered carcass was found alongside a road near Detroit five months after the Kansas City Massacre.

Adam Richetti and Pretty Boy Floyd would remain at large for more than a year before being nabbed.

Meanwhile, just as the 1920s had an enforcer in the form of Machine Gun Jack McGurn, who took his weapon as a nickname, the 1930s folklore includes George "Machine Gun Kelly" Barnes. Born in Chicago, he did federal time in Leavenworth Penitentiary for his bootlegging activities on an Indian reservation in Oklahoma. Released in 1928, he changed his surname to Kelly and married a woman named Kathryn Thorne.

In retrospect, she should have earned the nickname, rather than bestowing it upon her husband. Although the folklore does not, we should call her "Machine Gun Kate," because, as it is stated officially by the FBI, "she encouraged Kelly to become deeply involved in a life of crime, bought him a machine gun, and gave him the nickname."

Despite the colorful nickname, George and Kathryn earned their bread and butter mainly from petty crimes and illicit booze. While they did the occasional bank job, George had not actually killed anyone with his tommy gun. They probably would have been just one more pair of Depression-era bandits had Kathryn not had the brainstorm that they should kidnap two prominent Oklahoma City businessmen, Charles Urschel and Walter Jarrett, on July 22, 1933.

Jarrett was released the following day, but Urschel was well known as a millionaire, so the Kellys issued a ransom demand for him. The ransom was

Drive-by shooting, 1930s style. An FBI special agent practices firing his Thompson
submachine gun from a moving vehicle at the FBI range near Quantico, Virginia.
In Chicago, they had been firing tommy guns from cars since the 1920s.
(Courtesy of the FBI)

paid and Urschel was released after nine days. His recollections of the place
where he had been held led Bureau of Investigations agents to the Kellys,
who were arrested in Memphis on September 26.

If J. Edgar Hoover can be accurately credited for popularizing—if not
inventing—the term "public enemy" for referring to villains, George Kelly
added a now-immortal term for government agents to the lexicon of popular
culture. When surrounded by Bureau of Investigation men on his last day as
a free man, Kelly is reported to have shouted "Don't shoot, G-men!"

From this plea, the term "G-men" became synonymous with federal law
enforcement agents, although the FBI now disavows the "Don't shoot, G-men!"
story, which Hoover's public relations department used to build up its reputation at the time.

Two years later, the term would be adapted as the title of the blockbuster
film starring Jimmy Cagney as a "G-man" on the trail of a "Public Enemy
Number One," played by Edward Pawley.

Meanwhile, George Kelly was getting his justice. Charles Urschel's prominence and Kelly's unfortunate nickname combined to make the subsequent trial a major media event. Machine Gun Kelly and Machine Gun Kate were both sentenced to life in prison and sent away without having ever had the opportunity to explore the deadly potential of their namesake. Kelly died in prison in 1954, and Kate was released four years later.

If George and Kate did hard time for the unfulfilled potential of an ill-considered nickname, another couple would pay the ultimate price for living such potential to the fullest. Chicago crime writer Joseph Geringer described Bonnie Parker and Clyde Barrow as "Romeo and Juliet in a Getaway Car," which explained their particular media appeal.

The promo line from Arthur Penn's 1967 biopic said simply, "They're Young . . . They're in Love . . . and They Kill People!"

That just about says it all.

When the young Texans met one another in January 1930, Clyde was twenty and Bonnie was nineteen. Her husband of three years was then in prison for burglary, and she fell for Clyde. He was a safecracker and petty criminal who had done time in the Texas prison system, against which he harbored a deep and lifelong grudge. Bonnie, meanwhile, had been a well-liked honor roll student.

For Clyde, their meeting was probably love—or at least lust—at first sight. For Bonnie, it was the beginning of a deep obsession with this dark stranger, at whose side she stayed most of her remaining short life.

Clyde's first capital crime, murdering a deputy sheriff who tried to hassle him for being drunk and disorderly, came in August 1932 in Oklahoma while Bonnie was visiting her mother. By the time his crime spree was over, Clyde would be connected to ten homicides, while Bonnie is, for all her aiding and abetting, not believed to have killed anyone.

The famous crime spree of Bonnie and Clyde got under way around the time that Clyde's brother, Marvin "Buck" Barrow, was released from prison in Texas in March 1933. Together with Buck's wife, Blanche, and William D. "Deacon" Jones, they formed what came to be called the Barrow Gang. For the next four months, until Buck was fatally wounded near Dexter, Iowa, on July 24, the gang committed a string of robberies and killings across several states.

In the 1967 film about the notorious "Romeo and Juliet in a Getaway Car," as well as in the publicity stills for that movie, both Faye Dunaway and Warren Beatty are seen brandishing Thompson submachine guns. However, Clyde Barrow favored not the Thompson, but the BAR. He stole several from the National Guard Armory in Beaumont, Texas. Photographs that Bonnie took of Clyde show him posing with as many as three, including one on which he shortened the stock and the barrel in order to use it as a concealed weapon.

Clyde famously used a BAR in the July 18, 1933, shoot-out at the Red Crown Tourist Court near Kansas City, Missouri, in which the Barrow Gang was nearly captured. They had been tracked to the motel by Sheriff Holt Coffey, who attacked late that night. The sheriff and highway patrol reinforcements opened fire at a distance, firing Thompsons beyond their effective range. The Barrow Gang returned fire using the BAR's superior range capability and managed to escape.

After Buck's death a short time later, Bonnie and Clyde continued their reign of robberies through Texas and the Midwest, earning them numerous headlines, and the coveted public enemy title. They cleverly crisscrossed multiple states, exploiting the inability of the authorities from the various jurisdictions to cross state lines.

Clyde's insistence on raiding the Texas prison farm at Eastham in January 1934 brought the wrath of the embarrassed Texas Department of Corrections down upon the colorful pair. For a time, Bonnie and Clyde were seen by the mass media as colorful Robin Hood characters. However, the murders of three police officers in Oklahoma and Texas during the first week of April began to turn public opinion against them.

Every tale of villains deserves a corresponding good guy, and that lawman was retired Texas Ranger Captain Frank Hamer, a twenty-seven-year veteran. As described in a June 4, 1934, article in *Time* magazine, Frank Hamer stood over six feet tall, wore "a big black hat and his trousers outside his boot tops, speaks little and that little in a slow, courteous drawl. In Texas his marksmanship and speed on the draw are famed. His favorite revolver he calls 'Betty' and some 60 badmen have died at his hand."

Why had Hammer left the Rangers?

"When they elected a woman governor for the second time," he explained in the *Time* report, "I quit." The woman in question was Miriam Amanda "Ma" Ferguson, who served two non-consecutive terms in 1925–1927 and 1933–1935.

For three months, Hamer tracked Bonnie and Clyde, finally picking up their trail as they passed through Shreveport, Louisiana. At that time, Hamer's posse included both Texas Rangers and Louisiana lawmen, notably Bienville Parish Sheriff Henderson Jordan and his deputy. On May 23, 1934, Bonnie and Clyde were driving in a stolen Ford sedan along Highway 154, a country road in Bienville Parish, when bullets began to fly.

Without warning, Hamer and the others unleashed a fusillade of small-arms fire from a variety of weapons, including Thompson submachine guns and BARs supplied by the federal government. Well over 150 rounds were fired into the four-door Ford.

There are varying accounts as to whether Bonnie and Clyde were each hit fifty times, or whether the pair was hit with a total of fifty rounds. In any case, neither survived. Bonnie was said to have been screaming for several moments during the shooting, indicating that she did not die instantly.

As reported in the June 4 issue of *Time*, "Barrow was found with the door of the car half-open and a sawed-off shotgun in his hand. Bonnie Parker, wearing a red dress, was doubled up with a submachine gun in her lap. There were two other machine guns, another sawed-off automatic shotgun, six automatic pistols, a revolver, a saxophone, sheet music, a half-eaten sandwich, a bloody package of cigarets, and $507 in cash in the car."

The submachine guns mentioned were actually Clyde's three Browning Automatic Rifles.

Reported in *Time* in 1934, and repeated in a 1959 interview with the *Austin American*, Hamer justified his decision to open fire on Bonnie Parker without warning, and to continue shooting until she stopped screaming, by saying that "I hated to bust a cap on a woman, especially when she was sitting down, but it was her or us."

While Clyde Barrow used a Thompson submachine gun only in the movies, the equally notorious John Herbert Dillinger wielded a tommy gun for real—and effectively. From September 1933 until July 1934 he and his violent gang terrorized the Midwest, robbing banks and police arsenals, and staging three jail breaks, while killing ten people and wounding seven others. During those months, which coincided with the Barrow Gang's heyday, John Dillinger also lived on the front pages of the nation's media, frightening, titillating, and selling papers.

A cruel sociopath despite what some perceive as dashing good looks, Dillinger was just a kid when he started his life on the dark side as a petty criminal in Indianapolis. It continued when the family moved to a farm near Mooresville, Indiana. As often happens in such cases, John reacted no better to rural life than he had to that which he experienced in the city. After a stint in the U.S. Navy, Dillinger joined forces with a small-time hood and pool hustler named Ed Singleton. The dream now was for fast, easy money, the Holy Grail of all small-time hoods.

The chief difference between small-time hoods and successful criminals is the knowledge born of experience that fast money is almost never easy and that easy money rarely comes fast. Usually money comes neither fast nor easy. In September 1924, the Singleton-Dillinger gang chose, as their first "job," a grocery store holdup in Mooresville. The robbery went down with a small take and a pistol-whipped grocer. Dillinger and Singleton were quickly apprehended.

The erratic and violent Dillinger became a tortured, deeply bitter man in prison. After a mere eight and one half years of his twenty-year sentence, he was paroled on May 10, 1933. Many things had happened while he was in the Indiana State Prison. The prosperity of the 1920s had been replaced by the darkest years of the Great Depression. If John Dillinger was unemployable in 1924, he was hopeless in 1933.

Dillinger knocked over a bank in Bluffton, Ohio, within weeks of walking free of prison. As had happened eight and a half years earlier, he did not have long to enjoy his loot. Busted by the police in Dayton, Ohio, on September 22, he was thrown into the county jail in Lima to await trial. On October 12, several of Dillinger's friends—including three who had just broken out of the Indiana State Prison—freed him from the Lima lockup, leaving the sheriff to die in a pool of blood.

Dillinger and his gang promptly pulled several successful bank robberies. They also plundered the police arsenals at Auburn, Indiana, and Peru, Indiana, stealing several Thompson submachine guns, as well as a number of rifles and revolvers, a quantity of ammunition, and several bulletproof vests.

The five gangsters on the run were now a small, well-equipped army. They had withering firepower, and several new men joined to become part of the action. Through the winter they ranged from Chicago to Florida, robbing banks, spraying .45-caliber ACP rounds, and killing cops. Like Bonnie and Clyde, they exploited their ability to elude authorities by crossing state lines. Also like Bonnie and Clyde, they attracted a cult following as the media followed their progress. The media reported each installment in their crime waves as though they were the games in a grisly world series or installments of a radio soap opera.

It was in Tucson in January 1934 that the crime spree might have ended. Dillinger and three gang members were recognized from newspaper photos, arrested, and relieved of their arsenal of tommy guns. Dillinger was extradited and sequestered at the "escape proof" county jail in Crown Point, Indiana, to await trial for the murder of an East Chicago police officer. On March 3, Dillinger cowed the guards with what he claimed later was a wooden gun he had whittled, forced them to open the door to his cell, grabbed two Thompsons, locked up the guards, and fled.

It was then that Dillinger made the mistake that would cost him his life. He stole the sheriff's car and drove across the Indiana–Illinois state line, heading for Chicago. By doing that, he violated the National Motor Vehicle Theft Act, which made it a federal offense to transport a stolen motor vehicle across a state line. Dillinger had, in a phrase of the vernacular that is still with us, "made it a *federal* case."

This brought J. Edgar Hoover's Bureau of Investigation into the picture. A complaint was sworn charging Dillinger with the theft and interstate transportation of the sheriff's car, which was recovered in Chicago. After the grand jury returned an indictment, the Bureau became actively involved in the nationwide search for Dillinger.

Nothing would have pleased Hoover more than to nab such a high-profile bad guy. John Dillinger had just become J. Edgar Hoover's new best friend.

In Chicago, Dillinger joined his girlfriend, Evelyn "Billie" Frechette, and they moved to St. Paul, Minnesota. It was here that Dillinger would team up with Homer Van Meter, Eddie Green, Tommy Carroll, and the notorious, tommy gun–brandishing psychopath, Lester "Baby Face Nelson" Gillis. This new edition of the Dillinger Gang was even more violent than the previous year's version, and their seemingly endless bank robberies were netting them trunkloads of cash.

By now the newspapers were following the story with rabid enthusiasm. The parallel crime sprees of Bonnie and Clyde and John Dillinger were exactly the kind of thing that captivated the public, however lurid and however dangerous it was for the people in the upper Midwest.

J. Edgar Hoover even joined in the media frenzy by naming Dillinger "Public Enemy Number One," the first man to hold that exalted title since Frank Loesch placed Al Capone atop his own enemies list. The stunt sold papers, but it also put the Bureau of Investigation on the front page of those papers, which is exactly where Hoover wanted it. Of course, what the Bureau of Investigation now had to do was to actually *catch* the Dillinger Gang.

On March 31, acting on a tip and their own subsequent surveillance, Bureau of Investigation agents and local police caught up with John and Billie at the Lincoln Court Apartments in St. Paul, Minnesota, where they had registered as "Mr. and Mrs. Hellman." The police recognized Homer Van Meter outside the apartment, but as they approached, he opened fire and got away.

Suddenly, the door of the "Hellman" apartment opened and the muzzle of a Thompson submachine gun began spraying the hallway with .45 caliber lead. Under cover of the machine-gun fire, Dillinger and his girlfriend fled through a back door. At the apartment, the Bureau found a Thompson with the stock removed for easier concealment, several other guns, and plenty of ammunition.

Dillinger and Frechette split up, with him going to Mooresville, Indiana, where his father lived, while Billie made the mistake that may have saved her life. She went to Chicago to visit a friend—and was arrested by the Bureau of Investigation. She was taken to St. Paul for trial on a charge of conspiracy to harbor a fugitive. Meanwhile, Dillinger and Van Meter had robbed a police station at Warsaw, Indiana, of guns and bulletproof vests and eluded the police as they lay low on the Upper Peninsula of Michigan, and later northern Wisconsin.

In April 1934, John Dillinger, Baby Face Nelson, and the gang checked into the Little Bohemia Lodge, about fifty miles north of Rhinelander, Wisconsin. Here they were recognized and reported to the Bureau. Late on the cold afternoon of April 22, a Bureau of Investigation task force set out from Rhinelander in rental cars. They surrounded the Little Bohemia, but Dillinger and the others spotted them and opened fire.

Under the withering fire of the bad guys' Thompson submachine guns, the G-men could do little but try to keep their heads down. Before the gangsters made good their escape, however, Dillinger reportedly buried $200,000 in several suitcases in the thick woods behind the Little Bohemia. The loot was never found, but it has provided countless hours of theorizing and treasure hunting, not to mention numerous television documentaries, in the decades since.

Acting on a tip, Bureau of Investigation agents Sam Cowley and Melvin Purvis—special agent in charge of the Chicago office—tracked Dillinger to a whorehouse in Gary, Indiana. Here they spoke with a Romanian lady of the night named Ana Cumpanas, who called herself Anna Sage. The federal agents exploited her fear of deportation as an undesirable alien and got her to tell them that she and another woman would be attending the movies at one of two theaters in Chicago the following evening—with John Dillinger.

On Sunday, July 22, G-men surrounded both Chicago theaters. At 8:30 P.M., Purvis watched Anna Sage and Polly Hamilton stroll into the Biograph Theater with John Dillinger. Two hours later, as Dillinger and his two female companions walked out of the theater, the feds closed in. Dillinger quickly realized what was happening, grabbed a pistol from his right trouser pocket, and ran toward the alley. Five shots were fired from the guns of three Bureau of Investigation agents.

None of them ever admitted who had actually killed Dillinger.

After Dillinger's demise, Baby Face Nelson remained on the loose, but only for four months. Having replaced Dillinger as J. Edgar Hoover's Public Enemy Number One, he continued robbing banks at a rapid pace until Bureau agents finally caught up to him on November 27, 1934, near Lake Geneva, Wisconsin, about sixty miles northwest of Chicago. He fled, but the news that he was headed for Chicago was phoned ahead to Sam Cowley, who immediately sent Agents Bill Ryan and Tom McDade to intercept Nelson. Cowley, along with Agent Herman "Ed" Hollis, followed in a second car.

Near Barrington, Illinois, first Ryan and McDade, then Cowley and Hollis, overtook Nelson, his wife, and their fellow gangsters. A running gun battle sputtered to a standoff when the radiator of Nelson's car was punctured. Next, Nelson forced Cowley and Hollis to abandon their bullet-riddled sedan.

With tommy guns on both sides, it was a shootout straight from the movies. Dodging Bureau lead, Nelson attacked, killing Hollis and fatally wounding Cowley.

Escaping in the damaged Bureau car, Nelson and his gang headed south. Badly injured himself, however, Nelson was dead before the car reached Chicago.

Meanwhile, Pretty Boy Floyd and Adam Richetti had hid out in Toledo for a few months after the Kansas City Massacre, but later relocated to Buffalo, New York. Here they lived for a year with their girlfriends, the Baird sisters, Bulah (who went by the name Juanita) and Rose. In October 1934, the foursome decided to make a move to Oklahoma, and had made it as far as Wellsville, Ohio, when Floyd drove the car off the road, wrapping it around a telephone pole. While Rose and Juanita took the car into town to be repaired, the men hung out in the woods, looking suspicious to any passers-by who happened to take a second look.

Alerted to a pair of strangers in the woods, the Wellsville sheriff went to investigate. Floyd and Richetti opened fire, but the police got the best of them. Richetti was captured with an empty gun. A wounded Pretty Boy found himself on the run without a car and low on ammunition.

The Bureau of Investigation's Melvin Purvis, who had helped bring down John Dillinger, now went after Floyd. Two days later, Purvis, with police backup, located their quarry, hiding on an Ohio farm with a stolen car. Though he was still armed, the fugitive gave up after exchanging fire, telling Purvis, "I'm done for; you've hit me twice."

He was right. He died of his gunshot wounds later the same day.

Less than three months later, Ma Barker and her son Fred were killed in Florida during a four-hour gun battle with the G-men. Fred was every bit the criminal—in addition to his numerous bank jobs and other mayhem, he had once murdered a police chief and a sheriff in the space of just six weeks—but it was another case for poor Ma Barker. She was more of a willing accomplice than the criminal mastermind that Hollywood would make her out to be. After the shootout, she was found to be clutching a Thompson, but some skeptics have suggested that the federal agents posed her with the gun to validate their having gunned her down. Ma's son Arthur "Doc" Barker was arrested the same month that his mother was killed, but he died in 1939 while trying to escape from Alcatraz. Creepy Karpis was captured by Bureau agents in May 1936, the last member of the notorious Barker-Karpis Gang still at large, and the last man whom J. Edgar Hoover named as "Public Enemy Number One."

Karpis spent twenty-five years at Alcatraz before being transferred to the McNeil Island Penitentiary. It was here that he befriended a young inmate—born in 1934, the heyday of the Public Enemy crime sprees—named Charles Manson. Again, the word "creepy" comes to mind, but that, as they say, is another story.

The enduring pop culture image of the public enemies of the 1930s, while not always precise in the details, is more or less accurate. They all did live fast, most died young, and they nearly all carried tommy guns—or died with .45 ACP rounds in them.

PART THREE

Wheelers and Dealers

CHAPTER 12

Deaths in the Family

General John Taliaferro Thompson turned sixty-nine on the last day of 1929. The decade had begun with immense excitement and promise for the invention for which he was mostly—albeit not exclusively—responsible. It ended with Tom Ryan's death and with Thompson's losing control of "his" company just as the advent of the M1928 had brought the best sales figures in company history.

If it hadn't been for Thomas Fortune Ryan, Thompson's brainchild would have been just one more unremembered and unfulfilled promise buried in the drifting sands of time. If it hadn't been for Ryan, Auto-Ordnance never would have made it from the disappointment of 1921 to the revival of orders that came with the renaissance embodied in the M1928. As *Time* magazine summarized it in the June 26, 1939, issue, "Between 1921 and 1928 Auto-Ordnance, doing a small, tidy business, sold more than 6,000 Thompsons for a gross of $1,330,000."

Ryan was generous with Thompson. Being among the top ten richest men in America, he could afford to be. His personal art collection contained a Donatello and several Rodins. What made the latter especially significant is that Auguste Rodin himself sculpted Ryan's likeness three times.

Though Ryan had officially retired in 1912, he continued to dabble in those investments that interested him. He allowed Auto-Ordnance to operate out of his Manhattan offices for years, and kept the checks coming, although he seems to have had little hands-on involvement with the company and its products.

Eventually, Ryan began spending less time at his palatial Manhattan town house and settled in at Oak Ridge, his country place in Virginia, with its private golf course. His wife, Ida Mary Barry Ryan, preferred the other family estate in upstate New York, so he occasionally brought his widowed friend, Mary Townsend Lord Cuyler, down to Oak Ridge to keep him company. On

October 29, 1917, twelve days after Ida passed away, Ryan and Mary were married.

According to Edwin Slipek Jr., writing in the January 19, 2005, issue of *Style*, Ryan's son, Allan, called the marriage "the most disrespectful, indecent thing I have ever heard of."

When Thomas Fortune Ryan died at the Manhattan town house on November 23, 1928, he left an estate worth a billion and a half in today's dollars. Mary was well compensated, of course, as were most of Tom Ryan's progeny, but Allan received only a set of pearl shirt studs.

Within his vast fortune lay Ryan's share of the Auto-Ordnance Corporation—into which he had invested more than $15 million in today's dollars. As viewed by the Ryan family, the estate's share in the company was tainted goods, tainted by the image of the Auto-Ordnance tommy gun as the "gangster gun." It was as though a family of prohibitionists had inherited a distillery. For Auto-Ordnance, Ryan's death could not have come at a worse time, coinciding as it did with the apogee of bad publicity from the streets of Chicago.

The official executor of Ryan's estate was the Guaranty Trust Company of New York (which merged with J. P. Morgan & Co. in 1959 to form the Morgan Guaranty Trust, which in turn merged with Chase Manhattan in 2001 to become JPMorgan Chase Bank). To manage his affairs, Ryan had picked Wall Street lawyer Elihu Root, the 1912 Nobel Peace Prize laureate who was a well-connected former United States senator and a former secretary of state under Theodore Roosevelt. Despite his association with the pistol-packing, cowboy groupie Roosevelt, Root shared the disdain that most of Tom Ryan's heirs felt toward the gangster gun. As *Time* put it in the June 26, 1939, article, "In kindly Pacifist Root's scheme of things, the sale of man-killers had no place. Quietly he put Auto-Ordnance on the shelf."

One of Root's first moves was to fire Marcellus Thompson and install Thomas Ryan's nephew, Walter Ryan, as president of the Auto-Ordnance Corporation. His tenure was intended to be short, and the plan was to liquidate Auto-Ordnance as quickly as possible—for pennies on the dollar if necessary—and to bury the gangster gun once and for all.

Although Walter Ryan and the Ryan family were nominally in charge, they did not hold *all* the cards. Marcellus and his father did not have the financial resources to buy out the Ryan family interests and take back "their" company, but they still owned enough Auto-Ordnance stock to block an outright liquidation of the company at a deep discount. A stalemate of an entirely different sort had been the catalyst for General Thompson's greatest brainstorm. Now, he and his son found themselves on the horns of another stalemate, one that would bring them a long, difficult decade of their greatest anguish.

The late 1920s were not the best of times for Marcellus. He was out of a job and he owned shares in a company where sales had been pitiful for most of the decade, and which was now under the control of interests whose goal was to kill it just as the M1928 was coming on line. Not only that, Marcellus's long-pending divorce would not be final until early in 1929.

Nor were the late 1920s the best of times for Marcellus's estranged wife. Dorothy's father, Ambassador George Brinton McClellan Harvey—the man who had introduced Marcellus's father to Tom Ryan back in 1916—had died on August 20, 1928, three months before Ryan's passing.

Despite this, things were looking up for Dorothy. A pampered daughter of Manhattan society, she was cruising in all of the right circles while the lawyers worked to undo her marriage. She had been dating forty-four-year-old New York banker Augustus Smith Cobb, who was in the process of untying the knot of his own thirteen-year marriage to Mary Christine Converse.

Marcellus and Dorothy finally received their divorce decree on February 9, 1929, and she married Augustus on Valentine's Day, the *same* Valentine's Day in which Marcellus's submachine gun was being used most notoriously in that Chicago warehouse. Eight years later, Dorothy herself died of a gunshot wound to the head. It was a pistol, not a tommy gun. Augustus said she was upset about having contracted tuberculosis. Her demise was ruled a suicide.

Seven months after Dorothy's ill-fated wedding day, Marcellus also remarried, to a young lady a few years less than half his age. Evelyn Allensworth was a twenty-two-year-old graduate of the Louisville Conservatory of Music in Kentucky, and the daughter of attorney James Butler Allensworth.

So long as the Thompson and Ryan families were at odds, Auto-Ordnance remained in limbo. The Thompsons had no control save to thwart the Ryans' liquidation plan.

Both sides sought a means to tip the balance. Walter kept after the brokers whom he knew on Wall Street, trying to find a buyer for the company. Meanwhile, Marcellus Thompson, who had no money, beat the Wall Street pavement for a venture capitalist who could back him in a bid to buy out the Ryan interests.

In 1930, John Thompson would thrill to the birth of Evelyn Southgate, his first grandchild, and mourn the death of his wife of forty-eight years, Juliet.

After Juliet's death, General Thompson resigned his reserve commission, left the home in Connecticut where he had lived with her for more than a decade and moved in with Marcellus and his young bride on Long Island.

In 1931, his second grandchild was born. She was named Juliet, for her grandmother.

CHAPTER 13

The More Things Changed

Walter Ryan found himself in the peculiar place of running a "family business" that sold a product that the family loathed.

It didn't help that by 1930 Hollywood had discovered the tommy gun,
and was acting to immortalize its infamous role in Prohibition-era lawlessness. One of the first of the truly great gangster pictures was Mervyn Le-
Roy's classic *Little Caesar* (1931), starring Edward G. Robinson in the Capone-like
title role as a mob boss, with Douglas Fairbanks Jr. as an enforcer amid plenty
of tommy gun action.

At the same time, sales to ostensibly responsible private entities continued to spark controversy and breed negative publicity for Ryan and Auto-
Ordnance. Guns sold to private security firms often found their way into the
hands of those involved in strikebreaking and union busting on the railroads, within garment factories, and at mines. Indeed, selling guns to the
police forces in company towns—of which there were many in the early
twentieth century—was the same as selling them to strikebreakers. News
reports of goons attacking strikers with tear gas were one thing, but when
the goons started wielding tommy guns, the publicity shadow cast upon
Auto-Ordnance was worse than when Al Capone was using the company's
products.

In October 1930, one year after the stock market crash, and twenty-three
months after Thomas Fortune Ryan's death, Walter implemented a policy
restricting sales to the armed forces only. He certainly saw the value in the
U.S. Navy contract for the M1928. He had previously included law enforcement agencies and banks among permissible customers, but now he closed
the door on them as well.

He even went so far as to close down the sales department at Auto-
Ordnance. No longer were Auto-Ordnance salesman calling on customers.
Potential customers knew how to reach them. The call came in March 1932.

It was not just any customer, it was *the* customer. Eleven years after rejecting the Thompson submachine gun, the U.S. Army announced that it was adopting the weapon. So as to sidestep any critics who might say "I told you so," the army qualified its acquisition, describing it as "limited," and characterizing the Thompson as "nonessential." The "limited procurement" specified that one submachine gun be assigned to each motorcycle and each armored vehicle of an armored car or mechanized cavalry regiment, and then "subject to availability." The numbers were small. According to Leland Ness, writing in *Jane's World War II Tanks and Fighting Vehicles,* between 1932 and 1935, the U.S. Army acquired just 40 armored cars, 41 combat cars, 19 light tanks, and 8 medium tanks.

For the Thompson family, it was vindication. For the Ryan family, it only meant that they would have to keep Auto-Ordnance in business. Of course, who could argue with the fact that the company was actually earning a little money now? The family, via Tom Ryan's estate, had more than a million dollars tied up in the company—never mind interest—and business was business.

At this time, Auto-Ordnance was still selling through existing inventory. No Thompson submachine guns had been manufactured for more than a decade. The company was relying, for the most part, on what was left of the stockpile of fifteen thousand parts and assembled guns that dated back to 1921. Indeed, as late as 1938, nearly a third of the original inventory remained unsold.

A month after the U.S. Army order, Walter Ryan decided to formally outsource the marketing and distribution of Thompson submachine guns. That way he did not have to take calls from arms purchasers.

As his new sales agent, Ryan picked a firm that specialized in dealing arms and related merchandise to police departments and national armies. That company, located near Pittsburgh, Pennsylvania, was known as Federal Laboratories. Despite the term "Federal," this firm (like the much later Federal Express) was not a government agency, but a private company that used "federal" in its name for the flavor of officialdom. Now headquartered in Casper, Wyoming, Federal Laboratories is still a manufacturer and distributor of various law enforcement products, especially tear gas and antiriot equipment. In 1998, the company was acquired by Florida-based Armor Holdings, Inc., which had been founded in 1969 as American Body Armor and Equipment. In 2007, the combined entity became part of BAE Systems PLC (BAE), a British defense and aerospace company headquartered at Farnborough in England, which also includes such subsidiaries as British Aerospace (BAe).

During an October 1942 visit to FBI headquarters in Washington, D.C., General
Manuel Benítez y Valdez, head of the Cuban National Police, stopped by the shooting
range to empty a magazine using one of the Bureau's M1928s.
(Courtesy of the National Archives)

In 1932, Ryan's mandate was that Federal Laboratories sell only to constituted governments, but this did not mean that the company was always
dealing with the most peace-loving of characters. A case in point was Cuba.
As in Nicaragua, politics in Cuba were reminiscent of the world of Chicago
bootleggers, where tough guys from rival gangs battled it out. Consisting of
either freedom fighters or terrorists—depending upon one's perspective—
these gangs were constantly gunning for one another. Since 1925, the country had been run by the iron-fisted General Gerardo Machado y Morales,
who occupied the post of president, but who was called a dictator anywhere
but in his palace. The brutality of his secret police was matched only by the
ruthlessness of the gangs who wanted him out of power. Such gangs and
gangsters included Carlos Manuel de Cespedes y Quesada, the son of Cuba's
first president, and the secret ABC, a group that took its name from the let-
ters used to designate its hierarchy of inner circles.

The more things changed after Thomas Fortune Ryan's death, the more things remained the same with respect to nefarious characters having access to Thompson submachine guns.

Federal Laboratories found Machado y Morales—the head of a constituted government—an eager customer. He and his chief of police, Captain Miguel Calvo, were anxious to arm the palace guard with Thompson submachine guns, which, thanks to Capone's colorful example, was the gun of choice for ruling the mean streets of contested cities.

As might have been expected, the weapons also found their way into the arsenals of those who sought to undo the president's hold on power.

As reported in the July 18, 1932, issue of *Time* magazine, "As Captain Calvo rode down the broad Malecón with two Havana policemen one day last week, a submachine gun suddenly began to spat-spat. The two policemen were instantly killed. Captain Calvo was rushed to a hospital, died with 36 slugs in his body. The submachine gunners escaped unidentified."

In August 1933, Carlos Manuel de Cespedes y Quesada finally succeeded in ousting Gerardo Machado y Morales. However, he lasted only three weeks until he, in turn, got the boot from Ramón Grau and General Fulgencio Batista. Alternating between being the power behind the throne and the man on the throne, Batista ran Cuba for a quarter of a century before he was finally toppled by the tommy gun–wielding gang led by Fidel Castro.

Having a Batista man in power by no means diminished the violence on Havana's streets. On June 25, 1934, *Time* reported that Thompson submachine guns had spoken "from a red Pontiac sedan that suddenly rolled alongside a monster Havana parade of ABC men, women and children. The guns killed twelve, four of them women, wounded more than 60. The parade went on but stiff-jawed ABC men stepped out of line and went in pursuit. They shot and burned four men in the red car, shot three in another."

The article does not mention whether or not General Batista was present.

While Cubans burned cars and hammered at one another with tommy guns, Federal Laboratories salesmen were heading farther south—selling more Thompsons to more constituted governments. Simultaneous with the well-remembered public enemy street wars and the vaguely remembered gang warfare in Cuba and Nicaragua, a major war raged in South America, a conflict of which few North Americans have heard. The Chaco War of 1932–1935 took place in the Gran Chaco, a vast, but remote, landlocked plateau the size of Texas that had been claimed by both Bolivia and Paraguay for more than a century.

A smug Fulgencio Rubén Batista Godínez, the ten-year-old son of Cuban president
Fulgencio Batista, happily observes the target that he peppered with rounds from
an M1928 Thompson submachine gun in 1943. He fled Cuba when his father was
overthrown by Fidel Castro in 1959 and died in Coral Gables, Florida, in 2007.
(Courtesy of the National Archives)

The premise for the two countries going to war over the Gran Chaco was
simple. The place was supposed to contain immense oil reserves. It didn't,
but neither side knew that at the time.

When the war began, Bolivia commanded most of the Gran Chaco.

When the war ended, most of the Gran Chaco was within Paraguay's borders, where it remains to this day.

Military historians recall the Chaco War as being the first western hemisphere war in which airpower played a significant role, and the only (to date) western hemisphere war in which tanks were used to cross an international border. As they had in Cuba, Federal Laboratories also played a part, selling Thompson submachine guns to both governments. A number of Bergmann Maschinenpistole 18 submachine guns also showed up in the Gran Chaco during the conflict.

The more things changed with Walter Ryan's attempts to rein in access by the bad guys to Auto-Ordnance products, the more things remained the same.

How ineffective Walter's policies were is illustrated by an article by Edgar Sisson in the May 19, 1934, issue of *Today* magazine, coincidentally the issue that was on newsstands the week that Bonnie and Clyde were killed. In a checklist of customers of an unnamed New York armsmaker—presumed by historians such as Bill Helmer to be Auto-Ordnance—it is noted that 83 of 785 guns sold in a particular period went to "fictitious buyers." Sales to law enforcement agencies amounted to less than 40 percent of the total, and military sales were just 4 percent. Gun dealers bought more submachine guns than the marines.

As Bill Helmer points out, the entry for "fictitious buyers" is "impressive." It also is indicative of the way things were still being done five years after the St. Valentine's Day Massacre and six years after Walter Ryan took over at Auto-Ordnance.

That same year, with John Dillinger, Pretty Boy Floyd, and Baby Face Nelson—not to mention Bonnie and Clyde—in the midst of well-publicized rampages across America's heartland, there was a growing sense in the United States that "something had to be done." Washington politicians began talking about gun control, although the object in 1934 was not to ban firearms, but to restrict distribution.

Not wanting to infringe on what their constituents might construe as an inappropriate action against legitimate gun ownership, the congressmen narrowed their focus only to the guns that the gangsters had made famous though media accounts of their exploits. These included sawed-off rifles and shotguns with barrels shorter than eighteen inches, as well as silencers and machine guns.

Counterintuitively, the sanctimonious Ryan family found it appealing that the Congress was choosing to restrict the despised product of the family business. Walter dutifully took the train down to Washington to testify on Capitol Hill, where he told Congress that gun control had been *his* idea all along.

"We have studied the bill fairly carefully and we believe that the provisions of it will materially aid in the disarming of the criminal," Ryan told the House Ways and Means Committee. "The policies of the company itself have been exactly those as embodied in the pending bill for a number of years."

The National Firearms Act of 1934 became law on June 26, as John Dillinger was hiding out in Chicago. The act imposed an excise tax on the manufacture and transfer of sawed-off shotguns and Thompson submachine guns, mandating that owners register these weapons. The transfer tax, applied to each weapon regardless of the price tag, was roughly $3,000 in today's dollars. Al Capone may have purchased his first tommy gun over the counter, but men such as Dillinger didn't acquire their weapons through taxable channels. Nor did the much-heralded new law apply to men such as Fulgencio Batista or Anastasio Somoza García—or to self-styled holy warriors such as the late Augusto Sandino.

The "policies of the company itself," of which Walter Ryan bragged to Congress, no doubt met with a positive response in uptown drawing rooms, but downtown at the company's offices at 302 Broadway there was a different reality. Walter Ryan still presided over and managed Auto-Ordnance, the company was still in the machine-gun business, and Federal Laboratories was still south of the border marketing Auto-Ordnance products.

The international arms trade, of which Federal Laboratories was certainly part, caught the attention of the United States Senate that same summer that the House of Representatives was debating gun control. The senators appointed a committee, headed by Gerald Nye of North Dakota, to look into the American munitions industry, and scheduled hearings. Federal Laboratories was not only willing to appear, but also brought some exhibits for show-and-tell. As *Time* reported on October 1, 1934, "President John W. Young of Federal Laboratories, Inc. brought gifts for the committee—one wooden model of a Thompson Submachine Gun, two sample gas bombs, one packet of sickening-gas crystals."

On the stand, Young explained that he had advised and supplied both sides in the ongoing trouble in Cuba and that he had received a $12,000 retainer to reorganize the Cuban police force. The Senate then adjourned to go home and take care of the midterm elections. Said Chairman Nye, "The committee feels that it has thus far only scratched the surface."

Issued on February 24, 1936, the *Report of the Special Committee on Investigation of the Munitions Industry* (U.S. Congress, Senate, 74th Congress, 2nd session), known as the "Nye Report," had harsh words for Federal Laboratories, pointing out that "attempts to sell munitions frequently involve bribery, which, to be effective, must go to those high in authority. This is apt to involve the companies in the politics of foreign nations. Federal Laboratories, by putting itself at the disposal of the administration of Cuba and two opposing factions, all at the same time, is a case in point."

The more things changed, the more they remained the same.

CHAPTER 14

In the Movies

The story of Auto-Ordnance Corporation in the 1930s was like the screen-play of a movie. For Marcellus Thompson, it was a horror film. He spent his time trying, without success, to find a way to regain control of the company that had cost him his first marriage, and to which he had devoted his entire life since leaving the U.S. Army at the end of the Great War.

For Walter Ryan, it was a science fiction film. Auto-Ordnance had become the thing that would not die. Ever since his uncle's death in 1928, he had sought to rid the family of this company, but he found that the orders from the U.S. Navy for M1928s kept alive a company that otherwise would probably have collapsed.

As reality imitated the movies, the image of the Thompson submachine gun continued to be kept alive in the newsreels. Hollywood had discovered the public fascination with Prohibition-era gangsters, and they had not—nor have they yet—faded from the forefront of popular culture. As *Time* magazine said so eloquently on June 26, 1939, "To most U.S. cinemaddicts the Thompson submachine gun is a gangsters' weapon. The late black-browed John Dillinger, potbellied 'Killer' Burke, the late Charlie Birger of Southern Illinois were virtuosos with the Thompson, called it, with utility in mind, a chopper."

Indeed, the tommy gun, especially the M1921 with the big fifty-round drum magazine, became a staple of the gangster movie during the 1930s. So, too, did certain Hollywood leading men. Having starred in *G-Men* in 1935, Jimmy Cagney was wielding a tommy gun again in Michael Curtiz's *Angels with Dirty Faces* (1938), another Warner Brothers release, and the story of two tough Irish kids growing up in New York's Hell's Kitchen. Naturally, the two—played by Cagney and Pat O'Brien—go their separate ways as adults in order for there to be the requisite tension. O'Brien's character goes into the priesthood, while Cagney's becomes a gangster. Humphrey Bogart also appeared in the film as the crooked lawyer.

Hi-Yo Silver! The Lone Ranger takes a turn at emptying an M1928's drum magazine.
Clayton Moore was the best-known actor to have portrayed the Masked Man,
but he was preceded by many others, including Robert Livingston.
(Courtesy of the National Archives)

Cast as a mob boss in MGM's *Little Caesar* (1931), Edward G. Robinson earned his credentials for "tough guy" roles and went on to carry tommy guns in several of these. Robinson's characters brandished tommy guns on both sides of the law. William Keighley, who directed *G-Men*, cast Robinson in *Bullets or Ballots* (1936), and Edward Ludwig put a tommy gun in Robinson's hand in *The Last Gangster* (1937). Robinson was not, however, the "last gangster." Hollywood had more waiting in the wings.

Like Robinson, Humphrey Bogart alternated between bad guy and good guy roles, although most of the latter came in the years after he was cast as Sam Spade in *The Maltese Falcon* (1941) and in his landmark role as Rick Blaine in *Casablanca* (1942). During the 1930s, he was typecast mainly as a hard-boiled tough guy. Three 1939 films are cases in point. He had the title role in Lewis Seiler's *King of the Underworld* from Warner Brothers, was a partner in crime with George Raft in Lloyd Bacon's *Invisible Stripes* from First

National, and in a speakeasy with Cagney in Raoul Walsh's *Roaring Twenties* during the era which Warner in the film's advertising called "the shock-crammed days G-men took ten whole years to lick!" Of course, the tommy gun also starred.

As the Southern California motion picture industry mushroomed during the 1920s, so, too, did the ancillary businesses that supported it. As moviemakers began producing action-adventure pictures that required guns, entrepreneurs bought collections of firearms and set up rental companies to provide them to the studios. One such man was James Sidney Stembridge, born in Georgia a few years after the Civil War.

After serving in the Spanish-American War, Stembridge came to Hollywood, where he worked as an actor and coached other actors to behave realistically as soldiers. After playing small roles in several Westerns, such as *The Trail of the Lonesome Pine* (1923), Stembridge began renting guns around 1920. He became a close friend of blockbuster filmmaker Cecil B. DeMille, who was a gun collector. Soon Stembridge found himself in a business that was far more lucrative than being a bit-part actor. He founded Stembridge Gun Rentals, setting up shop at 5451 Marathon Street on the back lot at Paramount Pictures in a facility that was well known as the "Gun Room." While Stembridge served as the figurehead, the day-to-day management of the business was in the hands of Fritz Dickie, who is recalled as having been the backbone of the company from 1927 to 1974. By the end of the 1930s, the arsenal within the Gun Room had grown to 7,000 rifles, 1,200 revolvers and pistols, and about 200 machine guns. The latter once included 72 Thompsons, mainly M1921s and M1928s. Indeed, the Stembridge company logo was a musket with its barrel crossing that of a tommy gun.

While the Thompson was required equipment for the plethora of Roaring Twenties gangster films, it also started appearing in action-adventure films set in locations thousands of miles from the North Side of Chicago. One such instance was Tay Garnett's *China Seas* (1935), an MGM release. Clark Gable played the captain of a freighter plying the waters of the South China Sea with Wallace Beery as his sidekick. The plot thickens when Gable's ex-girlfriend, Dolly "China Doll" Portland (Jean Harlow), wants him back. Other antagonists range from tropical storms to Malay pirates, against whom the tommy gun is most effective.

While the movies were a popular diversion during the 1930s, a centerpiece of popular culture during the 1930s were the funny papers, the comic strips that appeared in daily newspapers in black ink, and the large comic section that appeared in color on Sundays. The movies may have cost less than a dollar, but during the Great Depression, when money was scarce, the funny papers were available to everyone. They cost pennies and could be passed around. A kid could keep the Sunday funnies in his room and digest them all week long. Among the popular strips that captured the imaginations of all ages during the 1930s were *Alley Oop, Blondie,* and *Lil' Abner.* One of the most popular was *Dick Tracy.*

Created by newspaper illustrator Chester Gould, the Tracy strip had its debut in the *Chicago Tribune* in October 1931. Dick Tracy, who remains a part of popular culture to this day, was a heroic, crime-fighting detective who used high-tech gadgets to pursue and thwart villains. However, when the gadgets had done their job, Dick Tracy would be the first to tell you that there are some things only a tommy gun can do.

Gould, who probably drew more pictures of more tommy guns from more angles than anyone during the 1930s, got his ideas from life. All around him, and especially in the pages of the Chicago newspapers, gangland violence ruled. His idea was to create a hero who could not only outshoot the bad guys, but outthink them as well.

So popular was Gould's crime buster that Dick Tracy began his radio career in 1934, appearing in various serials on several networks, including ABC, CBS, NBC, and Mutual Broadcasting. One anecdote that illustrates how thoroughly Dick Tracy became ingrained in popular culture involves the Academy Award for Best Actor in 1937. Spencer Tracy won the Oscar, but as the story goes, when the statue was delivered to him, it was engraved "Dick Tracy." The Academy quickly fixed its error.

Coincidentally, it was in 1937 that Dick Tracy first reached the silver screen. Ralph Byrd was cast by Republic Pictures in the title role in a fifteen-part serial, which in turn, became a feature-length film. This was followed by two additional fifteen-part serials starring Ralph Byrd, *Dick Tracy Returns* (1938) and *Dick Tracy's G-Men* (1939). Further films and a television series came after World War II. Until his death in 1952, Ralph Byrd was the favorite for the title role, although others played the part. Since 1952, perhaps the definitive Dick Tracy was Warren Beatty—late of a title role as tommy gun–cradling Clyde Barrow—who portrayed Gould's hero opposite Madonna in 1990.

John Taliaferro Thompson had intended it as a weapon "on the side of law and order." He had neither planned nor imagined that its reputation would be—despite the best efforts of Dick Tracy—exactly the opposite. Even if the St. Valentine's Day Massacre had never occurred, Hollywood and the colorful villains that came to life on its sound stages had assured that the tommy gun was *the* gangster gun.

Actor Gary Cooper is obviously enjoying the chance to shoot a tommy gun during his visit to the indoor range at FBI headquarters. *(Courtesy of the National Archives)*

As the 1930s neared their end, both Walter Ryan and Marcellus Thompson were reaching the climactic scenes of their own personal bad movies. The suspense was about to be broken. The next scene in their drama would be the climax.

CHAPTER 15

Dark Angel

In 1938, even as Jimmy Cagney squeezed the trigger of a tommy gun in Curtiz's *Angels with Dirty Faces* on screens all over the country, Marcellus Thompson was about to make the acquaintance of an angel of his own. Whether or not John Russell Maguire was an angel of good or ill has been debated for years by those who have studied his involvement with the Auto-Ordnance deal. It has been said of Russell (he went by his middle name) Maguire that, although his face was clean, his past was not exactly that way.

Like Thomas Fortune Ryan, Maguire was a financier. He'd made fortunes, lost them, and come back to earn fortunes anew. He had run afoul of the federal Securities and Exchange Commission (SEC), the agency created by Congress in 1934 to regulate the stock market and to prevent the sorts of securities and corporate malfeasance that had led to the stock market crash and the Great Depression. As later summarized in the December 8, 1952, issue of *Time,* he had operated principally as a Wall Street broker until the SEC forced him out for "flagrant violations" of the law.

But Maguire was a persistent man. He'd been banished from Wall Street, and he'd gone through personal bankruptcy, but he had risen from his misfortune. He'd owned and operated several firms, and had helped to underwrite initial public offerings. More than that, he was a turnaround expert. As with many such people even to this day, Maguire trolled for opportunities, looking for companies that are, for want of a more delicate term, "circling the drain." He would then snap up the virtually worthless entities and return them to profitability. During the Great Depression, many such opportunities presented themselves.

One of Maguire's success stories was the Alco (for Automatic Liquid COntrols) Valve Company. Founded in St. Louis in 1925, the company had originally been formed to manufacture a recently patented automatic constant-pressure expansion valve to control the flow of ammonia used as a refrigerant. The valve was a revolutionary innovation then, but by the time Maguire came into the picture, the firm was in need of help. Maguire turned Alco around—boosting profits more than four thousand percent in the first year. During World War II, Alco flourished, branching into aircraft hydraulic controls, radio direction finders, and aircraft windshield wipers as well as refrigerant flow controls. Acquired by Emerson Electric in 1967, the company still exists as Emerson's Flow Controls component.

By the time Russell Maguire became aware of Auto-Ordnance in 1939, it looked a lot like Alco had when he'd first knocked on its doors. Auto-Ordnance was a relic of a past era, whose product once had a certain cachet, but seemed now to have run its course. There were barely enough orders to keep the company struggling along. When Matthew Hall, a Wall Street deal maker who had worked on and off through the years with both the Thompsons and the Ryans, mentioned what Maguire had done with Alco, Walter Ryan was ready to listen.

For Walter Ryan, Auto-Ordnance was a cup half empty. For Marcellus Thompson, who still imagined the immense potential of the gun, it was a cup half full. Russell Maguire could sense this.

What Marcellus saw was that the world in 1939 was a very different place than it had been back in 1921 when Thomas Fortune Ryan had told John Taliaferro Thompson that the company should go ahead and build a huge inventory of M1921 Thompson submachine guns. Back then, national governments were not in the market for new or innovative weapons. Nineteen thirty-nine was also a much different time than the early 1930s, when wars were nasty little potshot conflicts on the streets of Chicago or Havana.

In 1921 or 1931, thoughts of the terrible days of 1914 were just a distant, unpleasant memory. By 1939, though, things were starting to look a lot like 1914 all over again.

The clouds of war had been gathering over Europe throughout the decade. In Germany a man came to power who, in any other circumstances, might have been written off as just another gangster. In many ways he was. However, he would soon rule one of the world's most technologically and industrially advanced countries.

An Austrian rabble-rouser with an uncanny gift for mesmerizing oratory, Adolf Hitler became Germany's chancellor in 1933. Germany had been humiliated by the terms of the Treaty of Versailles that concluded World War I, and Hitler promised a face-saving rise to greatness. The German people went for it.

Though few people noticed or took him seriously at first, Hitler had already laid out his grandiose plan for Germany's future in his book *Mein Kampf* (My Struggle). In a nutshell, he planned not just for Germany to overcome the disgrace of Versailles but to remold the nation as Europe's preeminent power, a *Grossdeutschland* (Greater Germany) that would be the centerpiece of a new German *Drittes Reich* (Third Empire). The English-speaking world called it the Third Reich, but in Germany, Hitler extravagantly referred to it as his "Thousand-Year" Reich. In order to accomplish his scheme, Germany would need to incorporate more *Lebensraum* (living space) into the Third Reich, and the only way to accomplish this was through conquest. Many a European country would pay a price for ignoring Hitler's plan.

Having taken power, Hitler soon began the steps that led to the rearmament of Germany, in violation of the Treaty of Versailles. In 1936, when German armies occupied the German Rhineland in direct violation of the treaty, the lack of active opposition by Britain and France encouraged Hitler. In 1938, he annexed Austria and the Sudetenland regions of Czechoslovakia, making them part of Germany. Britain and France complained, but at a summit conference in Munich, Hitler promised no further land grabs. To avoid war, Britain and France acquiesced.

With twenty-twenty hindsight we know how this decision turned out, but in the first months of 1939, it was just one of those world crises, like the world crises before and since, that lives on the front pages and does not affect any American's daily life. In March 1939, it was still possible to turn to the comics page, read today's installment of *Dick Tracy*, and forget the bickering under the headlines.

However, Marcellus Thompson was reading those headlines. He had that foreboding that comes from being able to see what is going on in the world and to sense what will happen next, and in the coming war he could anticipate a suddenly increasing demand for weapons such as the tommy gun.

He was not alone. There was already speculation about a major war in Europe and the possibility that the United States might be sucked into it. President Franklin D. Roosevelt was among those who saw preparation for war as a cautionary step. Even in 1938, Roosevelt had been talking about American industry gearing up for what would be called "National Defense."

In 1921 there had been little interest in the maxim of Publius Flavius Vegetius Renatus "Let him who desires peace prepare for war." By 1939 opinion had shifted. Roosevelt called for huge increases in the number of warplanes of the U.S. Army and U.S. Navy, using this as symbolic of what he meant by National Defense.

Marcellus Thompson correctly predicted that soon the United States armed forces would be in the market for Thompson submachine guns in numbers that would make the original fifteen thousand M1921s seem small.

When Marcellus at last sat down with Russell Maguire for their very auspicious first face-to-face meeting, facilitated by Matthew Hall, he told him so.

Both men saw opportunity.

Maguire and Thompson decided that it was time to make a deal. They agreed to create and incorporate a company that would be called Thompson Automatic Arms, and Maguire dialed Walter Ryan's phone number.

As *Time* magazine reported on June 26, 1939, "For $529,000 the heirs of Thomas Fortune Ryan agreed to sell their Auto-Ordnance stock, write off $1,090,000 in notes for money advanced to the old company. Other stockholders (including the heirs of Commander Blish) agreed to trade their shares for stock in new Thompson Automatic Arms Corp. Today Thompsons can be made for $50 to $60 each, sold at $200 to $225. Well-grounded in military tactics, well-acquainted with soldiering men, rumpled, Kentucky-born Colonel Marcellus Thompson sees the day near when there will be a Thompson in every infantry squad, a chopper or two in every armored car. Pacifists still object to war, but few of them still object to arming against it."

Even with his taking the write-down, Walter Ryan had to be feeling a sense of relief once he'd freed himself from the unprofitable company that manufactured a product his family found so objectionable.

As of January 1939, a total of 25,630 shares of an authorized 40,000 Auto-Ordnance shares had been issued. Guaranty Trust, as Tom Ryan's executor, held 72 percent on behalf of the Ryan family, while Marcellus Thompson held 19.5 percent, and the heirs of John Bell Blish held 6 percent. Both Marcellus's wife and his ex-wife had one hundred shares.

The Thompson Automatic Arms Corporation was officially registered as a Delaware corporation on March 3 with the intention of absorbing the assets of Auto-Ordnance. Thompson Automatic Arms received its New York State business license on May 15.

For Marcellus Thompson, it had to have seemed like a dream come true. In essence, Russell Maguire became to Marcellus Thompson in 1939 what Thomas Fortune Ryan had been for the elder Thompson in 1916, the man who would pay him to control the family business. There was, however, a big difference. Ryan had been rich, but Maguire had no money. He did, however, have a scheme, one that would involve other people's money.

According to official records of the Supreme Court of Delaware in a case that later arose involving Thompson Automatic Arms, the company entered into an underwriting agreement with Maguire's firm, Maguire & Company, on March 29, 1939. Under this agreement, Maguire agreed to purchase or find purchasers for 300,000 shares of Thompson Automatic Arms stock at $2.00 a share net to Thompson Automatic Arms after registration of the shares with the Securities and Exchange Commission. According to the Delaware Court, "The offering price was $3.00 per share, leaving a gross spread of $1.00 per share or $300,000 for Maguire & Co. Maguire & Co. was given an option to purchase 64,000 additional shares."

First, Maguire had to get the deal underwritten by Guaranty Trust, the official executor of the Thomas Fortune Ryan estate. This covered the Ryans in case Thompson couldn't make two equal payments of $264,500 to the Ryans in July and September 1939. If Maguire did not, the bank would take over, sell Auto-Ordnance, and split the proceeds with the Ryans.

In essence, Marcellus was making an all-or-nothing bet. So, too, was Maguire, but only in dollars and cents. For Marcellus, it was an all-or-nothing bet involving a company that was engrained in his soul.

For nearly eleven years, Marcellus and his father had watched as Auto-Ordnance Corporation was managed by Walter Ryan, a man whose interest in the firm and its product hovered between ambivalence and disdain. They watched as the submachine gun that bore the Thompson name was sold around the world. They looked, but could not touch. They owned enough of Auto-Ordnance that they could force Ryan into a stalemate, but not enough to control the company.

Now, at last, after a decade of bleakness, Marcellus had reason for hope. In doing a deal with Maguire, and by creating the Thompson Automatic Arms Corporation, he had reason to be optimistic that the control of "his" company that had long eluded him was just weeks away. In Russell Maguire, he had found his angel. Only as those weeks progressed would Marcellus begin to learn he was a *dark* angel.

CHAPTER 16

Roller Coaster from Hell

On July 21, 1939, Marcellus Thompson would have to pay the Ryan family more than a quarter of a million dollars, or nearly four million today. If he failed to make that deadline, he would forfeit his family's minority interest in the company his father had founded.

But the Thompsons didn't have the money. All they had was Russell Maguire, and all Russell Maguire had was a plan.

As the initial payment deadline loomed, there was good news, and there was bad news. In due course there would be more of both as Marcellus rode the roller coaster toward the third Friday in July.

The bad news had come from the federal Securities and Exchange Commission. The commissioners had looked at Maguire's proposal for Thompson Automatic Arms, and had given the thumbs-down to the notion of allowing this corporation to sell its stock. The commissioners could be forgiven for raising an eyebrow over this proposal of a company without assets that depended for its very existence on buying out another company that it could not afford. To the commissioners, it did not seem like a sound basis upon which to build a business. It looked like a house of cards.

All that Russell Maguire had was a plan, and that plan was starting to unravel. Maguire had none of his own money at stake, but poor Marcellus felt as though he had his whole being at stake.

The good news that followed was so fortuitous and so unanticipated that it read like a good scene from a bad novel. On the day before Independence Day, the U.S. Army suddenly sent Auto-Ordnance a rush order.

The service was developing a new tactical doctrine involving the deployment of mechanized cavalry operating in armored scout cars. The Thompson submachine gun was seen as the ideal weapon with which to equip these vehicles.

The army's order, for 900 Thompson submachine guns (some sources say 950) plus spare parts and miscellaneous gear, is said to have totaled nearly half a million dollars. In 1939 that was a lot of money. For Auto-Ordnance, which was barely afloat, it was an unbelievable windfall.

Marcellus Thompson was ecstatic, but it was just the start of a roller coaster ride from hell. At first, he figured that a single order that amounted to more than 85 percent of the total agreed valuation of Auto-Ordnance would be all that the Securities and Exchange Commission would need to see that Thompson Automatic Arms was legitimate.

It was like a movie where the protagonist runs up the corporate steps with the paperwork that proves his case. But this was no movie, and Marcellus Thompson was not Jimmy Stewart. The government officials turned up their noses and dug in their heels. The answer, they said, peering at poor Marcellus over the tops of glasses perched on beaklike noses, was no.

This order, they sneered, seemed to them to be nothing more than a one-time fluke.

All that Russell Maguire had brought to the table was a plan, and that plan now seemed to be hopelessly unraveling. There were less than three weeks left to raise the capital and do the deal.

Marcellus decided that he had to take matters into his own hands.

Marcellus had to get the money.

With four days to spare, Marcellus found himself beneath the marble pillars of the vast banking lobby of the Marine Midland Bank (now owned by and operated as the Hong Kong and Shanghai Banking Corporation).

It was Monday, July 17, and the first payment to the Ryans was due at midnight on Friday.

The proposal looked familiar, the Marine Midland banker told Marcellus as he scanned the outline of the deal that Thompson needed to finance.

It *was* familiar. It turned out that none other than Russell Maguire had approached Marine Midland the week before, asking for a loan to do the same deal for him. The banker said that he was working with Maguire, and his loan was already in the works. He then told Marcellus that Maguire would be picking up his check on Friday afternoon, the deadline. Just when Marcellus had decided to take matters into his own hands, he discovered that Maguire had taken matters into *his* own hands!

Maguire had originally hoped to do the deal using other people's money, but when that did not work, he reached into his own pocket, and pledged his own money as part of the collateral. Marcellus realized that he could not have matched the deal even if he had arrived at Marine Midland before Maguire.

The Marine Midland loan would cover not just the first payment due on Friday, but both payments, plus $10,000 in additional cash. After four months of beating the pavement, the money would be in Maguire's hand on Friday afternoon with just hours to spare.

An exhausted Marcellus Thompson left the bank, his head spinning.

How could this be happening?

On Wednesday, the son of the inventor sat down across the table from Maguire, who explained how things would work as they went forward toward Friday.

Russell Maguire explained that, by pledging his own money, he had personally arranged the financing that was necessary to buy Auto-Ordnance from the Ryans. In exchange for this, he told Marcellus that he now expected to receive a much larger share of the Thompson Automatic Arms Corporation than they had agreed when they had formed the company in March.

Marcellus Thompson had no choice but to agree to give Maguire nearly half of the stock in the company.

All that remained was the immense task of getting the paperwork in order, which involved sorting though two decades of Auto-Ordnance records.

On Friday morning, with mere hours to spare, Marcellus Thompson and his attorney, Tom Kane, were coming off an all-nighter in the lower Manhattan offices of the law firm that represented Russell Maguire.

Suddenly, the blood vessels serving Thompson's overworked brain seized and he tumbled to the lushly carpeted floor, surrounded by a swirling cloud of onion skin.

The roller coaster had crashed.

Marcellus was still breathing when his attorney got him to the nearest hospital, a recently bankrupted institution later described in the July 8, 1940, edition of *Time* as a "rickety little Broad Street Hospital." The hospital had originally been founded in response to the never-solved 1920 anarchist bombing of the J. P Morgan headquarters on Wall Street, the worst terrorist attack in Manhattan until 2001, and by now it was an underfunded shell of what it had been in the prosperous 1920s.

Here Marcellus rested as Kane hightailed it to Maguire's offices.

Knowing that Marcellus was fighting his way back from a stroke and that the deal must be done within hours, Maguire approached Tom Kane with a new proposal.

Recalling his insistence on having nearly half the stock in Thompson Automatic Arms, Maguire said that he'd been giving it some thought. He told Kane that he had done a lot of work to make the deal happen, and he had now, as of Monday, put his own money on the line. He was feeling short-changed.

Having gotten the stock for which he had previously asked, Kane wondered, how could he feel shortchanged?

Maguire explained to Marcellus's attorney that he was a businessman. He ran businesses. He might have had some ups and downs, but he had certainly turned Alco Valve around. Marcellus Thompson, on the other hand, was a retired U.S. Army officer who had run a business for a time, and had not had his hands on the helm for eleven years. Now, Maguire said callously, the stricken Marcellus might never be able to work again in any capacity.

Maguire put it bluntly. He had his own money on the line and he wanted the best-qualified man running Thompson Automatic Arms—himself! He felt that in order to go forward, he needed to up the ante and to receive *controlling interest* in Thompson Automatic Arms.

Timing is everything, they say, and Maguire evidently felt that he had Kane over a barrel, with Marcellus at death's door and it being the eve of the deadline. However, Kane could not abide such audacity. Kane told Maguire to go to hell and stomped out.

Russell Maguire had wondered for a moment whether he had miscalculated, but he put on a brave face and headed over to the bank, where Walter Ryan and his attorneys were waiting to sign the papers. The waiting and pacing continued all afternoon as Maguire's emissaries shuttled back and forth to Tom Kane.

When Ryan left to get dinner, nothing had yet been resolved. He dined knowing that if Maguire, Kane, and Thompson did not have their ducks in a row by midnight, the Ryans would own Auto-Ordnance outright and Walter could liquidate it without interference first thing on Monday morning.

Ryan returned to Marine Midland around eight o'clock to find the situation unchanged. Then, about two hours later, a document arrived with Marcellus Thompson's signature on it, agreeing to the deal. It was handed over by Matthew Hall, the broker who had first introduced Russell Maguire to Walter Ryan and Marcellus Thompson. Apparently, he had thought to sneak over to Broad Street and call on the bedridden son of John Taliaferro Thompson.

Marcellus had decided that the only thing worse than submitting to the Dark Angel's demand was to allow Walter Ryan to win.

In cinematic fashion, the deal was finally consummated with minutes to spare.

Walter Ryan left the room as the clock tolled midnight with more than half a million dollars.

Russell Maguire woke up the following morning the president of a submachine-gun company.

Marcellus Thompson woke up in the hospital, critically ill, a beaten man.

CHAPTER 17

Cash and Carry

The wheelings and dealings between Messrs Ryan, Thompson, and Maguire during the spring and summer of 1939 were dwarfed by the far larger negotiations going on in Europe.

Here the man who held the best hand at the big geopolitical negotiating table in 1939 was Germany's chancellor. Britain's prime minister, Neville Chamberlain, and France's president, Edouard Daladier, were willing to go to almost any lengths to appease Adolf Hitler and avoid war.

Back in September 1938, at the now infamous summit conference in Munich, Hitler said he wanted Czechoslovakia's Sudetenland—and promised peace if *only* he could have just this region incorporated into his Third Reich. Britain and France let him take it, and Chamberlain flew home, happily announcing that he had helped to negotiate "peace for our time."

In March 1939, as Maguire and Thompson were organizing Thompson Automatic Arms, Hitler decided that he wanted the rest of Czechoslovakia. The price tag for peace had gone up.

As Russell Maguire had with Marcellus Thompson, Hitler had received a concession, then demanded more. Czechoslovakia was chopped into bits, with part of it becoming a protectorate of the Reich and the other part a satellite of Germany. Chamberlain and Daladier complained, but did nothing.

Two months later, on May 22, as Maguire and Thompson were courting the Securities and Exchange Commission, Hitler inked a deal with Italy's Fascist "Duce," Benito Mussolini. Known as the Pact of Steel, it called for cooperation in time of war, a war that seemed all that much closer because of the agreement.

On August 24, as Marcellus Thompson lay in his bed on Long Island, trying to recover from his stroke, Hitler sent his foreign minister to Moscow. There Joachim von Ribbentrop signed a nonaggression pact with the Soviet Union.

A week later, German bombs began falling on Poland on the morning of September 1 as German troops raced across the border. In London, Neville Chamberlain proposed more negotiations, but Hitler had decided that the time for negotiating was over.

Chamberlain consulted with Daladier, and on September 3, Britain and France declared that a state of war between them and the Third Reich had existed for two days.

World War II had begun.

At the time Germany invaded Poland, its army and Luftwaffe were the best-trained and best-equipped military force in the world, superior overall to all others. Their coordinated air and ground offensive, known as blitz-krieg (lightning war), was the most rapid and efficient mode of military attack the world had ever seen. The use of fast tanks, mobile forces, dive bombers, and paratroop units, all working together as one tight, well-disciplined force, stunned the world, especially the Polish defenders. Germany was able to subjugate Poland in just four weeks.

In the aftermath of Poland's collapse, Britain and France dispatched bombers over Germany, but, for the most part, took no other offensive action. A lull in the action of World War II descended over Europe. Throughout the winter of 1939–1940, Allied and German troops sat and watched one another across the heavily fortified Franco-German border. So little was happening that newspaper writers dubbed the situation the "Sitzkrieg" or the "phoney war."

Meanwhile, in the United States, by an overwhelming margin, the American people wanted to stay as far away as possible from "Europe's War."

During the long winter of 1939–1940, the governments of Britain and France quickly and nervously ramped up their acquisition of the weapons of war, soon outstripping their domestic manufacturing capacity. As in 1914, their gaze drifted to that industrial giant across the Atlantic.

Earlier Neutrality Acts passed by the United States Congress in 1936 and 1937, in reaction to the Spanish Civil War and the war between Japan and China, had placed restrictions on American businesses and individuals assisting the combatants, although the Neutrality Act of 1939, which was passed in November, two months after World War II began, opened the door to nations at war being able to buy arms from American factories on a cash-and-carry basis. The term was derived from the wholesaling business in which the seller does not offer billing or credit terms, and the buyer must therefore pay in cash and arrange for shipping. This new law was passed with the understanding that it was to benefit mainly Britain and France, who were seen as "Western democracies" involved in a war with Germany, seen as a totalitarian foe.

With the passage of the cash-and-carry legislation in November, British and French military acquisition teams began flooding into the United States on shopping trips to American arms factories. Heading the French delegation was J. Frédéric Bloch-Laine of the international financial services company Lazard Frères & Company. Coincidentally, M. Bloch-Laine had led the French arms shoppers to the United States a quarter century earlier during World War I. For the British purchasing commission, it was the president of Canadian Industries, Ltd, Arthur Blaikie Purvis, who had been the first British munitions buyer to reach the United States in 1914. They and their staffs visited California plane makers, placing orders for Douglas DB-7 (A-20) and Consolidated LB-30 (B-24) bombers. They bought trucks from White Motor Company and Studebaker. They ordered tanks and they bought small arms.

The governments represented by Bloch-Laine and Blaikie Purvis had no domestic source of submachine guns, so they turned to Auto-Ordnance. Delegations swept into New York, where they sat down with Russell Maguire. Conspicuous by their absence when the Europeans came calling in November and December 1939 were the men whose surname was synonymous with the famous gun. The general, who was approaching seventy-nine and losing his eyesight, was mainly confined to a wheelchair at his son's home on Long Island. As for Marcellus, his chair at the Auto-Ordnance conference room table was permanently empty. He had seen the family business recovered from the Ryans, but he would not live to enjoy the fruits of the long and arduous battle that achieved the victory.

Marcellus had lived to see the Battle of Poland, the opening battle of the war in which the family gun would finally have its vindication. He did not, however, live to see the passage of the liberalizing Neutrality Act of 1939 that would make it possible for the Thompson submachine gun to be part of the war he had seen coming.

Three months after the Thompson Automatic Arms Corporation absorbed all the assets of the Auto-Ordnance Corporation, Marcellus Thompson was dead. He had never fully recovered from his first stroke in July, and more followed. The last took his life on October 17. He was survived by his young wife, his two young daughters, and his invalid father.

Initially, Russell Maguire had decided to make Auto-Ordnance a subsidiary of Thompson Automatic Arms Corporation. However, in October 1941, a year after the death of Marcellus, Maguire folded the short-lived

Thompson Automatic Arms back into Auto-Ordnance. The name on the door once again read "Auto-Ordnance Corporation." Nevertheless, it was a vastly different company than the Auto-Ordnance the Thompsons and Walter Ryan had guided between 1921 and 1939. The big difference—and the difference that really mattered—was that it had orders, *big* orders.

The U.S. Army order for more than nine hundred submachine guns on July 3, 1939, was a very big deal. Though most of the records are lost, this order easily exceeded the number of Thompson submachine guns sold in most years during the preceding two decades. However, this sale was small compared to all that World War II would bring.

The European shoppers were in Maguire's office even as the Neutrality Act was working its way through Congress. The British came to express interest. Despite numerous overtures from John Taliaferro Thompson in the early 1920s—before his son's indictment on gun-running charges—Auto-Ordnance had failed to sell its guns to His Majesty's government. It was partly the "gangster gun" image, but mainly it had been Marcellus Thompson's alleged duplicity in selling tommy guns to the Irish Republican Army for use against British soldiers. Now that Marcellus was gone, the Brits were ready to consider normalizing relations with Auto-Ordnance and its new management. More important, there was a war and a need for arms.

The English would not submit their first order for Thompsons until February 1940, but the French had anxiously put pen to paper in November. *Time* magazine reported that they bought 3,750 Thompson submachine guns at $200 apiece, although other sources say it was 3,000 Thompson submachine guns for $250. In any case, their order was the largest yet for Thompsons, but it would soon be dwarfed by others.

In the meantime, representatives of yet another country also knocked on Russell Maguire's door, a country that would in fact remain neutral throughout World War II. As Gordon Herigstad told me, Sweden ordered 500 Model 1928A Thompsons in January 1940. Sandwiched between Finland, which had just been invaded by the Soviets, and Norway, which would soon be invaded by the Germans, the Swedes took to heart the classic fifth-century maxim of Publius Flavius Vegetius Renatus to preserve peace by preparing for war. They decided that the best way to stay neutral was to prepare to fight a war. Their strategy worked.

The M1928A guns that the Swedes ordered were like the M1928 Navy, but without the Cutts compensator.

"They could save $25 on a gun by not having a compensated model, so they saved $12,500," Herigstad told me with a chuckle. "They ordered two million rounds of ammo, two thousand twenty-round stick mags and one thousand L drums. That order was paid for by the Swedish government. A friend of mine found the records in an archive in Sweden. . . . All the serial numbers were in the 14,000 serial number range. These were probably the last Colt Thompsons to go out. More than twenty M1928As are now in the Swedish military museum, all of them numbered in the 14,000 range."

The present locations of the other Swedish Thompsons are unknown.

It was when Marcellus Thompson had told him that the inevitable war would bring with it an immense market for submachine guns that Maguire had first gotten serious about Auto-Ordnance. Now the customers were getting serious with him. Marcellus hadn't lived long enough to see his prediction come true, but he died knowing that it would.

Marcellus had not been alone in foreseeing war. Many in the American arms industry could see what was coming. On November 20, 1939, *Time* punned, combining the terms "profiteer" and "seer," writing, "When Congress gave Franklin Roosevelt the kind of Neutrality Act he wanted fortnight ago, profiseers dusted off their crystal globes, looked hard and long, saw a billion dollars worth of lush war orders for U.S. industry. To the U.S. came seven foreign missions, ready to take advantage of Cash & Carry. Up to this week their checkbooks still bristled with unused checks."

Russell Maguire went home on the evening of the day that he took the French order and toasted his good fortune. However, he woke up the following morning to a new reality. Be careful what you wish for, the old admonishment goes. So it was for Maguire. For two decades Auto-Ordnance had responded to their trickle of orders with basic equipment that had been manufactured by Colt back in 1921. The M1928s that Auto-Ordnance had been marketing since 1928 were basically modifications of M1921s taken from stock. To meet the new orders, Auto-Ordnance would have to start building new guns, but it did not own a factory.

Russell Maguire's first call was to Colt in Hartford, Connecticut, where General Thompson had outsourced production of the M1921, and indeed where all the production series guns had been manufactured to date.

The tooling for the Thompson submachine guns had been stored at Colt's facility for eighteen years. It was time to pull it out and put it back to work.

Colt's answer was an unexpected no.

Maguire had assumed he could just phone up and say "run me another thousand or three." However, Colt had endured years of embarrassment through having their name associated with the "gangster gun." Besides, with

World War II having now begun, and with the warring powers on their shopping sprees, Colt was not hurting for work to keep its production lines busy.

Russell Maguire's subsequent knocking on doors led him, at last, to the Savage Arms Corporation in Utica, New York. Founded in 1894 by Arthur Savage, the company was a well-established maker of ammunition and bolt-action hunting rifles, among other products. Having merged with Driggs-Seabury Ordnance, Savage had manufactured Lewis machine guns during World War I. Were they interested in building Thompson submachine guns under contract?

Yes, but with conditions. Just as the arms buyers from Europe shopped on a cash-and-carry basis, so, too, Maguire. Auto-Ordnance was known in the industry as a nearly moribund company that was snatched at the midnight hour for a bargain-basement price. Savage Arms was in no mood to extend credit to Maguire. The deal that Maguire signed with Savage on December 15 called for an initial payment to cover half the total bill for manufacturing. The tooling for the Thompsons was moved to Utica from Hartford, and four months later the first of an initial order of ten thousand new Savage tommy guns began rolling off the line.

Savage had offered a hard bargain, but it could not be refused.

As soon as the guns were in production in Utica, though, Maguire started looking around. Auto-Ordnance ought to have a factory of their own. Rather than parting with a great deal of cash in the form of down payments to Savage, he should be investing some money in means of production over which he had control.

In thinking ahead to finding a location for a Auto-Ordnance factory, Maguire was betting that World War II, which had stalled at an uneasy stalemate in the winter of 1939–1940, would restart and grow into a wider and more serious conflict. Though no one knew what Hitler would do next, it was a safe bet that he would not limit his lust for Lebensraum to the former Czechoslovakia and Poland. The French and British arms buyers were taking that bet, and so was Russell Maguire.

CHAPTER 18

Serious Business

On April 9, 1940, the other shoe finally dropped. Germany went on the offensive. Sitzkrieg became blitzkrieg once again.

The German combined armed forces, the Wehrmacht, quickly occupied Denmark, and by the end of the month Norway had also been taken. On May 10, the Germans began an offensive in the west that duplicated their advance on Belgium and France in 1914. The best-equipped of the units in the still relatively small British army had been dispatched to France as the British Expeditionary Force (BEF), and were on hand to help the French stem the German tide.

By the end of May, Luxembourg, Belgium, and the Netherlands had surrendered and German forces were pouring into France. The Wehrmacht moved so quickly that hardly any of the matériel acquired in the United States during the previous winter had time to reach frontline troops.

The French army and the BEF were outmaneuvered and quickly routed by the German blitzkrieg. Elements of both armies, but mainly the British, found themselves surrounded at the French port of Dunkirk, with their backs to the English Channel. The only good news to come out of the ensuing disaster was how much worse it might have been. Between May 26 and June 4, a hastily assembled fleet of more than eight hundred boats, including fishing boats, pleasure craft, and lifeboats, made numerous crossings of the English Channel to rescue nearly 200,000 British troops and more than 100,000 French soldiers, saving them from capture by the Germans.

Large parts of the French army were not so lucky. By June 14, Germany had seized control of Paris, having accomplished in five weeks what it had been unable to do in four years of protracted fighting in World War I. France surrendered a week later, leaving Britain alone to face the onslaught of the German blitzkrieg.

Dunkirk was one of those pivotal battles in British military history, not so much for what happened, but for what did *not* happen. The men of the BEF were not captured by the Germans and an incalculable catastrophe was averted. However, most of their equipment was lost. While replacing gear is easier than replacing men, it is still a task easier said than done.

Only the English Channel separated Germany's crack troops from a British army lacking weapons. The trickle of British purchases quickly became a torrent as His Majesty's government sought to prepare for the inevitable invasion. By the end of 1940, more than 100,000 Thompson submachine guns were earmarked for delivery to the United Kingdom. From these alone, the Auto-Ordnance Corporation, which had been bought for half a million dollars just the year before, grossed $21.5 million.

On June 22, the attention of the global media was on the fall of France. Hitler had smugly arranged for the French to formally surrender at Compiègne Forest near Paris, in the same spot and in the same railway car where the Germans had surrendered in 1918. Hitler had achieved an astounding victory, and he would gleefully rub French noses in defeat.

As the world's headlines blared the obituary of the French Third Republic, a few people noticed a much smaller obit in the back pages. On June 21, Brigadier General John Taliaferro Thompson, aged seventy-nine, the U.S. Army's director of arsenals in World War I and the inventor of the Thompson submachine gun, had died of a heart attack in Great Neck, on Long Island.

General Thompson, who had watched his son literally kill himself over Auto-Ordnance, would not live to see the company that was his brainchild arise to glory.

PART FOUR

Guns and Glory

CHAPTER 19

I Could Do with Some Machine Guns, Too

By the end of the summer of 1940, Mussolini was so impressed by Hitler's conquests that he sent the Italian army to invade southern France—though he did wait until after the Germans had vanquished the French army. Across the globe, Imperial Japan was so awed by Hitler's conquests that they asked to join Germany's alliance with Italy. In September, the Tripartite Pact was signed, creating the three-nation Axis alliance.

The noose was tightening on the United Kingdom. In August, Germany had declared unrestricted submarine warfare against Britain. Any ship of any nation that came into British waters was subject to being sunk. Many were. Hermann Göring, the boss of the Luftwaffe, insisted that his air arm would destroy the British will to carry on the war. He declared August 13 as "Adler Tag" (Eagle Day), the beginning of a no-holds-barred air offensive against British industrial centers and air bases.

In the United States, the majority yearned to remain separate from the bloodshed of Europe's War. However, some people, from President Franklin Roosevelt on down, were reluctantly preparing for a worst-case scenario.

In May 1940, Roosevelt resurrected the World War I–era Council of National Defense and its Advisory Commission. He also established the Office of Emergency Management to coordinate and direct new agencies such as the National Labor Relations Board, the Office of Civilian Defense, the Office of Defense Transportation, and so on. The budgets for the American armed forces were on the rise as the president called for—and Congress approved—a gradual expansion of the services.

The event that best underscored Roosevelt's thinking on the subject of National Defense came on May 16. Two days after the Netherlands government fled their homeland in disarray, Roosevelt went before Congress and proposed that it authorize funding for fifty thousand new aircraft for the U.S. Navy and the U.S. Army Air Corps. In 1939, a total of just 921 military aircraft had been built in the United States. It is a testament to American industry that manufacturers were nearly able to meet Roosevelt's goal by 1942 and to double it by 1944, but that, as they say, is another story.

The stream of matériel from the American arms industry had moved lazily through the 1930s, but it would soon rush forward like whitewater rapids. The British arms industry was also running at full capacity, and His Majesty's ordnance department waited anxiously for additional weapons to flow in from across the Atlantic.

As Göring's Luftwaffe was bombing Europe's cities and airdromes, the British people waited anxiously. Their shores were the obvious next stop for the blitzkrieg that had swallowed Western Europe in less than three months. It was not a question of if, but *when*.

While Hitler's forces prepared for their cross-channel invasion of Britain, the English people rallied around Prime Minister Winston Churchill, who had taken office on May 10, telling them he had "nothing to offer but blood, toil, tears and sweat." He defied Hitler by informing him that his troops would meet relentless opposition "on the beaches, on the streets and in every village."

However, to meet the Germans on an equal footing, the British army desperately needed small arms. Auto-Ordnance was ready to oblige. At the end of July, the prime minister attended a photo op at a military post in Yorkshire, where he had a chance to see the Thompson submachine gun up close. In the company of military brass, Churchill not only inspected, but handled, many of the weapons he was shown. A soldier was standing by with a new-production M1928A1, equipped with a drum magazine. The prime minister asked to see it, and the soldier raised the weapon obligingly, the trace of a grin on his lips.

Churchill cautiously touched the weapon, caressing the Cutts compensator between his thumb and forefinger. He didn't actually mean that he wanted to *see* it. He wanted to *touch* it.

There may have been a "May I?"

The next thing we know is that Churchill had the tommy gun in his hands, posing for photographs, his signature cigar clamped in his teeth, a grin on his face, and a gangster gun cradled in his arms.

The photograph was seen by many as a defiant image of Britain standing firm, ready to defend itself. Others saw it as grandstanding by Churchill. The London editorial writers had a lark, dubbing him "Cigarface," a pun on "Scar-

Prime Minister Winston S. Churchill was photographed in Yorkshire in July 1940
holding one of the first M1928A1 Thompson submachine guns delivered to Britain
after the start of World War II. *(Collection of the author)*

face." In Germany, Dr. Joseph Goebbels, Hitler's propaganda minister, climbed
on the same bandwagon, labeling Churchill a Chicago-style gangster.

What many articles and news reports about Churchill's famous photo
op failed to mention was that one of the prime minister's American cousins,

Frederic A. Willis, was now an Auto-Ordnance vice president. A former U.S. Army officer, Willis had come to Auto-Ordnance in mid-June 1940 from his post as assistant to the president of the Columbia Broadcasting System.

It seems that there may have been more than one tommy gun circulating in the hands of British civilians during that uncertain summer. In an article in the June 19, 2006, issue of *The Guardian*, Midge Gillies tells the interesting story of the Women's Home Defence groups that were formed to defend England against the Nazi invasion.

These were, she writes, "uniformed, private armies whose members trained in unarmed combat and learned how to fire a tommy gun, while using opera glasses to scan the skies for German paratroopers. Technically, these groups were illegal but there seems to have been no attempt to disband them."

As Ms. Gillies explains, Lady Helena Gleichen, a grandniece of Queen Victoria, set up her own private army to protect her stately home near Much Marcle in Herefordshire. She then presumptuously demanded that the Shropshire Light Infantry give her eighty rifles with ammunition, adding, "I could do with some machine guns, too, if you have any to spare."

When her request was denied, Midge Gillies writes, Lady Helena resorted to her own collection of antique weapons.

CHAPTER 20

Guns for Armies

As the summer of 1940 wore on, things went from merely uncertain to truly frightening for Winston Churchill's beleaguered Isle. However, in the United States, things went from good to better for Russell Maguire and Auto-Ordnance. It is a pity that Marcellus Thompson and his father could not have lived to see the numbers.

In 1939, when an order from the U.S. Army for nearly a thousand submachine guns arrived, it was the momentous event that probably saved Auto-Ordnance from collapsing. A year later, against the backdrop of World War II, it was a whole new company. In 1940, the U.S. Army cast aside nearly two decades of indifference to the Thompson, placing orders totaling 20,450, a number that would soon go even higher. This tally was topped by the 107,500 that were ordered by the United Kingdom that year.

"Outside Germany, the Thompson Gun was the only submachine gun in the world," Thompson authority Doug Richardson pointed out. "It was the only submachine gun that the U.S. Army could get into production *today*. Right now. They had a design, they had a gun, they had a manufacturing facility. All the U.S. Army had to do was place the order. They had no choice. They had no other option. The Thompson was the only submachine gun they could get, and it was pretty obvious by that point in time that a submachine gun *was* necessary."

Initially, the U.S. Army saw the Thompson as a weapon for an armored vehicle crew, first in armored scout cars, and eventually in tanks. The idea here was to give the tank crew a weapon that could be used to knock off "tank riders," enemy soldiers who climbed aboard with the intention of shoving a hand grenade or a gun muzzle though one of the tank's ports. The Thompson was seen as an ideal weapon for such an application. It had a high rate of fire and a large magazine, but more important, it was about a foot shorter than a main battle rifle and could be more easily maneuvered in the confined space within a tank. It was only later that the Thompson evolved into one of America's signature infantry weapons of World War II.

The production rate at Savage Arms ramped up quickly. Having completed just 201 tommy guns in April 1940, and 627 in May, the Utica plant topped 5,000 units monthly in August and reached 9,937 in December. By the end of the year, Savage had delivered 43,811 Thompson submachine guns to the United States government alone.

In September, things were going so well that the company, on the edge of collapse in 1939, suddenly and unexpectedly paid a dividend. It was a substantial dividend, $5.50 a share, for a total of $1.39 million. As Vice President Fred Willis put it, the suddenness of the unannounced dividend was "to avoid speculation" in Auto-Ordnance stock. In fact, the share price jumped 18 percent overnight. Not everyone was happy. Many on Wall Street felt blindsided by the surprise announcement, and Thomas Kane unsuccessfully sued Russell Maguire on behalf of the Thompson Estate, claiming that paying the dividend amounted to siphoning money out of the company.

In the United States, National Defense was a buzzword, an organizational concept, and a potential for profits from investments in industry. In the United Kingdom, it was a matter of life and death. Somewhere within the British arms procurement establishment, someone was scribbling on a piece of paper, calculating what proportion of the 107,500 tommy guns on order would reach Britain without being sent to the bottom of the Atlantic by a German U-boat.

In the summer of 1940, as Britain teetered on the abyss, surrounded by U-boats and hammered by the Luftwaffe, Russell Maguire presided over an arms company that was no longer teetering on the brink of collapse as it had been one year earlier. Indeed, it was at that critical juncture that he visited an old industrial plant located along the New York, New Haven & Hartford Railroad tracks in Bridgeport, Connecticut. He took out a Connecticut business license on July 3, then shook hands with the realtor and agreed that Auto-Ordnance Corporation would lease the factory.

Though it would take a year before the Bridgeport plant was turning out tommy guns, it would give Auto-Ordnance a proprietary production facility that was separate from the contract production that would continue in Utica.

The winter of 1940–1941, like the previous winter, was marked by a pause in major offensive action by Hitler's legions—aside from the relentless air campaign against Britain. The word "sitzkrieg" had, however, vanished from the media lexicon. The blitzkrieg was no longer something to joke about.

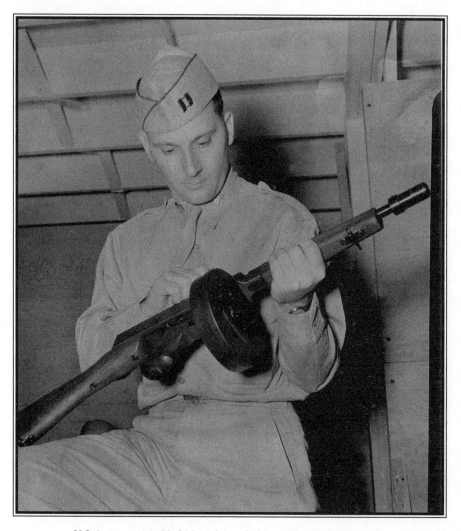

U.S. Army captain Ned Moorehouse holds an M1928A1 Thompson
submachine gun with a fifty-round drum magazine, September 1942.
(Courtesy of the U.S. Army via the National Archives)

In March 1941, as Russell Maguire was supervising the installation of
machine tools at Bridgeport, the restless Wehrmacht and its Italian compa-
triots came to life for spring offensives. The focus was on the Balkans, and
on Greece, where Mussolini's forces had been bogged down after invading
the previous fall. North Africa was now shaping up as a major front. Hitler
and Mussolini owned most of the Mediterranean's southern shore already.

Libya was an Italian colony, and Tunisia, Algeria, and Morocco were French colonies that Hitler acquired by way of beating France in 1940.

This left Egypt, where the smallish British garrison was all that stood between the Axis and the Suez Canal, Britain's lifeline to its colonies. Taking the canal would not only be a blow to Britain, it would open the gate to the oil fields of the Middle East and put an end to the Wehrmacht's fuel worries as they streamed out to conquer the world.

A year earlier, when the British arms buyers had been in the United States, they had run up large orders and an immense tab. By the beginning of 1941, His Majesty's government was running out of ready money. Roosevelt feared Hitler as much as anyone, and he knew that the United States was not, despite the buildup for national defense, ready to fight the Wehrmacht. He wanted to keep the British fighting, and to keep the British between the United States and Hitler.

Perhaps the second to last thing that Roosevelt wanted to see was Britain unable to pay for all the planes, tanks, rifles, and tommy guns they had ordered during 1940, so he came up with a plan. The plan was called Lend-Lease. The idea was that the United States would "sell, transfer title to, exchange, lease, lend, or otherwise dispose of" weapons and matériel to any government whose defense the president deemed vital to the safety of the United States. The way it worked was the United States government would purchase the weapons from the manufacturers and then deliver them to the Allies.

On March 11, as Germany's General Erwin Rommel prepared to begin his first offensive in Libya, driving the British eastward toward the Suez Canal, Roosevelt was signing the Lend-Lease Act. Sympathetic countries other than Britain, including China and the Soviet Union, were later included as well.

Probably the most colorful explanation of Lend-Lease was that made by Roosevelt at a press conference several months later.

"What do I do in such a crisis?" Roosevelt quipped, likening World War II to a fire at his neighbor's home. "I don't say. 'Neighbor, my garden hose cost me $15; you have to pay me $15 for it' . . . I don't want $15—I want my garden hose back after the fire is over."

Payment for the Lend-Lease goods, or their return to the United States, was to be made after the war. In fact, few of the garden hoses that survived the war were actually returned, and repayment was delayed. Britain finally settled up its bill, deeply discounted, at the end of 2006.

Against the backdrop of the rapidly emptying British purse, and

A group of U.S. Army Air Forces guards train with M1928A1 Thompson submachine guns at Mitchel Field, New York, in 1942. All but one of the weapons are without a magazine. *(Courtesy of the U.S. Army via the National Archives)*

discussions of Lend-Lease, rumors swirled around the British need for more and more Thompson submachine guns. Were the 107,500 not adequate? On January 20, 1941, *Time* had reported, "Recently Great Britain was reported eager to buy 250,000 to 500,000 from the U.S.—if they could be made fast enough."

Speed of production would footnote everything that happened at Auto-Ordnance for the next three years. Quantities would have been unimaginable by prewar standards. For Maguire's company, Lend-Lease would be a boon. Auto-Ordnance would continue building guns for both American and British customers under Ordnance Department purchase orders with Uncle Sam picking up the tab. Production of submachine guns at Utica mushroomed.

Beginning in March 1940, Auto-Ordnance delivered more guns every month than its total deliveries in all the years between the world wars. Between November and January, deliveries had been averaging 9,612 units per month. From March through May, the monthly average jumped to 19,523. In

August, as the Bridgeport plant began delivering Thompsons, the monthly production had risen to 29,946. Consider these numbers in comparison to the fact that it previously had taken Auto-Ordnance the better part of two decades to get through just 10,000 units of General Thompson's initial inventory.

On December 27, the business section of *The New York Times* reported all this under the headline "Savage Arms Will Speed Up." Indeed, during that last month of 1941, the output of Thompson submachine guns was just a shade under 40,000 units. Of course by the time this article appeared, the United States had been in the war for nearly three weeks.

CHAPTER 21

Americans at War

Even before World War II began, there were those in the United States who had predicted American involvement in the war as inevitable. A few had even suggested that the catalyst for America going to war with the Axis would be, not an egregiously aggressive act by Hitler, but an attack by the Japanese in the Pacific. As we know, it was the latter, and it came on the morning of Sunday, December 7, 1941.

The attack, centering on the U.S. Navy's base at Pearl Harbor in Hawaii, was a complete surprise and an immense success for the enemy. When it ended, more than 2,400 Americans were dead, nearly 200 aircraft had been destroyed, and the Pacific Fleet had been decimated. Eight of the nine battleships anchored in Pearl Harbor had been put out of commission.

The following day, President Roosevelt asked Congress for a declaration of war. On December 11, Germany and Italy declared war on the United States and Japan declared war on Britain. The United States was now embroiled in World War II, and American industry was ready to meet the challenges that lay ahead. That was a good thing, because the armed services were woefully unprepared in terms of matériel.

Despite many months of the National Defense buildup, the United States armed forces were caught flatfooted at Pearl Harbor. So inadequate were America's defenses in December 1941 that extreme measures were required. People in the big urban areas of Southern California, where a Japanese attack like Pearl Harbor was now dreaded, felt like sitting ducks. So did their defenders. On the afternoon of December 7, Fritz Dickie at Stembridge Gun Rentals in Hollywood received a phone call from the U.S. Coast Guard. It was well known that the Stembridge "Gun Room" on the Paramount Pictures lot was one of the biggest private arsenals anywhere, and the Coast Guard needed guns—especially tommy guns.

"We loaded them on trucks and, by night, the guns which had been

used mostly in gangster pictures were ready for the feared Japanese invasion," Dickie recalled after the war in a story printed in a Stembridge company brochure. "During the next few days, we also loaned rifles to the Coast
Guard stationed at Catalina and machine guns, pistols and shotguns to the
California State Guard. It was several months before all of the weapons were
returned. Subsequently, we received a letter from the Harbor Defenses command which said, in part: 'Due to the critical shortage of such weapons on
Dec. 7, 1941, those provided from your stock were a most welcome addition
to our defenses.'"

Though the feared invasion of California never materialized, the Japanese advance in the western Pacific was unstoppable. Their military suc-
cesses were reminiscent of the German blitzkrieg of 1939 and 1940. Within a
month of Pearl Harbor, they had captured Wake Island, Guam, Hong Kong,
and Manila. Then, just five weeks later, they conquered the supposedly impregnable British fortress at Singapore.

Across the globe, Hitler now dominated all of continental Europe. His
armies had invaded the Soviet Union and reached the gates of Moscow. The
Axis controlled all of North Africa from the Atlantic, nearly to the Nile River,
and they were poised to assault Cairo and the Suez Canal.

For America, and for its Allies in Britain and the Soviet Union, it was the
worst of times. Failure, disappointment, and defeat seemed to emanate from
every battlefront.

It was also a time of heros—and a time for tommy guns.

After landing in the Philippines, the Japanese quickly put the once-
cocky Americans on the run. It couldn't happen, the Yanks thought. But it
did. The Americans abandoned Manila by New Year's and withdrew west-
ward into the Bataan Peninsula, hoping to hold off the Japanese until help
arrived from the United States. It never came.

The American and Filipino defense of Bataan is one of the most tragic
and most heroic events of World War II, as a vastly outnumbered force held
out against General Masaharu Homma's Fourteenth Army for more than
three months.

One of the many stories to come out of the defense of Bataan is that of
the trusty tommy gun wielded by Captain Arthur W. Wermuth, the man
whom the media called a "One-Man Army." Assigned to the 57th Filipino
Scout Regiment, this officer had "a Vandyke beard, a .45-caliber tommy gun,
a Garand rifle, and an unerring eye."

A graduate of the Northwestern Military and Naval Academy in Lake
Geneva, Wisconsin, Wermuth became one of America's first World War II

Sergeant W. Emerick trains with an M1928A1 Thompson submachine gun in September 1942. By this time, the M1 Thompsons were starting to reach the troops.
(Courtesy of the U.S. Army via the National Archives)

heros thanks to reports filed by Clark Lee of the Associated Press, who escaped from Bataan before the final American defeat. According to Lee, the One-Man Army was wounded three times, killed more than a hundred Japanese soldiers and spent more time behind enemy lines during January 1942 than within his own. Lee had the unique perspective of having interviewed the captain as the battle was still raging. In turn, his dispatches appeared in newspapers across the United States, as well as in the February 23, 1942, issue of *Time*.

"On one of his reconnaissance patrols Captain Wermuth, from a foxhole, spotted a long line of Japanese crossing a ridge," Lee wrote.

"I worked them over with my tommy gun," Wermuth told Lee, "and got at least 30 like ducks in a Coney Island shooting gallery."

For his readers, Lee explained that, "attracted by the shooting, five Filipino scouts rushed to the scene, [and] helped Arthur Wermuth polish off 50 or 60 more" of the Japanese.

"On January 14," wrote Lee, "[Wermuth] volunteered to burn the enemy-held town of Samal. He crawled through the Japanese lines before dawn with five gallons of gasoline and walked behind the shacks where the Japanese were sleeping. He sprinkled the gasoline, threw a lighted match and fled. He formed a 'suicide antisniper' unit with 84 volunteers to eliminate 300 enemy snipers who had infiltrated behind the American lines. . . . The unit cleaned up one sector of the sniper area every morning between daybreak and 8:30. They killed at least 250 and also wiped out a number of Japanese machine-gunners with hand grenades."

When the United States and Filipino units surrendered on April 9, they were forced to endure the starvation and torture of the horrible Bataan Death March. It is estimated that a quarter of the captives died before reaching the prison camps. Wermuth was among those who survived, and one of the luckier few who survived four years of Japanese captivity. After the war he served as sheriff of Jefferson County, Colorado. In June 1959 he was famously photographed presenting Vice President Richard Nixon with a white cowboy hat.

While working on this book, I exchanged correspondence with historian John Fredriksen, who has been researching Wermuth. According to Fredriksen, much of what Clark Lee gave posterity was exaggeration.

"Many of Wermuth's contemporaries dispute that he did any of the deeds recorded in the newspapers," Fredriksen told me. "The country was hungry for heroes, imaginary or otherwise, and the newspapers obliged. . . . Not only was he a creature of the press, in captivity he was predatory and constantly stole food from other prisoners. His wartime reputation notwithstanding, after his release in 1945 the army gave him the choice of immediate discharge, or immediate court martial. He chose the former."

The part about Wermuth wielding a Thompson submachine gun, however, is true. There are photographs that prove it.

CHAPTER 22

Send Them In with an M1A1

American infantry soldiers went to war in 1941 and early 1942 with M1928 and M1928A1 Thompson submachine guns. "One-Man Army" Wermuth brandished such a gun in Bataan, and all of the Thompsons shipped out of Bridgeport and Utica in the weeks after Pearl Harbor were M1928A1s. Essentially, it was the same gun carried by the troops when the United States had "sent in the marines" back in the late 1920s. Soon this would change.

The M1928A1 was an old gun, with a design that dated back to 1921, but its age was not really relevant. The U.S. Army still equipped infantry companies with Browning automatic rifles that dated back to 1918. Though the semiautomatic M1 Garand, firing standard .30-'06 rifle ammunition, had been adopted as the U.S. Army's standard service rifle in 1936, it took five years to build enough to reequip the army, and there were still plenty of M1903s and M1917s being used in 1942.

It was not the age of the Thompson submachine gun design that became an issue as Auto-Ordnance and Savage ramped up production in late 1941, it was the Thompson's complexity. The U.S. Army Ordnance Department decided, and Savage concurred, that the gun had to be redesigned.

A few years earlier, the government bean counters trimmed requisition requests, but by the time the United States entered World War II, the only questions on the lips of those who acquired weapons of all kinds were "how many?" and "how quickly?" Therefore, speeding up production was an important priority. Simplifying the intricacies of its design would make it faster and easier to manufacture.

Redesign a classic? Russell Maguire balked. The man who had gone into the tommy gun business because Auto-Ordnance was an undervalued company with growth opportunity had become a fan of the gun itself.

At Savage the theory—first articulated a quarter century earlier by Theodore Eickhoff—was that the Blish lock was not essential to the operation of the gun. Many people had agreed with this assessment, and Savage engineers had proven it. The same blowback principle on which the BAR worked could be utilized in the Thompson. However, the Blish lock was so much a part of the essence of the Thompson submachine gun's image, and so much a part of its technical mystique, that Maguire dug in his heels.

He lost. The government insisted, and the customer is always right.

The Blish lock was out. So, too, were a number of other features. The Ordnance Department also decided that the Cutts compensator was unnecessary, and the stock was greatly simplified and made nondetachable. The complex Lyman gunsight, which afforded rifle accuracy to a weapon that was not used like a rifle, was replaced by a simpler sight that took only a fraction of the production time. The finish on the gun would be a dull black, a far cry from the carefully blued patina of the original M1921 Thompsons.

The prototype redesigned Thompson submachine gun was completed around the time of Pearl Harbor, evaluated by the Ordnance Department over the next several months, and officially adopted in April 1942. By then, the U.S. Army had dispensed with the practice of designating new weapon types as the model of the year it was adopted, but rather new weapons were now numbered within their class. Because the "Model of 1942" Thompson submachine gun was the first U.S. Army submachine gun adopted under this system of nomenclature, it became the "United States Submachine Gun, Caliber .45, Model 1" or simply "M1."

The then-current service rifle, the Garand, was adopted in 1936 and designated "United States Rifle, Caliber .30, M1," or "M1," rather than "M1936." The name was that of the rifle's designer, John Cantius Garand of the Springfield Armory.

When the armed forces took the M1928 and M1928A1 into the field, the heavy fifty-round L and hundred-round C drum magazines were determined to be too clumsy to be practical, and most guns were fielded with box magazines. With this in mind, the new, redesigned M1 Thompson submachine gun would accommodate only box or "stick" magazines. Both the twenty-round Type XX magazine and the Type XXX thirty-round magazines would be used during World War II.

Many people see the removal of the Blish lock from the Thompson submachine gun as a reasonable step toward simplifying the weapon, but this is not a unanimously shared perspective. As Bill Helmer points out, the engineers at Savage considered the Blish lock "a frill, if not a fraud." At the opposing pole of the spectrum, design engineer and Thompson aficionado

U.S. Army sergeant Sterling Hester strikes a classic pose with his M1 Thompson submachine gun in January 1943. Note the absence of the Cutts Compensator on the muzzle, and the actuator knob on the side, rather than the top, as it had been on earlier model Thompsons. *(Courtesy of the U.S. Army via the National Archives)*

Doug Richardson told me quite emphatically that abandoning the Blish lock was tantamount to a step back into the Dark Ages.

"The Blish lock is what makes the M1921 Thompson the greatest submachine gun ever made," said Richardson, who has spent a lifetime studying the inner workings of Thompsons of every model. "If you don't believe that, just try taking the Blish lock out of your M1921 and you'll probably blow the back out of your gun. Every design change made to the M1921 Thompson degraded the performance, increasing the problem of assembly and disassembly. The Blish lock works perfectly. It created a gun that was very controllable. The Thompson submachine gun is predicated on the Blish lock. The reason for removing the Blish lock was to make the gun cheaper and easier to manufacture. The Blish lock is complicated. It makes the receiver difficult to manufacture. It makes a great submachine gun, but it doesn't make a good *military* submachine gun. The military wants things that are cheap and easy to make, but the M1921 Thompson is not that gun. The M1A1 Thompson is a far better military gun than the M1921 or the M1928, but it's a different gun. It's a simpler gun. They eliminated the Blish lock and went to a straight blowback system."

Meanwhile, as Auto-Ordnance was gearing up to supply large quantities of Thompsons for the U.S. Army, the Secret Service joined the FBI among federal law enforcement agencies to put the gun into service.

"The Thompson submachine gun was available for use by the Secret Service at least as early as January 1941," Secret Service archivist Michael Sampson told me. "[It] probably existed earlier, [but I've been] unable to locate on-site documentation that notes specific date of introduction. [The] firearm of choice at this time was a side arm. Rifles and Thompsons were on hand depending on the heightened nature of the event or trip. For example, the Thompson was available to the White House detail agents accompanying President Franklin Roosevelt during his January 1943 visit to North Africa to participate in the Casablanca Conference. In addition, the White House police had access to the Thompson while guarding the Executive Mansion."

Meanwhile, the Border Patrol had already started using the Thompson to enforce roadblocks set up to stop booze smugglers during Prohibition. Seth Nadel, a U.S. Customs agent with whom I spoke at length while writing this book, had a friend whose father had been in the Border Patrol during World War II, and who had used a tommy gun while guarding prisoner of war camps in the United States.

At this point in the narrative, it might be useful to provide a brief snapshot of the small arms that would be carried by American infantrymen during World War II. The basic weapon was the M1 Garand service rifle, which was carried by most soldiers and marines. In situations where a lighter weapon was required, such as on missions where a great deal of equipment was being carried, or with paratroopers, many men would carry the M1 carbine. It was shorter and lighter and easier to handle than a Garand, but it fired a lower velocity .30 caliber round and had less hitting power.

Each infantry company had several Browning automatic rifles, and officers usually carried an M1911 automatic pistol as a sidearm. Most sergeants were assigned a Thompson submachine gun. As we will see in later chapters, an informal, random look at infantrymen who earned the Medal of Honor during World War II indicates that a majority of the men who did so while carrying a Thompson submachine gun were sergeants.

In actual practice, however, most infantrymen eventually got their hands on, and kept their hands on, their weapons of choice. Not infrequently, half the men in an infantry squad were armed with Thompsons.

The Marine Corps, meanwhile, had flirted briefly with going in a different direction. In the late 1920s and early 1930s, when circumstances demanded that the United States "send in the marines," they had, as we have seen, gone in with Thompson submachine guns. However, on the eve of World War II, the Corps chose to adopt an entirely new submachine gun as a hedge against the uncertain availability of the Thompson under the recent and largely untested manufacturing arrangement with Savage Arms.

The new gun was designed by Eugene Reising, a gunsmith who had spent sixteen years with Colt, and according to *Time* magazine on January 20, 1941, held around sixty patents and had "enough marksmanship medals to clutter his home at Hartford."

Patented in 1940, the Reising gun was manufactured under the designation M50 by Harrington & Richardson of Worcester, Massachusetts. It had a single-piece wooden stock and looked at first glance like a rifle. It weighed only seven pounds and fired .45 caliber ACP cartridges from a twenty-round magazine. The basic M50 was complemented by an M55 with a folding stock, and the M60, which was semiautomatic.

Embraced by the U.S. Navy and Marine Corps, it was also auditioned by the U.S. Army, in whose testing it was seen to compare favorably to the Thompson. In the field, however, there was no comparison. Under battlefield conditions, the Reising proved to be a finicky piece of equipment with a propensity for jamming and breaking. Individual marines quickly exchanged their Reisings for Thompsons or other guns as soon as the opportunity presented itself.

Before the United States entered the war and the marines had those experiences, however, the Reising had actually looked like the solution to the problem of building Thompsons fast enough.

Also in its January 20, 1941 issue, *Time* veritably gushed about Reising's gun and its ease of production. "Last week a new submachine gun that looked like the answer to the speed problem began coming in quantity from the Harrington & Richardson Arms Co. plant at Worcester, Mass. The new gun weighs only six and a half pounds (to the Tommy's ten), fires 200 shots a minute [actually it was more than twice that rate]. Its biggest feature: it has only three moving parts, is designed to be mass-produced at about $50 (Tommies cost $200-225)."

The report stated that Harrington & Richardson had bragged that it would "produce 500 a day by next month, 1,000 a day by April." The U.S. Army made no commitments, but its Ordnance Department predicted that the new gun "will play no small part in military events of the future."

It didn't. Because of the complaints from men in the field who were actually using the Reising, the U.S. Army went back to the Thompson, at least for the moment, and pursued the M1 variant.

In the history of the Thompson submachine gun, the M1 was actually a relatively short-lived iteration. A further simplification occurred almost immediately after the M1 was officially adopted. This redesign involved reducing the number of moving parts in the firing mechanism, including incorporating the firing pin directly onto the bolt. Perhaps these steps were influenced by competition from the Reising gun.

This new Thompson was designated as M1A1, with the suffix standing for "Alteration One," and was officially adopted in October 1942, only half a year after the M1. Outwardly, the M1 and M1A1 were essentially identical, and can be distinguished from M1928A1 by the simplified muzzle without the Cutts compensator, and by the actuator knob being on the side, rather than on the top as it is in earlier Colt Thompsons.

Doug Richardson reminds us that there has been some discussion of a stainless steel M1A2 Thompson, of which some prototypes were made under a U.S. Navy contract, but he insists that the M1A2 never existed. Savage did, however, make several dozen experimental aluminum M1928A1 Thompsons with an eye toward a lighter gun. This concept never entered large-scale production.

Another experimental Thompson variant was an M1 that was retrofitted with a longer, .30 caliber barrel, with its receiver redesigned to accept a Browning automatic rifle magazine. This, like the other experiments, never entered production.

Almost all of the M1s were built at the Auto-Ordnance plant in Bridgeport, beginning in July 1942. Savage continued to manufacture mainly

Two GIs pose for the camera with their M1 Thompson submachine guns at Camp Chaffee, Arkansas, in October 1942. *(Courtesy of the U.S. Army via the National Archives)*

M1928A1s until December 1942, when this facility converted over to full production of the M1A1. By this time, monthly production was running around or above 50,000 units. In October 1942, 60,504 Thompsons were produced. The year was the biggest ever, with 594,910 units delivered, and a gross income of $42.6 million for the company—up nearly 250 percent since 1939.

Essentially all of the guns delivered to the United States government went to the Army Ordnance Department, and from there some went on to the U.S. Navy and Marine Corps. Bill Helmer writes in *The Gun That Made the Twenties Roar* that at least 183,973 were transferred thusly. As noted earlier, sizable quantities that were acquired by the U.S. Army after the passage of the Lend-Lease Act in March 1941 were passed along to Allied countries, especially the nations of the British Empire.

A large number of Lend-Lease Thompson submachine guns, along with millions of rounds of .45 caliber ACP ammunition, were sent to the Soviet Union. Few, if any, of these guns were actually used by the Red Army, although they remained in storage for over half a century.

"By the time the Russians got all this, they didn't need it anymore. Their own production [of indigenous submachine guns] had caught up," firearms advisor Idan Greenberg told me. "In my opinion, none of the Thompsons were used by the Russian forces. Unlike our own government, which destroyed [surplus war materiel] that it couldn't immediately use or give away, the Russians kept everything in cold storage in Murmansk until just a few years ago. . . . That's where all the mint-condition parts kits are coming from [in the early twenty-first century]. I have a collector friend in Austria who got some brand-new, unissued M1928A1s from Russia."

On the assembly lines, the M1 and M1A1 were boons for Auto-Ordnance. They took half as long to manufacture, and they could therefore be delivered at a fraction of the cost of a prewar M1928A1. The unit price of an M1928A1 in 1939 was more than $200, but mass production got that number down to $70 by 1942, and eventually, Auto-Ordnance was able to sell an M1A1 to the Ordnance Department for just $45.

CHAPTER 23

Britain Stands Alone

The German invasion of Britain, which had seemed to be a foregone conclusion in the summer of 1940, never happened, and the Wehrmacht never had to face Lady Helena.

The Germans had assembled the men and the tanks, and they brought together coasters and river barges for use as landing craft for what they called Operation Sea Lion, a massive amphibious operation that would have put three field armies ashore along the English Channel coast between Dorset and Kent. But Hitler pulled the plug on September 17 because of the failure of the Luftwaffe to achieve air superiority and the approach of winter weather. Initially, it was understood that the suspension was merely a postponement, but Hitler gradually lost enthusiasm for the operation, and forces earmarked for Sea Lion were gradually reassigned.

For Britain, 1941 was a better year than it might have been, but not a great year. The worst thing was Germany's unrestricted submarine warfare against British supply lines. The best thing that happened was Hitler's ill-considered Operation Barbarossa, the invasion of the Soviet Union in June—on top of his having to intervene in the Balkans in April to save Mussolini from humiliation. Though Barbarossa went splendidly for the Wehrmacht at first, a combination of vast distances and bad weather late in the year turned the Eastern Front into a quagmire. The British, and later the Americans, benefited most from Hitler's eastern folly as it siphoned resources away from other fronts.

Had it not been for the Eastern Front, 1941 might have been much worse for Britain. Hitler might have rethought his decision to cancel Sea Lion and he would certainly have devoted more resources to General (later Field Marshal) Rommel and his effort to capture the Suez Canal and the Middle Eastern oil fields beyond.

In December 1941, the attack on Pearl Harbor was a mixed blessing for

Britain. On one hand, it brought into the war a powerful ally, the United States, but it also unleashed a powerful foe, Imperial Japan.

As we have seen, 1942 saw immense gains for Japan against both British and American interests in Asia and the Pacific. It was also a time when Britain continued, for the most part, to stand without much in the way of American help against the Germans. It was not until November, eleven months after Pearl Harbor, that the United States finally made a major commitment of ground forces against the Axis in North Africa.

This coincided with the best news that the British had since the war had begun. Between October 23 and November 5, in the climactic Battle of El Alamein, in the deserts of western Egypt, British Empire divisions turned the tide against Rommel's Afrika Korps and his Italian sidekicks. In this massive battle, British forces were augmented by those from such empire nations as Australia, New Zealand, South Africa, and India as well as Greek and Free French units.

In the battle, the M1928A1 Thompson submachine guns that had been acquired by Britain over the preceding two years played an important role. Take for example, the case of Sergeant William Henry "Bill" Kibby, who earned the Victoria Cross—the highest medal for valor awarded by the British Empire—at El Alamein.

Born at Winlaton in England's County Durham, Kibby had emigrated with his family to Australia, where they settled in Adelaide. A husband and father of two daughters, he joined the Australian Militia in 1936, and was assigned to 2/48th Infantry Battalion when World War II began and sent to North Africa with the Second Australian Imperial Force. The "2/" prefix in the designation of the battalion was used to identify the unit as part of the Second Australian Imperial Force (2nd AIF) of the Australian Army. The 2nd AIF was formed in September 1939 and was comprised of volunteer personnel. Under the Australian Defence Act of 1903, the personnel of neither the part-time Militia nor the Permanent Military Force could serve outside Australia or its territories unless they volunteered to do so. Originally the 2nd AIF was to consist of just one division, but during World War II, it grew to be comprised of five divisions, the 6th, 7th, 8th, and 9th, as well as the 1st Armoured Division. The divisions numbered 1st through 5th were Militia divisions, as were the 10th through 12th, and the 2nd and 3rd Armoured Divisions. The units of the 2nd AIF used the "2/" prefix to distinguish themselves from the Militia units. The 2/48 Infantry Battalion, Australia's highest decorated unit of the war, was originally part of the 7th Division, but in early 1941, it became part of the 9th Division. Deployed initially to the Middle East, the 2/48 redeployed to the South West Pacific Area of Operations in 1943.

On October 23, as the battle opened, Bill Kibby went out with No. 17 Platoon in the assault against Miteiriya Ridge on the northern end of the battlefront. Very soon in the fight, the platoon leader was killed, and Kibby assumed command. Almost immediately, No. 17 was ordered to attack some particularly stubborn enemy machine-gun positions that were holding up the battalion's assault.

Leading from the front, Kibby ran forward, his Thompson blazing as he poured lead into the Germans. With his men running to keep up, he blasted his way into the enemy strongpoint, killing three and taking a dozen prisoners.

Over the next several days, he proved himself to be the sort of inspiring leader that men look up to and remember. As reported in *The London Gazette* of January 28, 1943, "Sergeant Kibby moved from section to section, personally directing their fire and cheering the men, despite the fact that the Platoon throughout was suffering heavy casualties. Several times, when under intense machine-gun fire, he went out and mended the platoon line communications, thus allowing mortar concentrations to be directed effectively against the attack on his Company's front. His whole demeanor during this difficult phase in the operations was an inspiration to his platoon."

On the night of October 30, 2/48th Battalion struck behind enemy lines, with No. 17 Platoon pushing through heavy German machine-gun fire to take its objective. As the heavy machine guns took their toll, Kibby and his blazing Thompson took the lead, and one by one the enemy fell. Just as he assaulted the last enemy holdout, alone and with hand grenades, Bill Kibby was caught in the sights of the German gunners.

The morning after he died, the Australian battalions, concentrated in the thickest part of the battlefront, began to break the back of German resistance. Within a few days, the Afrika Korps began a long retreat to its ultimate defeat in North Africa.

The British infantry battalion of this period consisted of four rifle companies comprising 100 to 120 men, plus other units, such as administration, signals, and a mortar platoon. In turn, the rifle companies consisted of three rifle platoons, each commanded by a lieutenant and each containing three rifle sections. As the standard infantry rifle in the U.S. Army was the M1 Garand, that of the British rifle platoon was the No. 4 Mark 1 .303 caliber Lee-Enfield rifle, the latest iteration in a long line of bolt-action Lee-Enfields of that caliber that had been standard with the British army since before World War I.

The rifle sections were each commanded by a corporal, who by 1941 had his Lee-Enfield officially replaced by a Thompson submachine gun. Eventually, the Thompson was also routinely issued to sergeants. As with American soldiers, the tommy gun became an integral part of the arsenal of the British infantry at a very basic level.

The sections were also each armed with a Bren .303 caliber light machine gun. Weighing roughly twenty pounds, the Bren gun had a role with British infantry in World War II that was generally analogous to that of the U.S. Army's BAR. It took its name from a combination of Brno, the Czech city where it was designed, and Enfield, where it was made at the Royal Small Arms Factory. Unlike the BAR, the Bren gun had a very long career, and would still be in service with the British through the Falklands in 1982 and Gulf War I in 1991—and it was still being manufactured in India in the twenty-first century.

In addition to its role in infantry battalions, the Thompson submachine gun was also adopted by the British and British Empire armies for use by Commando teams and units such as the Long Range Desert Group, because a high volume of sustained fire was seen as essential to their work.

Originally formed in the summer of 1940, the Commandos were elite units roughly analogous during World War II to the U.S. Army's Ranger Battalions and precursors to modern Special Operations units. The Commandos were created secretly to conduct clandestine raids and operations behind German lines in Scandinavia and occupied Europe, sometimes in conjunction with regular infantry.

As Doug Richardson once explained in a conversation with me, the British government did not like the drum magazines on the Thompson guns "because the cartridges rattle inside the drum when it's loaded because they're loose between the rotor arms. They were concerned that the British Commandos would be heard by the Germans. The Commandos said that one of their greatest weapons was making that noise because the Germans were so afraid of that noise they would abandon their outposts. The Commandos are said to have claimed that they liked the noise the gun made because they didn't even have to shoot."

Perhaps the most successful of the Commando raids was the March 1942 destruction of the battleship-sized drydock at St.-Nazaire on the French Atlantic coast, while one of the most infamous was the August 19, 1942, assault on the French coastal port of Dieppe. The latter mission involved more than

1,000 Commandos and Royal Marines, 50 American Rangers, and nearly 5,000 members of the 2nd Canadian Infantry Division. The object of this exercise, called Operation Jubilee, was to capture the town, hold it for a short time, then withdraw having taken German prisoners. The point of this was to test German responses to the eventual Allied invasion of northern Europe.

One of those self-assured young men with a tommy gun that day was Corporal Harold Scharfe of Windsor, Ontario. A section leader, he landed with a Thompson submachine gun under his arm and enough rations for three meals.

"We were real confident," he told Tom Berg of *The Orange County Register* in an August 2006 interview. "We'd been in England training for two years and we wanted action. . . . We were supposed to go in for a day, do our jobs, and get picked up by the ships, then go back to England."

In 2006, an eighty-four-year-old Scharfe packed up the portable oxygen concentrator that his son bought him, left his home in Anaheim Hills, California, and flew back to Dieppe to help dedicate a memorial on the rocky beach.

"I saw guys getting it as we jumped out," Scharfe told Berg. "We jumped over dead bodies, arms flying, and stomachs. . . . There were all kinds of wounded. Guys were crying. Guys were saying, 'Shoot me.' I had a very close buddy—we held hands and said, 'This is it.'"

At around 3:00 P.M., a Canadian officer held up a white flag, Scharfe put down his Thompson, and the Germans flooded into the areas where the Canadians had taken cover. By nightfall, he was headed for Stalag VIIIB near Breslau.

The Germans had repulsed a major raid on their domain and had inflicted heavy casualties that sent the bloodied Allies fleeing. The operation was a disaster. More than half of the men who landed were killed, wounded, or captured.

In August 1942, the Axis still held the upper hand from the rugged coasts of continental Europe to the sweaty jungles of the Pacific.

CHAPTER 24

Digging In Their Heels

The news from the fronts was bad. The defeat of the beleaguered men of Bataan was a serious blow to American morale, but in the context of the over-ocean blitzkrieg of Imperial Japanese troops, it was a wonder that it took General Homma's army so long. Having captured the jewels in Imperial Britain's crown from Hong Kong to Singapore with blistering speed, the Japanese captured most of the Dutch colonial empire that is now Indonesia, as well as most of the Australian protectorate that is now Papua New Guinea. They also began picking off the islands in the Solomons chain.

Strategically, the Japanese high command had decided to occupy New Guinea as a stepping-stone to neutralizing Australia. After capturing the port city of Rabaul on the island of New Britain in February 1942, the Japanese had quickly turned it into their principal forward operating base in the South Pacific.

The unlikely first land-war battlegrounds in the Pacific Theater were on New Guinea and the island of Guadalcanal in the Solomons. When he was forced out of the Philippines, General Douglas MacArthur vowed that he would return, but it would take the better part of three years to accomplish that. The main concern of the Allies in the Pacific in 1942 was not recapturing lost territory but merely *stopping* the Japanese advance.

Harry Horsman, who was with the 1st Marine Division on Guadalcanal, recalled using the Thompson submachine gun. As he told Lisa Craft in a 1998 interview that resides in the archives of the Marine Corps Oral History Branch, he recalled that the marines went into action in 1942 still equipped with M1903 rifles.

"We went through the first campaign entirely with the '03 rifle [but] we didn't think we were being deprived because we knew it was a good rifle," Horsman told Ms. Craft. "We knew it was true. It would take a lot of abuse in jungle conditions. It always works. . . . Of course, you did get a lot more

Private Richard Ryski of Chicago pauses in the Guadalcanal jungle on the day
after Christmas 1942 to view a grisly reminder of the terrible fighting that had
taken place on the island during the year. He has a bayonet fixed to his M1928A1
Thompson submachine gun, not a common configuration, but not unheard-of.
(Courtesy of the U.S. Army via the National Archives)

firepower with the M1, [but] we didn't get that until we got to Australia after
the Guadalcanal campaign. . . . We also had the Thompson submachine
guns. . . . The Japanese found out to their great discomfort that we *did* have
superior firepower."

In his 1949 Center of Military History study entitled *The War in the Pacific,
Guadalcanal: The First Offensive,* John Miller Jr. discussed the superiority of
small arms that the United States was finally able to bring to bear in the latter half of 1942.

"American weapons had generally proved to be both potent and practi-
cal," writes Miller, citing 1st Marine Division after-action reports by General
Alexander Vandergrift, the marine commander on Guadalcanal, and by
Captain John L. Zimmerman, USMCR.

"The U.S. Rifle, M1 (Garand) had shown itself to be superior to the

M1903 (Springfield), with which many marines had been armed," Miller observes. "Other small arms were less satisfactory. The .45 caliber automatic pistol found little use. The Marines' Reising Gun, a .45 caliber submachine gun, proved to be almost worthless. The .45 caliber Thompson submachine gun, while efficient, sounded too much like Japanese .25 caliber weapons, and could not be safely employed at the front."

To amplify Miller's observations: the Reising was prone to jam, and the folding stock of the M55 variant was likely to break when the weapon was fired; however, the tommy gun was not without a certain unexpected drawback. Stories of the similarity in sound between the Thompson and Japanese light machine guns are often heard among those told of the campaign on Guadalcanal. The problem came when an American was mistaken for a Japanese, and his own comrades opened fire on him. Among the marines, those who didn't care would have included the men of the Marine Raider Battalions, although they did not employ their Thompsons at the front. Instead they employed them well behind the front—but on the enemy side.

By the time the U.S. Army began arriving in the South Pacific in force, so too did weapons to finally supersede the M1903. Doug Richardson relates an interesting story that he was told by a man who grew up on a farm in downstate Illinois during the 1920s. The gangsters from Chicago would go down there to pick up bootleg booze and occasionally show up with a Thompson submachine gun. The man's father remarked that he'd like to have one of "them guns," and later they gave him an M1921 Thompson.

Fast forward to 1942, and the boy who learned to shoot a Thompson on an Illinois farm is now a soldier in the South Pacific.

"They arrived with their [M1903] Springfield rifles and were immediately told to put them into a pile," Richardson explained. "They were given one of three chits, either for a Garand, an M1 Carbine, or a Thompson. He didn't get a Thompson chit, but stood in the Thompson line anyway. They didn't bother to look at his chit when they gave him a Thompson gun—which he wanted badly. He was later involved in a firefight, and was on the ground when a Japanese soldier ran up and stuck him with his bayonet. He was able to raise his Thompson and pull the trigger, blowing the enemy and his rifle and his bayonet into the air. From that moment you'd never get that gun away from him!"

There are many stories about GIs whose first exposure to the Thompson was *not* after they went into uniform. Richardson tells of a young draftee who was not paying attention during a demonstration of how to fieldstrip a Thompson. The sergeant, wanting to make an example of this man for his inattentiveness, called him in front of the group, ordering him to strip and reassemble the weapon. This he did, quickly and nonchalantly.

"How did you know how to do that?" asked the sergeant, dumbfounded.

"I used to do it in the backseat of a Packard at night," the man replied casually.

How is it that New Guinea and Guadalcanal became such essential battlefronts of World War II?

It was almost by accident. They were just the first places where the Allies were finally able to dig in their heels and stop the heretofore relentless Japanese blitzkrieg. As they had for the Philippines and elsewhere, the Japanese had already printed currency to be used in Australia under Japanese occupation.

The troops who were sent here were mainly American troops—both soldiers and marines—and the Australian Imperial Forces. Ironically, many of the "Diggers," as the Aussies had called themselves since World War I, had gone to the Middle East and North Africa to serve under British command in 1941, and now the AIF was being rushed home to stop the enemy in New Guinea before they could start marching through Darwin.

New Guinea was an improbable slice of real estate to be fought over by the great world powers of the mid-twentieth century. The third largest island in the world after Australia and Greenland, New Guinea is more than three times the size of the United Kingdom and 20 percent larger than Texas. However, in 1941, when the Japanese first put troops ashore, the vast place had fewer people than the forty-nine square miles of San Francisco. It is a land of impossible terrain that even in the twenty-first century has yet to be bisected by a highway. It is a place of such remoteness that even after World War II, it was home to multitudes of plant and animal species not yet catalogued by biologists, and by numerous groups of Stone Age people whose languages had never been heard by anthropologists. New Guinea was such a difficult place to wage war that the troops who were fighting battles such as those on the Kokoda Track and at Buna had found it a triumph when they managed to march a mile a day through its jungles.

The jungles of the Pacific islands, with their slippery hillsides tangled in forests and foliage and where visibility was often measured in inches rather than yards, were literally hell on earth for most troops who dared to challenge them. Located barely south of the equator, New Guinea has a climate in which a medical textbook's worth of tropical diseases can flourish. The troops discovered that malaria was almost routine and maladies such as dysentery *were* routine.

Place names such as Buna, Gona, and Kokoda entered the headlines. Though today they have faded from the collective memory, they still have great resonance with the veterans who fought there, and with those who remember the men who did.

To carry the fight to the enemy in Buna, Gona, and Kokoda, Allied ground troops had to cross the seven-thousand-foot Owen Stanley Mountains from Port Moresby. It was a sixty-mile hike though terrain where there were no roads, only a very difficult, single-file trail known as the Kokoda Track. It climbs from equatorial heat and humidity near sea level at the two ends through frigid mountain passes in the middle.

In August 1942, Australia began to send elements of its 7th Division into New Guinea. They were soon joined by the U.S. 32nd Infantry Division. First to see action were the Australian 2/16th Battalion, who went onto the Kokoda Track shortly after disembarking at Port Moresby. They had had their baptism of fire fighting the French Foreign Legion—who fought on the side of the Axis after the fall of France—in Lebanon, and had fought Rommel in Libya.

The troops who fought in this difficult terrain did so with a variety of weapons. The Americans carried M1 Garands and not a few earlier model Springfields. The Australians, like the British, carried the .303 Lee-Enfields. Both the Yanks and the Diggers carried the Thompson submachine gun. As with the British and American armies, the Thompson was generally standard-issue for noncoms, but in the jungles of New Guinea, strict regulations gave way to the law of weapons of choice. For many, this meant Thompsons.

Japanese troops had captured every port of call along the northern coast of New Guinea, from Sansapor in the west to Hollandia to Lae in the east. Strategically, the next stop was Port Moresby, on the south shore. That was where their unstoppable forward charge stopped. The Aussies and the Americans were finally able to draw a metaphorical line in the jungle. Having amassed the resources to make a stand, they did so on the approaches to Port Moresby and turned it into a base of operations for offensive actions. With this the war entered a new phase in which the Japanese finally faced some serious resistance. The focus of the land battle would be along the north coast between Lae and Milne Bay—the eastern tip of New Guinea.

It was at Milne Bay that a young Queenslander named John Alexander French earned the Victoria Cross while carrying a Thompson submachine gun. It was on September 4, 1942, and Corporal French's 2/9th Battalion patrol was pinned down, taking fire from three Japanese machine-gun nests.

Directing the men to take cover, French inched forward to a place where he could lob hand grenades into one of the enemy strongholds.

Having blown it sky-high, he returned to his men, gathered up more grenades, and repeated the process with the second machine-gun nest. The third gun was not in a position where he could get to it with a grenade, so he rushed it head-on, firing his Thompson from his hip, Hollywood style.

The enemy brought their Nambu machine gun to bear on the young corporal. They managed a few hits, but still he came.

At last, he was upon them.

French raked the machine gun nest with .45 caliber ACP rounds, killing every one of the enemy.

Alas, French's wounds proved mortal, and his Victoria Cross was posthumous.

The Kokoda Track would see unbelievably awful fights. There were no gloriously sweeping battlefields, but there were many heros, and many of them preferred the Thompson. In his excellent book about the Australian serviceman, *The Spirit of the Digger: Then and Now*, Patrick Lindsay writes of Corporal Charlie McCallum of the 2/14th, who had already been wounded three times when his platoon was ordered to make a tactical withdrawal.

"Despite his wounds, Charlie held off the charging enemy, allowing his mates to pull back to another position down the Track," Lindsay tells. "Charlie held and fired his Bren gun with his right hand and carried a Thompson Submachine Gun in the other hand. When his magazine ran out on the Bren, he swung up the Tommy Gun with his left hand and continued to cut down the surging Japanese as he changed magazines on the Bren. When the Tommy Gun was empty he used the Bren gun again, and continued his one-man assault until all his comrades were clear. At least twenty-five Japanese lay around him. One got so close he actually ripped a utility pouch from Charlie's belt before falling dead at his feet. When he knew his mates were clear, Charlie fired a final burst and calmly moved off back down the Track."

McCallum received the Distinguished Service Medal, but his recommendation for the Victoria Cross was somehow lost in the shuffle of paperwork far from the Kokoda Track.

While working on this book, I had the pleasure of corresponding with Don Johnson in Brisbane, whose father, also Don Johnson, served with the 2/25th Battalion on the Kokoda Track. He shared with me the transcripts of a number of his father's stories about experiences with the Thompson in New Guinea.

According to "Men of Courage," memoirs penned by the elder Don, the Bren gun had been popular in North Africa because of its long-range accuracy on battlefields with vast unobstructed views, but the Thompson proved more popular in New Guinea.

"With the Bren it was possible to put three slugs in one man's head, at three hundred yards in a burst, which would blow the top off his head as he fell," he recalled. "This sometimes happened to [the Germans], some of their dead showed the signs after a Bren gun had been in action. It was a very deadly weapon to use in the desert campaigns, but in the Jungle close quarter fighting the tommy gun suited me better.

"I wasn't shooting at shadows. If I pulled off a shot there was a dead Jap at the other end of it," he said, discussing the effectiveness of the Thompson. "The Jap would fire all the 6.5mm bullets out of his Arisaka rifle, from his noisy five-round magazine. You would know it then, as he would come for you with his rifle, his bayonet fixed. . . . I would simply shoot him with a .45 calibre slug burst from the Thompson. Hit him in the brisket or between the kidneys with it. . . . I didn't have time to aim, just pointed the gun and fired, a reflex action. There was just the quick and the dead!"

Johnson added that the battalion had returned from North Africa with just forty-two Thompson submachine guns, but that the number was doubled as they transitioned through Queensland en route to Port Moresby, a fact that pleased the men.

In close combat, the Thompson almost invariably proved itself to be the soldier's best friend. Don Johnson tells of being attacked by a Japanese soldier with a fixed bayonet: "This Jap came at me with a fixed bayonet and I flogged it down with the Thompson gun but he kept trying to spike me so I shot him," he said. "I only had to hit him once in the chest and then he was clay."

While much of the Australian equipment was coordinated to British standards, the Diggers carried .45 caliber revolvers as well as the .45 caliber tommy guns. Though the calibers were identical, the men sometimes got into trouble mixing ammo. As Don Johnson said, "The .45 calibre submachine gun bullet would fit in a .45 revolver but the barrel of the revolver would eventually split like a banana, a bit too much power."

Some of the soldiers loved the power of the Thompson, but others did not. One of the criticisms that is often heard involves the low-velocity ammo. During firefights in the thick jungle, the .45 caliber ACP rounds would get stuck in tree trunks before reaching their targets. The .30 caliber rounds fired by Browning automatic rifles, on the other hand, could rip through more easily. When I discussed this with Don Johnson, though, he took exception to the negative remarks about the .45 round.

"No, mate," he said. "Mightn't go through a tree as far as a .303 would. . . . I guess the .45 is thicker and inclined to spread to the thickness of a penny on impact with something hard."

Indeed, the Thompson was a very popular weapon with the Diggers, as well as among U.S. troops in the New Guinea campaign. The evidence is in Ordnance Department records of ammunition that was fired. According to Lida Mayo, writing in *The Ordnance Department: On Beachhead and Battlefront*, "the highest expenditures in the campaign were of .30-caliber ball ammunition for the M1 rifle, .45-caliber ammunition for the submachine gun, and HE [high explosive] ammunition for the 81 mm. mortar, which was unexpectedly employed as a substitute for artillery."

She goes on to say, "The high expenditure of .45-caliber rounds for the submachine [tommy] gun was partly caused by the 32nd Division infantrymen's preference for the tommy gun over the BAR. In contrast to the marines on Guadalcanal, who swore by the BAR (and objected to the Tommy gun because it sounded like a Japanese weapon and drew friendly fire), the Army troops in Papua considered the BAR too heavy and clumsy for quick use in the jungle and too hard to keep in repair."

Repair and the availability of spare parts were, of course, key issues wherever the armed forces were engaged, and there were few areas of major operations where the supply lines were stretched thinner than in the Pacific during 1942–1943. Among the parts most in demand were main recoil springs for Thompson submachine guns, as well as rear sight and bolt assemblies for M1 rifles, driving springs and cocking levers for light machine guns, and firing pins for mortars. According to Ms. Mayo's study, "to obtain them the crews cannibalized arms and equipment left on the battlefield."

She added that the necessary process of cannibalization was "vigorously opposed" by Lieutenant Colonel Jonathan L. Holman, the ranking officer in the Ordnance Section of the U.S. Army's Forces in Australia command, "who advocated the evacuation of damaged weapons and vehicles to Ordnance service centers so they could be torn down and rebuilt. In later campaigns in the Pacific Holman was able to put this procedure into effect but in Papua cannibalization was often the only way to get parts."

As she points out, weapons parts had been extremely scarce in Australia ever since the 32nd Division, the first division-strength U.S. Army outfit to face the enemy in New Guinea, first arrived in May 1942. Within the Pacific islands, there was also the problem of bringing up supplies. In early

December 1942, during the American actions against Buna, on the New Guinea north coast, only seven jeeps and three one-ton trailers had been flown in. They were usable only when the roads were not a sea of mud.

"Most of the supply burden," Ms. Mayo notes, "was borne by carrier lines of Papuan natives, laden mainly with rations and ammunition."

Like the British Commandos and U.S. Army Ranger Battalions, the Marine Raiders of World War II are seen among the precursors of modern Special Operations units. Personally authorized by President Roosevelt, the Raiders were created as an organization in 1942 to conduct amphibious landings behind Japanese lines in the Pacific. The idea behind the concept can be traced to suggestions made to the president by Colonel (later General) William J. Donovan of the Office of Strategic Services (OSS)—itself the precursor of the CIA—and Major Evans Fordyce Carlson of the Marine Corps. As with Donovan, Carlson pitched the idea for his outfit to Roosevelt personally.

A veteran of World War I, Carlson had become a fan of the Thompson submachine gun while serving in Nicaragua in the 1920s, where he had earned the Navy Cross. In turn, he became an advocate of unconventional warfare techniques while with the 4th Marine Regiment in China. There Carlson had spent months traveling in the deep and rugged back country observing guerrillas such as Mao Zedong as they fought behind Japanese lines in the late 1930s.

Later in the 1930s, Carlson had done a tour as part of the marine detachment assigned to President Franklin Roosevelt during his vacations at Warm Springs, Georgia. It was here that the two men became friends, and it is how Carlson came to have the ear of the commander in chief years later.

Two battalions of Raiders were created in February 1942 for operations in the Pacific, and Carlson, promoted to lieutenant colonel, was given command of the 2nd Raider Battalion. In a letter to the president, dated March 2 and preserved in the Franklin D. Roosevelt Presidential Library, Carlson set out the details of the battalion organization, stressing the role to be played by the Thompson.

"I designed the organization and equipment with a view to providing a battalion capable of high mobility and possessing the maximum fire power compatible with such mobility," Carlson wrote. "The emphasis is on speed of movement on foot, endurance, self-sufficiency and great fire power. . . . The squad, consisting of a corporal and nine others, is armed with five Thompson submachine guns, four Garand rifles and one Browning automatic rifle. These nine men operate in three fire groups of three men each.

Each group, led by a scout armed with a Garand, is supported by two automatic riflemen. . . . The three fire groups, of course, are mutually supporting. A group so armed and so trained can cover a front of from 100 to 300 yards, as against the 50 yard front covered by the orthodox infantry squad of eight men, armed with the 1903 rifle and one BAR."

Carlson's Raiders, as the media dubbed the battalion, first achieved notoriety during their August 17, 1942, raid on the Japanese base on Makin Island (now Butaritari), an atoll in what is now the Pacific Ocean island nation of Kiribati. The tommy gun–armed Raiders landed by submarine and wiped out the enemy garrison, demonstrating the vulnerability of such island garrisons and the usefulness of the Thompson.

Carlson next achieved acclaim by leading a thirty-day "long patrol" behind Japanese lines on Guadalcanal in November and December 1942. During this mission, which established or illustrated many precepts of special operations doctrine that are still in use today, the marines killed nearly five hundred Japanese troops, while losing only sixteen of their own killed in action.

Also demonstrated by Carlson on Guadalcanal, as it was by the Diggers in New Guinea, was the value of a submachine gun in small unit actions set in difficult terrain where the front lines are ambiguous or functionally nonexistent. When a small patrol gets into a shootout with another small patrol, and the bad guy is charging at you through the bush, being able to hose him with a thirty-round magazine filled with .45 caliber ACP ammunition is a comforting thought.

CHAPTER 25

Giving Il Duce His Due

Benito Mussolini never thought it would come to this. For more than a decade, he had ridden the crest of power, running all Italy as though it was his own personal domain, and dreaming big dreams of a new Roman Empire. Il Duce followed Hitler into World War II as a whelp follows the alpha male in a wolf pack. He attempted to conquer Greece, but had to call on Hitler to save his bacon. After Italian forces suffered humiliating defeats at the hands of the British in Libya, Hitler sent Erwin Rommel into North Africa to salvage that situation. For a time, it looked as though Rommel's Afrika Korps would beat the Brits, but the tide had turned. In May 1943, the last Axis troops in Africa to elude capture retreated to Sicily.

On July 10, 1943, the Allies landed troops in Sicily, and within two weeks, King Victor Emmanuel III fired Mussolini and replaced him with Pietro Badoglio. By the end of the second week of September, the Allies had landed in mainland Italy and Badoglio had signed an armistice. This infuriated Hitler, who instituted a brutal military occupation of his former Axis partner's country. The armistice brought no end to World War II for the Italians, only the beginning of a horrible, bloody battle that would last for another year and a half and bring tremendous death and destruction to the peninsula as the Allies battled their way north.

As in all wars, the Battle of Italy was carried forward by the infantry, and in this case by British Tommies and American GIs carrying Thompson submachine guns.

Lieutenant David Waybur of Oakland, California, went ashore with the 3rd Infantry Division during the Operation Husky landings in Sicily. A week later, on the night of July 17, he was leading the 3rd Reconnaissance Platoon into enemy-held territory near Agrigento, an old Greek city on the island's southern coast. The mission that night, to find an isolated Ranger unit, took Waybur's three vehicles over roads that were probably heavily mined, and certainly defended by enemy machine-gun nests.

At they slowed to consider how to bypass a damaged bridge and get across a stream, Waybur's patrol came under attack and found themselves surrounded by a superior number of enemy troops. Not the least of their worries was that four enemy tanks managed to get in behind them, cutting them off from beating a hasty retreat to American lines.

Waybur immediately ordered the men and the vehicles to spread out. The more targets that they presented for the enemies, the better it was for them. He didn't have to tell them that the next order of business was to return fire with the large-caliber heavy machine guns they had.

In the ensuing firefight, four Yanks were wounded, including Waybur. The worst of their worries, though, came when they realized that they had burned through all the ammo for the large machine guns. Waybur still had his Thompson submachine gun, and he was determined to not let the mere lack of .50 caliber rounds let the balance tip irrevocably to the enemy.

By the light of the moon, Waybur went on the offensive, charging one of the enemy tanks that was about thirty yards away. He closed in, jumped on it, and poured .45 caliber rounds through an open hatch. It was an action like this that was tailor-made for the Thompson. The ACP rounds spattering around the interior of the hull were deadly. The driver died a noisy, painful death and the tank careened out of control, banging to a stop in the riverbed.

With this action, the men of the 3rd Recon rallied and the enemies hesitated. A small-arms firefight rattled through the night, but the enemies held back and the Americans kept them at bay until help arrived the next morning. For his actions that night, David Waybur would receive the Medal of Honor three months later. He never had the opportunity to go home to a hero's welcome. He was killed in action on March 28, 1945, during the Lorraine Campaign in what is now eastern France, near the border of Germany.

After landing at Salerno in September, the American troops found it slow going. The steep and rugged terrain greatly favored the German defenders. To circumvent this frustrating near stalemate, Allied planners decided on an end run. This involved a second amphibious operation, sending the British 1st Division and the American 3rd Infantry Division, along with British commando units and American Rangers ashore at Anzio, south of Rome. The force landed on January 22, 1944, but would be contained in the initial beachhead area for four months by wrathful German counterattacks.

One of the initial objectives in the Anzio operation was the town of Cisterna, where the 3rd Division met its first determined enemy resistance, and
where it was ordered to dig in. Technician Fifth Grade Eric Gibson was
among those caught in the first waves of German counterattacks against the
3rd that week. Born in Nascent, Sweden, he had emigrated to the United
States, and was living in Chicago when the war broke out. A cook, not an
infantryman, he was pressed into service during the German attack on
January 28. Gibson grabbed a Thompson submachine gun and soon found
himself leading a squad of five men as Germans attacked from the north.

To secure the flank against the German assault, Gibson and his men
went on the offensive, overwhelming enemy strongpoints while killing five
and capturing two of the enemy. By now, as his company was moving against
the Germans, Gibson was fifty yards ahead of his hastily assembled squad,
probing the German defenses and inching down a dry streambed known
colorfully to the locals as Fossa Femminamorta, "Dead Woman Ditch."

A German sniper, watching Gibson's approach, opened fire as the GI
was about sixty feet away, but he was not a very good shot and the young
Swede was able to take cover without being hit. Rather than staying down,
Gibson stood up and rushed the enemy gunner, firing short bursts with his
Thompson until he was on top of the German. Here he pointed his muzzle at
the shooter and cut loose with a burst of .45 ACP slugs.

As an artillery barrage began hitting the area, two other Germans
opened fire on Eric Gibson. Again, he rushed the enemy, popping off short
bursts with his Thompson. And again he managed to get within point-blank
range. He shot one German, but the other saw wisdom in dropping his weapon
and putting up his hands.

The literature of war is filled with stories of cooks who, when properly
seasoned with adrenaline, traded spatulas for guns to become killing machines. Such was the case with Gibson and the Thompson that he used so
well on that cold winter day south of Rome. After capturing the German, he
worked his way back to where the rest of his squad had taken cover from the
artillery.

He might have stayed in relative safety until the line had stabilized, and
he was able to return to his pots and pans. He had already done enough.
However, twice he had attacked and now he did it again.

Asking for his squad to cover him, Gibson crawled out into Dead Woman
Ditch. Crawling a distance longer than a football field, through machine-
gun fire and the ongoing artillery assault, he managed to get close enough to
attack one of the German machine-gun nests. He tossed in two grenades

and rushed the disoriented enemy with his blazing tommy gun. By the time its smoldering muzzle pointed down into the nest, two Germans were dead, and the survivor had his hands clasped atop his helmet.

Say what you will of a Thompson submachine gun, but there is something awfully terrifying about being on its receiving end at such close range.

Gibson's squad caught up with him here, and he told them that they should come when he called. He was going up around the bend in Dead Woman Ditch to scout further enemy positions.

Nobody saw what happened next, but they heard it.

There was the familiar thud of the Thompson coughing up .45 ACP rounds and the somewhat crisper sound of German MP40 submachine gun spitting 9mm slugs. Both sounds roared atop one another. Then there was nothing from around the bend, just the background crash of artillery and distant small-arms fire.

When the other Americans went to look, they found the Germans, as well as Eric Gibson, all lying dead. The young Swede from Chicago was posthumously awarded a Medal of Honor.

A week later, another young Allied soldier earned his nation's highest award for valor with a Thompson in his hand. His background was far from that of the Swedish kid who grew up in Chicago. Englishman William Philip Sidney, the son of the Fifth Baron de l'Isle and Dudley, was educated at Eton and Cambridge. As he studied to become a chartered accountant, he joined the Grenadier Guards as a reserve officer. When the war started, he went on active duty, and he went ashore with the Guards at Anzio as a major.

On February 7, he personally spearheaded a successful infantry assault against a German troop concentration near British lines. The following day, he again led the Guards into a close-range shootout with German troops. As reported in *The London Gazette* on March 30, he "dashed forward, engaging the enemy with his tommy gun at point-blank range, forcing a withdrawal. When the attack was renewed, Major Sidney and one guardsman were wounded and another killed, but he would not consent to have his wounds dressed until the enemy had been beaten off and the battalion's position was consolidated."

His wounds were grievous, but not mortal, and he survived to be awarded his Victoria Cross. After his recovery, he returned home, where he was elected to the House of Commons from Chelsea. Winston Churchill appointed him secretary of state for air in 1951, and he later served as the fifteenth governor-general of Australia.

After the war, Sidney feigned embarrassment over the fact that his most serious wound had been in his posterior. When asked where he was wounded, he would never say that he'd been "shot in the ass," but rather, with a wink, that he'd been "wounded in Italy."

The heroism of men like Eric Gibson and William Sidney notwithstanding, the Anzio beachhead became the kind of dreadful stalemate that soldiers hate; it reminded older soldiers of World War I. The breakout from that deadlock would not be achieved until the beginning of June, and then with enormous difficulty. When the offensive that finally led the breakout was launched on May 23, the 3rd Infantry Division, with whom Eric Gibson had fought, was still near Cisterna.

The following day, May 24, Sergeant Sylvester Antolak of St. Clairsville, Ohio, had a day like Gibson's. His tommy gun made it possible. He was with the 3rd Division's 15th Infantry Regiment, armed with a Thompson submachine gun, and leading a squad of the regiment's Baker Company against heavily entrenched German forces armed with all manner of small arms, as well as heavy machine guns. He was thirty yards ahead of the other men when he was hit by an enemy bullet. He went down, but got up, only to be hit again—and again.

The bullets had shattered his right arm, but he got up and continued marching against the machine-gun nest that was spraying fire into the advancing Americans.

Antolak gripped his Thompson under his left arm, but did not fire—that is, until he had gotten to within fifteen yards of the German position. Here, finally, he cut loose. What the Germans thought of this madman with a submachine gun is anyone's guess, but it had to be frightening to be attacked by this Amerikaner who couldn't seem to be hit again. Two of them died pondering Antolak the madman, but ten others threw up their hands.

When the rest of the squad reached this position, Antolak declined to have a medic take care of his arm, insisting instead on leading the men ever forward.

This time, as the one-armed man with the Thompson submachine gun inched forward, the German machine gunners got lucky. He was most of the distance to another enemy position when he went down for the last time. Like Eric Gibson, also of the 3rd Infantry Division's 15th Infantry Regiment, Sergeant Sylvester Antolak was posthumously awarded a Medal of Honor.

A week later, after relentless slamming by infantry and artillery, the German noose that had prevented the Allied breakthrough from the Anzio beachhead was on the verge of crumbling.

By the evening of June 2, the 15th Infantry Regiment had advanced to Valmontone, the site of the legendary Roman city of Labicum, when a dozen men in an American infantry patrol went out to probe the German lines. Among those Americans was a thirty-one-year-old private from Byersville, Ohio, named Herbert Christian. Older than most privates by a decade, he had joined the army in Steubenville and he probably shared the same hopes and fears as the others on his patrol, although they regarded him as the "old man."

At about 1:00 A.M., the patrol was suddenly ambushed by the Germans. Later it was estimated that the enemy had about sixty riflemen and three heavy machine guns. As they opened fire, the Yanks hit the dirt. There were also three German tanks concealed within a radius of about thirty yards. Suddenly, night turned to day in the eerie white-hot light of phosphorus flares launched by the Germans so they could see where to shoot. It was a ticket to annihilation for the GIs.

Maybe it was the wisdom of age, or sheer bravery, but Christian realized that their only chance was to beat a hasty withdrawal, *but* that fleeing in the face of such odds without covering fire was as bad as lying in the dirt waiting to die. With this in mind, he stood up, screamed for the men to run, and opened fire with his Thompson submachine gun.

Three Germans went down immediately as the .45 ACP rounds ripped through the enemy positions.

In the ghostly light, the men ran as Christian stood and fired, exchanged magazines, and fired some more. He hit some Germans and was hit himself.

It was a horrible scene. An enemy round—those who saw it say that it was a cannon shell—slammed into Christian's knee, severing his right leg and sending him tumbling in a heap.

Moments later, though, he was back up, his tommy gun blazing.

He advanced toward the German lines, taking painful steps on his left knee and the hemorrhaging stump of his right leg. In this manner, he inched forward an incredible twenty yards. Fueled by adrenaline and comforted by endorphins, his body did as his spirit willed it.

How he managed to avoid being blown to bits is anyone's guess. Perhaps the Germans were just staring in slack-jawed wonder. At least they were not staring at the other American soldiers who were now making their escape.

At last, Herbert Christian was just thirty feet from the German lines. He killed a German who was pointing an MP40 at him, slammed another clip into his Thompson, and began firing rounds directly into an enemy 20mm machine-gun nest. The Thompson at that range was the other side's worst nightmare.

This moment was the last that any of his comrades saw him alive.

"The courage and spirit of self-sacrifice displayed by this soldier were an inspiration to his comrades," read the understatement in Herbert Christian's posthumous Medal of Honor citation. "And are in keeping with the highest traditions of the armed forces."

Two other American GIs whose bravery near the Anzio beachhead on June 2, 1944, kept to that tradition came from a much different background. Both Tech Sergeant Yeiki "Lefty" Kobashigawa and Private Shinyei Nakamine were born in Hawaii of Japanese parents. Seen as pariahs by many Americans after Pearl Harbor, and as "enemy aliens" by their government, many of these American-born nisei, men who had grown up thinking they were as American as the next guy, enlisted in the U.S. Army to prove that they really were. The nisei from Hawaii who joined up early in the war were mainly concentrated into the 100th Infantry Battalion, which first went into combat in September 1943.

After these Hawaiian nisei had proven themselves in battle, the U.S. Army formed an entire regiment, the 442nd Regimental Combat Team, of nisei GIs from throughout the United States. The often-discussed irony is that most of the men in the 442nd were from the West Coast, from which their Japan-born parents had been herded into internment camps by a frightened United States government that feared they would become saboteurs. The feds never locked up the Japanese-born people living in Hawaii, though, for they formed too large a percentage of the total population.

Before the larger 442nd went overseas in the summer of 1944, the 100th Battalion was attached to the 133rd Infantry Regiment of the 34th Infantry Division for operations in Italy, and it was in this configuration that the unit participated in the breakout from the Anzio perimeter.

Born in Hilo, Lefty Kobashigawa had earned his nickname as a left-handed pitcher for several baseball teams in Hawaii, including the one sponsored by the Waianae Plantation Company. On the morning of December 7, 1941, he had been getting ready for a game on the west side of Oahu when he heard the news. On June 2, 1944, he was with the 100th as it helped spearhead the division advance northward toward the town of Lanuvio at the foot of the high ground of the Alban Hills.

Kobashigawa's platoon encountered strong enemy resistance from a series of German machine guns, including one that was about fifty yards away. With his eyes on this deadly gun, the southpaw pitcher crawled forward with one of his men. He tossed a hand grenade and then charged the enemy with his Thompson submachine gun while the other man covered him. He killed one German and took two prisoners.

When yet another German machine gun cut loose on them, Lefty pitched a couple of grenades at it, then raked the enemy position with his Thompson while the other GI circled around and finished them off. Over the ensuing minutes, Kobashigawa discovered four more enemy machine-gun nests and, tommy gun in hand, personally led the squad that took down two of them.

Meanwhile, Shinyei Nakamine's platoon became pinned down by German machine guns not far away, near La Torreto. The German gunners were on a small knoll two hundred yards to the front. Deciding on his own that something had to be done, he crawled toward one of the hostile machine-gun nests. Reaching a point twenty-five yards from the enemy, he stood up and charged, firing his Thompson as he ran. He killed three Germans and captured two. Before the day was out, he had wiped out another two machine-gun nests, but was killed in action.

For their heroism that day, both of these nisei men were awarded the Distinguished Service Cross. Lefty Kobashigawa lived to see the day, fifty-six years later, when both of these medals were upgraded to the Medal of Honor.

Three days later, the Allied objective in the Anzio landings was achieved. It was almost anticlimactic. On June 5, 1944, eleven months after the Sicily landings, and nine months after the American troops went ashore at Salerno in mainland Italy, the United States Fifth Army swept into Rome. The Germans were making the Allies pay dearly for every inch of Italy, but they had withdrawn from the Eternal City without a battle. As the Allies pushed north, it was back to business as usual, and the fighting was hard and vicious.

On June 14, the 36th Infantry Division was at Magliano a couple of hundred miles north of Rome. For a week, the going had been relatively easy and the division had pushed more than two hundred miles. However, as the official division history noted ominously, "Magliano was different; first-rate enemy troops were encountered."

Staff Sergeant Homer Wise was born in Baton Rouge, Louisiana, and it was there that he had enlisted in the army. As the 36th reached Magliano, he was serving with Company L of the division's 142nd Infantry Regiment. On June 14, as his unit was moving out to capture a ridge on which the Germans were entrenched, he found himself and his platoon pinned down by small-arms fire from those "first-rate enemy troops."

One of the men had been hit and was lying out in the open, desperate for medical attention. Wise knew what had to be done. Despite heavy German fire, he raced out into the open, grabbed the guy, and lugged him to relative safety where the medics could get to him.

As often happens, a show of bravery rallies the troops, and Wise's Company L platoon began moving forward. Again, heavy machine-gun fire from up ahead slowed the Yanks. Suddenly, a German officer and two enlisted men, armed with automatic weapons, attempted to hit the Americans on their right flank. They managed to get very close, but hadn't anticipated that Homer Wise would simply stand up and cut loose with his Thompson submachine gun. It was like the streets of Chicago. At that range the .45 caliber ACP rounds were deadly. All three Germans died quickly.

With this, Wise added a Garand to his tommy gun arsenal, picked up several antitank grenades, and became a one-man execution squad, spearheading his platoon, which was in the vanguard of a battalion advance. He shot up a German machine-gun nest and cleared a jammed gun on an American tank. In turn the tank was able to knock out further enemy positions. Wise survived the war and lived to see the Medal of Honor pinned on his shirt.

On July 7, it was the turn of a young soldier from Torrance, California, to prove himself to his fellow GIs, himself, and his folks back home. Well, his folks were not exactly back home. They had been shipped to the Rohwer Relocation Camp in Arkansas two years before. They were Japanese, and Tech Sergeant Ted Tanouye of the 442nd's Company K was leading a platoon of fellow nisei GIs in an attack to capture the crest of a hill in the ridgeline west of one of those many little Italian hill towns, known as Castellina because of its small castle.

Many stories told of this campaign, including those in this book, tell of Allied soldiers raked mercilessly by German machine guns on Italian hillsides. Ted Tanouye's tale begins as one about a GI having his first such experience. He spotted the Germans just as they were setting up their gun and got there first. His Thompson took three of the enemy out of the war, and .45 caliber lead sent two others running for their lives.

When another group of Germans opened fire, Tanouye gave them a taste of his tommy gun's wrath, and three more were no longer listed in Hitler's order of battle.

He wasn't through, though. A third German machine-gun nest felt the Thompson's sting, but in this attack, Tanouye felt German 7.92 mm lead. Still he persisted and again, he won.

Now under fire and out of ammo for his Thompson, the injured Californian might have taken cover and waited for the battle to end; instead, he crawled up to hurl a grenade at the nearest German machine gun and then crawled back twenty yards to get more Thompson magazines from another GI.

Back into the fray he went, raking another machine gun with the brutal fire from his tommy gun. Again, a German position fell silent, and then another. The medics reached him, but he waved them off, insisting on organizing a defensive position on the back side of the hill that he had almost single-handedly captured. He survived the day, but he would die of his wounds on September 6. Posthumously he was awarded a Distinguished Service Cross that would be upgraded to the Medal of Honor more than half a century later.

In the month after entering Rome, the Allies pushed the Germans northward about 150 miles to the Arno River, which flows east to west across Italy between Florence and coastal Pisa. A key to Allied success had been the arrival of more American troops, and among these were the 91st "Pine Tree" Infantry Division, which went into the line south of Florence in early July.

It was in the wee hours of July 12 that the 91st entered combat for the first time as a complete unit. Its objective that morning, as told in the official unit history, was "the high ground dominating the Arno River, [that] lay 15 miles away. Heavy opposition was expected because, the enemy had all the advantage of prepared positions in mountainous country that was ideal for defense and because the enemy was known to be massing a small force of tanks and mining every approach."

Covered by an artillery barrage, the division's inexperienced 362nd Infantry Regiment was deployed northward along the road leading from Casaglia to Capannoli. Among the men in the outfit was Sergeant Roy Harmon. Born in Talala, Oklahoma, Harmon had moved west with his family during the Dust Bowl years of the 1930s, when so many "Okies" made the giant migration to California's rich San Joaquin Valley. It was there that Harmon had joined up. By July 1944, he was a noncom and an acting squad leader in Charlie Company of the 362nd.

The regiment met stubborn resistance from the Germans that morning, but by the time the sun rose, they were inching forward. Charlie Company's advance came to a halt as they began taking fire from German heavy machine guns hidden in haystacks on the high ground above the road. One platoon in particular, badly exposed, was threatened with being wiped out. There were three enemy machine-gun nests. Between them they could hit every square inch of the terrain where the platoon was hiding in ditches and dying one by one.

When his lieutenant ordered Harmon to lead a rescue party, the sergeant knew the only way to save the men was to cut off the machine-gun fire at its source. Of course, easier said than done.

The closest gun was seventy-five yards away, the farthest more than three times that distance. First, the GIs tried setting fire to the hay using tracer rounds. When this idea fizzled, Harmon took some white phosphorus grenades, and crept forward, alone except for his Thompson submachine gun.

When he reached the first haystack, he turned it into a torch with the phosphorus, then hammered the German gunners with his Thompson as they attempted to flee.

Harmon at last reached the second haystack, and gave it the same treatment. Here, however, the enemy was able to exact some revenge before the Thompson made them breathe their last.

A wounded Roy Harmon dashed to a small knoll near the final German position and caught his breath. The last yards before he would be within throwing distance would be in the open. He would have to complete his mission without cover.

Wounded again, perhaps several times, he painfully inched his way to within 20 yards of the machine gun.

Here he sat up and raised the hand that contained the grenade.

It seems impossible that any human being could have survived the fusillade that knocked Roy Harmon to the ground at that moment.

But he did.

Again he rose. Again he raised his strong throwing arm.

This time, as the bullets tore him apart, the grenade flew.

For destroying all three machine-gun nests, Harmon was posthumously awarded the Medal of Honor.

In the weeks after Roy Harmon's death, Florence and Pisa were liberated as the Allied armies reached and crossed the Arno River, once seen as an important defensive line for the Germans. As summer turned to fall, the enemy withdrew northward into defensive positions in the steep and rugged Apennines which they would dub the Gothic Line.

Among the American units in action here was the 85th Infantry Division, which had been in action in Italy since April when the Allies were still battling the Germans south of Rome. Among the units spearheading the offensive within the 85th, as they moved northward amid the mud, rain, and German shells, was the 337th Infantry Regiment.

Born in Manchester, New Hampshire, Sergeant Christos Karaberis was a squad leader in Company L as the 337th advanced slowly toward La Martina, Casoni di Remagna, and the Idice River Valley on the first of October.

The Germans, in their carefully prepared defensive positions in the high ground above, had the tactical advantage and were able to rain mortar and machine-gun fire down upon the approaching Americans. So it was that Company L was pinned down that night. Karaberis was ordered to lead a squad to outflank the enemy on the left and to knock out the enemy positions.

It was tough going. The loose rocks on the steep slope were hard to cross without slipping, and the noise of men slipping on rocks made a stealthy approach impossible. Nor did the barren hillside afford the GIs any cover.

Nevertheless, Karaberis finally managed to creep above and behind one of the German machine-gun nests. Raising his Thompson submachine gun, he rushed the enemy position, hosing it with lead. He took eight prisoners, turned them over to his squad, and began crawling toward another machine-gun nest.

This time, however, the element of surprise eluded him, so he jumped up and charged, .45 caliber ACP rounds flying. The Germans valiantly returned fire, but four of five died and the fifth gave up.

A third machine gun turned its attention on Chris Karaberis, but he managed to crawl unscathed to within a few yards of it. Leaping up with a bloodcurdling shriek, he and his tommy gun descended upon the startled Germans, who immediately put their hands in the air. In a few minutes, this crazy GI had earned a reputation among the German gunners as indestructible.

An ordinary war hero might have called it a day at this point, but there were still more German machine guns on the ridge. There were still more sticks in Karaberis's magazine pouch, so he stabbed a fresh one into his Thompson and moved out.

There was a rock promontory up ahead on which there were two German positions with a commanding view of Company L. He charged the first one in an attack that even an official U.S. Army report called "savage." Four Germans died from tommy gun–inflicted lead, but three had the sense to give up.

The six Germans in the adjacent position did not even bother to resist. Clamping their hands atop their helmets, they became numbered among the twenty-two prisoners that Chris Karaberis captured that evening.

Within an hour or so, Company L had secured the ridge.

Karaberis, who later legally shortened his surname to Carr, survived the war and was awarded the Medal of Honor for his heroism.

* * *

The Allies continued to push north against the Gothic Line, tenaciously held by the Germans. On the western side of the Apennines, it was the mainly American Fifth Army, while the British Empire forces of the Eighth Army were on the east. Here young Richard Henry Burton of Mowbray, Leicestershire, was a private with the 1st Battalion of the Duke of Wellington's (West Riding) Regiment, at Monte Ceco on October 8. As we have seen, German machine guns controlled the high ground in the Apennines, and without the heroism of young Americans, fed up with being pinned down and picked at, the Germans might have controlled that high ground indefinitely.

Richard Burton was such a hero. He rose up and attacked a nest containing a German machine gun—identified in British accounts as a Maschinengewehr "Spandau" gun. He assaulted the enemy strongpoint with his Thompson submachine gun. Three gunners died.

The young soldier then turned the fury of his Thompson on a second group of German gunners. They, too, died trying to cut him down.

He ran though a hail of fire, trading .45s for 7.92 mm slugs, and a third group of gunners would bother the Dukes no more.

Thereafter, according to official accounts, "in spite of the fact that most of his comrades were either dead or wounded, he repelled two counterattacks, directing such accurate fire that the enemy retired."

Often in war, there is a crying need for someone to rise to the impossible challenge. Richard Burton was such a hero, and for his gallantry that autumn day, he took home a Victoria Cross. He survived the war, left the service as a corporal, and moved to Scotland.

Many Canadians also took home the Victoria Cross, and perhaps one of the most colorful of these heros was Ernest Alvia "Smokey" Smith, of New Westminster, British Columbia.

Before he joined the Canadian army, he had joined the army of young men that rode box cars across North America searching for work during the Great Depression. In March 1940, he enlisted in the Canadian army's Seaforth Highlanders in Vancouver, and saw his first combat two years later. Assigned to the 1st Canadian Infantry Division, the Highlanders went ashore in Sicily in 1943 and fought their way north the length of Italy. Smith was in the thick of it, his reputation alternating between hero—he was promoted to corporal *nine* times—and that of a unmanageable troublemaker. Drinking, carousing, and insubordination had gotten Smokey Smith busted back to private *nine* times.

On the night of October 21–22, 1944, the Highlanders were on the Savio River in northern Italy, west of Monte Fumaiolo. Private Smith was assigned to lead the force that was tasked with securing a bridgehead across the Savio. With him, he still carried both his Thompson submachine gun—a perk from his intermittent tenure as a corporal—and a PIAT antitank weapon.

The British-designed PIAT—for Projector, Infantry, Anti-Tank—was similar in purpose to the American bazooka, but unlike the rocket-propelled bazooka projectile, the PIAT used a spring-launched explosive charge, thus eliminating the backblast. The drawbacks of the PIAT were that it was cumbersome and hard to reload.

Smith's six-man patrol waded the river in driving rain and climbed up the high and slippery bank on the opposite shore, effectively isolating themselves from the rest of their unit. The enemy sent in some infantry, backed up by a Mark V Panther tank, to clean out the minor annoyance of having a half dozen Canucks on their side of the river.

The Germans cornered Smokey Smith and Jimmy Tennant in a ditch and attacked. A hand grenade exploded, its shrapnel injuring Tennant pretty badly. Then the Panther moved in for the kill.

Smith had another idea. Waiting until the tank was just thirty feet away, he cut loose with a PIAT round. In a moment, the tank was incapacitated—and if any of the crew had survived, they were incapacitated too.

The sheet of white hot blast illuminated the night, and Smokey Smith could see ten German infantrymen, and they saw him. Rather than bothering to reload the PIAT, he let his tommy gun do the work.

"They charged toward me," Smith explained in an interview published in Ed Marek's *Talking Proud* online magazine. "I killed four of them. I aimed for the middle body, where it hurts. The others turned around and fled, thank Christ. All the others knew was the tank was hit and then there's a big burst of fire and four guys drop. They weren't going to keep charging. . . . The four soldiers were badly hit, so they just died. I'm not sure about the guys inside the tank, but when a shell hits a tank in the side it makes a hole and the explosive goes inside and usually kills everyone inside or they'd be badly wounded and they'd burn. Sometimes, you'd hear yelling and hollering but you weren't going to open the door. I didn't wound many people; if I shot someone they were going to be dead."

At that range, a Thompson in the hands of the right man was a weapon that was capable of giving that right man the last word. Smokey Smith was one of those right men.

But the conversation was far from over.

The December 20, 1944, issue of *The London Gazette* continued the tale. "Almost immediately another tank opened fire and more enemy infantry closed in on Smith's position. Obtaining some abandoned Tommy Gun magazines from a ditch, he steadfastly held his position, protecting his comrade and fighting the enemy with his Tommy Gun until they finally gave up and withdrew in disorder."

With the Germans on the run, he carried Jimmy Tennant to safety, found him a medic, and reported that there was nothing in the way of enemy troops or tanks left to impede the Canadian advance across the Savio and beyond. The battalion got across and swept in to capture the town of San Giorgio di Cesena.

The Canadian army had a hero of some considerable significance on their hands, a man who was very soon recommended for the Victoria Cross. Also on their hands was the impossibly mischievous rogue. The higher authorities feared that the drinking, carousing, and insubordination that had gotten Corporal Smith busted back to private nine times could embarrass them. As the story goes—never confirmed or denied by Smith himself—he was taken to Naples (some versions of the tale say it was Rome), where he was literally locked in a jail cell until he could be flown to London to receive his Victoria Cross from King George VI personally.

Back home, Smokey Smith lived the image of a colorful hero, got married, and finally settled down. He died at his home in British Columbia on August 3, 2005, having lived to be the last surviving Canadian to have been awarded the Victoria Cross. He lay in state in the House of Commons, only the ninth person accorded such an honor, and his military funeral was the grandest seen in Vancouver in many years.

Just as Canadians were awarded the Victoria Cross, so, too, were other men from other far-flung corners of what was then the British Empire. One such man was Rifleman Thaman Gurung of the Indian Army's 5th Royal Gurkha Rifles. On November 10, Gurung was with this regiment's 1st Battalion on Monte San Bartolo, east of Perugia—and this Gurkha was not carrying a rifle. He had a Thompson submachine gun.

He and another man were scouting the German machine-gun positions along the crest of a ridge near San Bartolo. The rest of the battalion was farther down the slope, waiting to move out.

Ethnically, the Gurkhas are a mountain people living in the Himalayas of Nepal and northern India who had a long history of service with the British army. The Gurkha's aptitude for operating in rough mountainous terrain has long been valued by the British, and such skills permitted Thaman Gurung to creep unnoticed to within a few feet of the German position. The first they saw of him, he was standing on top of them pointing his tommy gun at their heads.

Seeing the gangster gun at close range left the Germans with no choice but to surrender without firing a shot.

Gurung then crossed the ridge, spotted another large concentration of Germans. He crept close, then attacked, squeezing off bursts from his Thompson as he charged. As he did so, the 1st Battalion moved out and up the slope. They crossed the ridge but came under heavy enemy fire.

Gurung reloaded and attacked again until he had no more ammo for his Thompson. He then lobbed two grenades, ran back to the battalion, and grabbed a Bren gun. From the ridgeline, he opened fire, burning through two magazines to keep the enemy pinned down as his battalion withdrew back down the slope. Just as he stood to turn and follow, Gurung took a round in the throat. His Victoria Cross was posthumous.

As spring came to the Europe in 1945, it seemed that war would soon be over. Allied armies were racing toward Berlin from the west, as the Red Army closed in from the east. In the Apennines, the German gunners that held the Gothic Line's high ground still fought like it was 1943, and as though Hitler's Thousand-Year Reich actually was going to last longer than a dozen years.

In the first week of April, the Japanese-American 442nd Regimental Combat Team found itself in the hills near Carrara, famous for the marble in the soil which made foxhole digging impossible. To call these "hills" is to belie their true nature. They were steep, most with sixty-degree slopes, and they were tall. Many topped three thousand feet, rising from valley floors that were not far above sea level. Among the last to remain in German hands, high ground beyond which the American troops could not pass, was imposing Monte Belvedere. Given the task of taking this mountain was the 2nd Battalion, and within that battalion was a sergeant from Koloa, on the "Garden Isle" of Kauai, named Yukio Okutso.

The attack jumped off at dawn on April 7, far from the peaceful shores of Hawaii on those Tuscan marble mountains.

German mortar and machine-gun fire cut the nisei men to ribbons. The air was filled with a hail of bullets, shrapnel, and fire. As the Americans took cover from the tracers, mortar shells churned up the rocks and dirt around them. In a particularly precarious place were the men of Company F. The interlocking fire from three machine-gun nests was so intense that nobody dared to raise his head. Nobody that is, except Yukio Okutsu. He could see that the fire from the nest just thirty yards up the hill could eventually wipe out the entire company unless something was done quickly.

Okutsu raised his head, and then his arm. In rapid succession, he heaved two hand grenades at the German gunners, and the three machine-gun nests raking the nisei had been reduced to just two. Using the boulders littering the hillside as cover, Sergeant Okutsu dashed up the hill, tossing another grenade into the second machine-gun nest, wounding two enemy soldiers. He then turned his attention to the third enemy strongpoint, advancing with his Thompson through withering fire.

A bullet was heard to strike his helmet, and the serious young man who had grown up on the Hawaiian island of Kauai crumpled into the dry, gravelly soil of Tuscany.

He was down, but he wasn't out.

Moments later, Yukio Okutsu miraculously staggered to his feet. The bullet had not penetrated his helmet, but merely glanced off it. He had been stunned and knocked down, but nothing more. The sergeant stood up and resumed his single-handed assault, his Thompson submachine gun blazing. Okutsu captured the machine-gun nest and its entire crew of four. Many, if not most, of the men of Company F owed their lives to the twenty-three-year-old from Koloa.

By the end of the day, the 442nd Regimental Combat Team had captured Monte Belvedere and had succeeded in not only piercing, but *breaking through*, the supposedly impregnable Gothic Line.

For his heroism, Yukio Okutsu was awarded one of the fifty-two Distinguished Service Crosses that were earned by men of the 442nd Regimental Combat Team in World War II. He received his medal in December 1945, but he donated it to the Kauai Museum. "My father was like that—a real generous man," his son Wayne Okutsu said in an interview with the *Honolulu Star-Bulletin* many years later. "He just wanted to give Kauai something to be proud of."

In June 2000, his medal was among those that were upgraded to the Medal of Honor; however, he was one of just a half dozen men so honored who would actually to live to see the day. On August 24, 2003, stomach cancer did what dozens of German gunners had failed to do fifty-eight years

A Hawaiian GI with an M1928A1 Thompson: Corporal Seikichi Miyashiro of Hilo
was assigned to the 100th Battalion of the Japanese American 442nd
Regimental Combat Team, which served mainly in Italy.
(Courtesy of the U.S. Army via the National Archives)

earlier, and Yukio Okutsu passed away at the Hilo Medical Center at the age
of eighty-one.

"He's bigger than life," said his son, Wayne Okutsu. "He's bigger than all
of us. He always was."

The heroism of these few Medal of Honor and Victoria Cross recipients offers merely a few examples among many. They have been singled out only to give a few illustrations of how the bravest of the brave utilized their Thompson submachine guns in difficult battles on one of the toughest battlefronts of World War II.

CHAPTER 26

The Setting Sun

By 1944 the Rising Sun that had heretofore been both the heraldry and symbol for the Japanese Empire had begun to set. The U.S. Navy had asserted its superiority throughout most of the Pacific Ocean. On land, after the long campaign in the New Guinea and the South Pacific islands, during which the Allies halted the Japanese and regained the strategic initiative, it was at last time for General Douglas MacArthur, as commander in the Southwest Pacific Area, to make good on his promise to return to the Philippines.

Here followed one of MacArthur's biggest battles, with the commander of the Pacific Ocean Area, Admiral Chester Nimitz, who favored Allied landings on Formosa (now Taiwan) rather than the Philippines. MacArthur insisted that America owed it to the Filipinos to liberate their country. President Roosevelt himself weighed in, and the liberation of the Philippines went ahead, beginning with the island of Leyte on October 20, 1944, and following with the main island of Luzon. Here Allied forces landed in January 1945, finally defeating the Japanese occupiers of Manila on March 3.

It was on Leyte that Private Harold Moon of the 24th Infantry Division earned the Medal of Honor with the help of a Thompson submachine gun. Born in Albuquerque in 1921, he had joined the army in Gardena, California, and went ashore on Leyte with George Company of the division's 34th Infantry Regiment. On the first night after the initial landings, George Company was beating off Japanese counterattacks on the beachhead at Pawig.

Dug in on the forward edge of the American lines, Moon watched as the Japanese infantry came through the darkness to assault the GIs. He sprayed the advancing enemy with his Thompson, firing burst after burst as the Japanese outflanked his platoon in the darkness. He watched as the men he knew fought and died. He saw the wrath of Japanese mortar and machine-gun fire.

Moon felt himself wounded, but still he held the line, hammering at the foe with his Thompson as he shouted encouragement to the men around him. As described in Moon's Medal of Honor citation, "A Japanese officer, covered by machine gun fire and hidden by an embankment, attempted to knock out his position with grenades, but Private Moon, after protracted and skillful maneuvering, killed him."

The young GI had become a rallying point for George Company, and a serious obstacle for the Japanese. They set up a light machine gun about twenty yards away and tried to use that to break the GI line. Moon bravely stood and shouted range corrections to an American mortar crew that eventually silenced the machine gun.

After four hours of bloody fighting, Moon was surrounded, but still he held his position. The Japanese then tried to wipe him out with a full-fledged bayonet charge, but he just stood up, aimed his Thompson into their midst, and let the .45 caliber ACP rounds do as they did best. After eighteen Japanese died trying, they gave up on their attack.

Off to the right, a Japanese machine gun opened up on the Americans.

Maybe Moon had come to think of himself as bulletproof, or maybe he just regarded the enemy as bad shots. As he stood to throw a hand grenade at the machine gun, a sniper got lucky, and Harold Moon died.

The Americans held the beach and eventually pushed the Japanese into the jungle. When they reached Moon's position, they discovered almost two hundred enemy dead within a hundred-yard radius of his foxhole. His Medal of Honor citation called it "magnificent heroism."

In April 1945 the 24th Infantry Division landed on the island of Mindanao, the last of the major islands of the Philippines to be liberated. Private First Class James Diamond was with Dog Company of the division's 21st Infantry Regiment. Born in New Orleans in 1924, he had entered the service at Gulfport, Mississippi.

On May 8, as World War II in Europe was coming to its close, the real war for Diamond was just beginning. Over the course of one week, Diamond would earn a Medal of Honor for repeatedly demonstrating what his citation would describe as "indomitable spirit, constant disregard of danger, and eagerness to assist his comrades, [that] will ever remain a symbol of selflessness and heroic sacrifice."

In the midst of a firefight near Mintal, as Dog Company was securing and holding a bridgehead, Diamond saw a Japanese sniper running toward the Dog Company GIs with a hand grenade. With the reflexes we admire in young men, Diamond raised the muzzle of his Thompson submachine gun

Davis Hargraves aims his M1A1 Thompson submachine gun at an enemy
position during the fighting on Okinawa's Wana Ridge on May 18, 1945. He and his
buddy Gabriel Chavarria were with the 2nd Battalion of the 1st Marine Division.
(Courtesy of the National Archives)

and cut down the enemy in a torrent of lead. He replaced his spent clip and
continued to work the battlefield with his Thompson, pouring sustained
bursts into the enemy, while at the same time directing fire for a battery of
105 mm howitzers.

During another gun battle the next day, he commandeered an abandoned vehicle to carry casualties to the rear. This he did, despite the fact that
the Japanese eventually shot up the truck so bad that it was almost not driv-
able. The day after that, he helped repair a bridge while taking enemy fire,
and on May 14, while leading a mission to evacuate the wounded, his patrol
was cut off, and he held off the enemy until everyone could get away. Everyone did, except James Diamond. His Medal of Honor was posthumous.

If the Marines in the Pacific had Carlson's Raiders as their precursor to
modern Special Forces, the U.S. Army in Burma had Merrill's Marauders.

Technically, they were the 5307th Composite Unit (Provisional), but when General Joseph Stilwell, the American commander of the China-Burma-India Theater, tapped Brigadier General Frank Merrill to lead the 5307th, the unit became Merrill's Marauders.

As with the Marine Raiders, the purpose of the Marauders was to operate deep behind Imperial Japanese Army lines in the mountainous jungles of Burma. The goal was the disruption of enemy communications from within and paving the way for the recapture by Chinese forces of the Burma Road, the only major supply route into China that was passable by motor vehicles. Another thing that the Marauders had in common with the Raiders was the Thompson submachine gun. Merrill himself carried one. So, too, did Stilwell.

At the beginning of 1942, Stilwell—who spoke fluent Chinese—was promoted to lieutenant general and tasked with organizing Allied operations in support of China's efforts against the Japanese, as well as a defense of Burma—the nation today often also called Myanmar, though the term "Burma" still persists (even the BBC still calls it Burma).

By late spring, when the Allies were on the run everywhere in the Far East and the Pacific, Stilwell was ordered to withdraw from Burma to India. Instead of allowing himself to be evacuated by air, Stilwell stayed with his troops and personally led their fighting withdrawal, which was completed by mid-May.

Reporting for *Time*, Jack Belden accompanied the "iron-haired, grim, skeleton-thin" Stilwell as he "walked into India with a tommy gun on his shoulder."

Along the way, in a dispatch published on May 11, 1942, Belden described the bespectacled general "in old khaki pants and shirt and a battered campaign hat . . . sitting on a log repairing his tommy-gun with expert fingers—cigaret between his lips, his big American feet dangling awkwardly from skinny shanks, hat tilted back. He did not look like a Napoleonic commander, performing a miracle of military endurance. He was only a plain, lanky, thin-lipped American, with a weather-beaten face, a dour smile, a sunburned neck: he might have been a hunter in the backwoods of his native Florida."

It was feared that the Japanese would conquer British India, or at least occupy large slices of it. They never did, although they reached the Indian border and threatened Imphal. Though their onslaught was blunted, the battle to reverse their gains of 1942—like the similar campaign in New

Guinea and the Solomons—took years. Indeed, the capital of Burma was still occupied by the Japanese when Nazi Germany surrendered.

As in New Guinea and the Solomons, the Burma Campaign was an infantry war, fought in difficult terrain where vehicles were largely useless and where a Thompson submachine gun was often a man's best friend. By 1945, Burma had become almost a forgotten front, except to those who lived its horrors on a daily basis.

One such man was Lieutenant George Arthur Knowland, a twenty-three-year-old platoon commander from Catford, in the English county of Kent. Having joined the Royal Norfolk Regiment in 1941, he served in Burma, having volunteered for the commandos. On the last day of January 1945, he was one of two dozen men of No. 1 Commando who were dug in on a 170-meter hill known simply as Hill 170 near the hamlet of Kangaw.

The troops had already been enduring Japanese artillery and small-arms fire for ten days when they were attacked by an estimated three hundred enemy troops. It was a moment that called for a hero. The crew manning the unit's Bren gun kept the enemy at bay for a while, but they were hit. The hero ran to man the Bren. Knowland then tossed grenades at the oncoming enemy and fired a few rounds from a two-inch mortar.

When the Japanese were a mere thirty feet away, this one-man army picked up a Thompson submachine gun and met them head-on. Faced with a man flinging those big .45 caliber dollops of lead at them, the Japanese faltered, fell back, then ran.

Just as the triumphant George Arthur Knowland watched them run, a stray round caught him. His Victoria Cross would be posthumous.

Another Victoria Cross awarded to a Thompson-wielding solder in Burma went to Naik (Corporal) Gian Singh of the Indian army's 15th Punjab Regiment. On March 2, 1945, a little over a month after Knowland's death near Kangaw, Singh earned his medal while leading an assault against the Japanese lines on the road to Myingyan. Despite his being wounded, the young Sikh warrior took the lead in attacking and knocking out one Japanese strongpoint after another, blasting them with his Thompson at close range.

Also taking place during that first week of March, the Battle of Meiktila would finally break the back of the Japanese forces in central Burma, paving the way for Allied victory in this stubbornly contested campaign. Among the units participating in the campaign was the Indian 17th "Black Cat" Infantry Division, comprising both Indian and British troops.

Within the division's 9th Battalion was a young Scotsman named George

Wearing a Chinese-style uniform, Captain Walter Mansfield of the Office
of Strategic Services instructs Nationalist Chinese troops on the reassembly
of an M1A1 Thompson submachine gun on January 25, 1945.
(Courtesy of the U.S. Army via the National Archives)

MacDonald Fraser, who would later go on to a career as a celebrated author
of both historical novels and nonfiction works. He is perhaps best remembered for his humorous, though meticulously researched, *Flashman* series of
novels.

Fraser is deserving of mention in any discussion of the Thompson submachine gun during World War II because of his eloquent, if disparaging,
discussion of the weapon. Not all who used it praised their Thompson.
Fraser, writing in his war memoir *Quartered Safe Out Here,* is among them.

Promoted to corporal at Meiktila, and made a section leader, Fraser was
issued a Thompson, as he put it, "much against my will.

"I had grown to love my old snub-nosed Lee Enfield, and resented having to part with it, but it was usual for a section [corporal] to carry a Thompson if one were available, so I accepted the thing and detested it. It was ugly,
ungainly, I hadn't been trained in its use or taught to regard it as a wife, and
it couldn't have come within ten feet of a falling plate at two hundred yards.

Its whole purpose was automatic, and my view was that if single aimed shots had been good enough for the Duke of Wellington, they were good enough for me. For some reason I felt like a bully, just carrying it, and it rusted like an old bed-frame. I threw it in a Sittang creek, eventually, but in the meantime I had to go about like Lance-corporal Capone."

The image of the Thompson as a gangster gun still prevailed, and certainly Fraser's comparison to the accuracy of the single-shot rifle is well taken. However, how did the Thompson stack up by comparison to other submachine guns that were available at the time?

CHAPTER 27

Burp Guns, Stens, and Other People's Submachine Guns

Marcellus and John Taliaferro Thompson saw it firsthand for two decades. Despite the immense publicity that swirled around the Chicago massacres, the armed forces of most of the world had shown very little interest in submachine guns after the Great War. Indeed, neither Britain nor France seriously pursued an indigenous submachine gun, and neither came shopping for tommy guns until after war was declared in 1939.

The big exception to this inattention was Germany, where a submachine gun was called a "Maschinenpistole," literally translating as "machine pistol" but actually meaning "submachine gun." As noted previously, it was in Germany that Theodor Bergmann had introduced the first Maschinenpistole, the MP18, back in 1918. The Treaty of Versailles forbade Germany to have an arms industry, but most laws have loopholes and some go unenforced. Then Hitler abrogated the treaty and announced a rearmament.

In the interwar period, even before rearmament became official German policy, many spin-offs of the MP18 were made in Germany. The Dusseldorf industrial firm Rheinmetall produced its S1-100, a similar gun, by using a front company in Solothurn in Switzerland. Theodor Emil Bergmann, son of the original Theodor Bergmann, meanwhile used a front company in Denmark in the development of his own MP34 Maschinenpistole.

There were no such charades for Hugo Schmeisser, who had been a key player in the MP18 design. He created an updated variant called the MP28, which was manufactured in Germany by Haenel Waffenfabrik of Suhl. Eventually, Bergmann's MP34 and its improved variant, the MP35, were manufactured in Germany by Carl Walther Waffenfabrik after Hitler decided to rearm the Reich.

A similar variation on the MP18/MP28 design was also developed by the Erfurter Maschinenfabrik (Erma), but Erma's fame would derive from a completely different design. It would become the standard submachine gun of the German armed forces during World War II. With its folding stock, the MP40 was a trim, compact gun that was more similar in appearance to the sleek Uzis and MP5s of modern times than to the clunky MP18 and its wannabes.

Preceded in the late 1930s by the similar MP36 and MP38 upon which it was based, the remarkable MP40 weighed eight pounds and carried thirty-two 9 mm parabellum rounds in a box magazine. More than a million MP40s were manufactured through 1945.

Like the Thompson submachine gun in the U.S. Army, the MP40 was routinely assigned to platoon leaders and paratroopers, but also might be used in the field by anyone.

In one of the enduring puzzles of World War II small-arms lore, Allied soldiers often referred to the MP40 as the "Schmeisser"—and it is still referred to as such in various accounts—although neither Hugo nor any of his family members had a role in its design. In fact, it was designed by Heinrich Vollmer, based on Bertold Giepel's MP36 design. Nearly as counterintuitive, guns actually designed by Schmeisser, such as the MP18 and MP28, were not called Schmeissers.

To GIs, the MP40 was also called the burp gun, because of the distinctive burping sound that it made when fired. This appellation is to be taken merely as descriptive and not as belittling, as we have heard numerous secondhand stories of American soldiers who adopted MP40s for their own use. It has even been said that many GIs threw away their Thompsons and used captured MP40s. The key problem in doing this was, of course, maintaining an adequate supply of 9 mm ammunition, which was nonstandard in the U.S. Army.

This author has fired the MP40 and has nothing but praise for the smoothness of its action. In contrast to other period submachine guns on full auto, the cartridges feel almost as though they are flowing through butter. However, my celebration of the fine German engineering stops short at the folding stock. Though more solid than the similar thin metal stock of the American M3 grease gun, it is obviously far more prone to bending or breaking than the solid walnut stock of the Thompson.

While Germany's signature submachine gun was not based on—or similar to—the MP28, those of several other countries, such as Finland's M31, were. The Soviet Pistolet-Pulemyot Degtyaryova (PPD) family of submachine guns, meanwhile, began as essentially a 7.62 mm knockoff of the MP28.

In 1941, at a time when the Soviet Union was in need of a large number of weapons quickly, the PPD was too complex for large-scale mass production by inexperienced factory workers. As was the case in the transition from the M1928A1 to the M1 Thompson submachine gun, simplification was needed. With this in mind, Georgi Semyonovich Shpagin created the renowned Pistolet-Pulemyot Shpagina of 1941 (PPSh-41). The "Peh-Peh-Sha," as Red Army troops called it, was, like the MP40, dubbed a "burp gun" by Americans who encountered it in the hands of Communist Chinese troops in the Korean War.

Chambered for 7.62 mm ammunition, the PPSh-41 was designed to accommodate either a 35-round box magazine or a 71-round drum magazine. Unlike the Thompson submachine gun, where the drum magazine was abandoned on World War II models, this option appears to have been the most commonly used configuration. Apparently the PPSh-41 met the mass production requirement, as an estimated six million were manufactured through 1945.

This author has never handled the PPSh-41, but I did speak with Mike Gibbons, the Hollywood armorer, who has a number of variants in his arsenal, and who has used one in his work more than most people alive today.

"I find it very crude, but it works," he told me. "The damned things actually work pretty good. They had a decent little drum so they have some firepower. They're not nearly as finely made as an MP40 or a Thompson, and as a result they suffer from problems, but we clean them up, take the burrs off and they work alright."

Alone among the major combatants in World War II, Japan never took the idea of a submachine gun seriously. While submachine-gun development was not a high priority with any army outside Germany before 1939, most countries raced to make up for lost time when the war began. Not so Japan. The Japanese Type 100, Model 1940 submachine gun was produced in very small numbers and was issued to combat troops in even smaller numbers.

Ian Hogg, writing in *The Encyclopedia of Infantry Weapons,* muses that "the thought of the Japanese Army armed with a cheap and simple submachine gun such as the Russian PPSh is quite terrifying; the combat in the Far East would have been a good deal more bloody, and one or two touch-and-go affairs might well have gone the other way."

Either through lack of foresight or lack of imagination, Britain and France went to war without a submachine gun in production and turned to Auto-Ordnance to make up for their shortcomings. As France fell, Britain kept the Thompson orders flowing, but also turned toward developing an indigenous submachine gun.

The first such effort was actually a collaboration between the Royal Navy and the Royal Air Force. The fastest route to a submachine gun was to do what the Soviets did with their PPD, and that was to knock off the German MP28. The task was delegated to George Lanchester at the Sterling Armament Company, and therefore this short-lived 9 mm model became known as the "Lanchester" submachine gun. The occasional reference to a "Lancaster" submachine gun that one hears from time to time is a misnomer.

Long-term, the British plans paralleled those of the Soviets. The goal was to create a weapon that would be easy and fast to manufacture. Just as the PPD gave way to the PPSh-41, Britain developed an all-new submachine gun that was some orders of magnitude simpler than the Thompson.

A 9 mm gun like the Lanchester, this new gun was the Sten. The name was an acronym for "Shepherd-Turpin-Enfield," that combined the initials of Major Reginald Shepherd and Harold Turpin, the men who developed it, with a reference to Royal Small Arms Factory at Enfield, where most of the roughly four million total units would be stamped out. Indeed, they were mostly stamped, as this process of metal forming is easier and simpler than machining all the parts with lathes and other industrial equipment.

Of the two men whose names are memorialized in the Sten's appellation, Shepherd was inspector of armaments with the Ministry of Supply at the Royal Arsenal in Woolwich, while Turpin was a senior draftsman in the design department at Enfield.

The first production series Mark I Sten guns were delivered from Enfield in June 1941 and issued to troops soon after. With its simple metal stock, fixed sights, and unrefined lines, the Sten was an ugly duckling when compared to the Thompson, but it weighed only around seven pounds and it was indeed fast and easy to make. The Mark II and Mark III Sten, which accounted for most of the production run, were even sparer than the Mark I, dispensing with the first mark's wood foregrip and flash hider. Also simplified were the barrel shroud, ejection port, and receiver. A wooden stock and grip were reintroduced in the later Mark V, however, but the gun was not widely produced or deployed. The miniaturized Mark IV, intended for paratroopers, never passed the prototype stage, and the Mark VI was a version specially equipped with a silencer.

The simplicity of the Sten, which looked crude to those who were used to the Thompson, was appreciated by some, while being derided by others.

There were numerous epithets hurled at the Sten by those who called it, among other names, the "Plumber's Nightmare" or the "Stench Gun."

In addition to the Sten becoming the standard submachine gun for British and Canadian troops from 1942 on, large numbers were air-dropped to partisans and resistance fighters in France and elsewhere across continental Europe. Its size and ease of use made it ideal for such operations. Indeed, the Sten was so simple that several thousand of them were built from scratch by the underground in secret backroom factories from Poland to Norway—under the very noses of the occupying German troops.

Aboveground factories outside Britain also built the Sten during World War II. Both the Mark II and Mark III Sten guns were manufactured in Canada at various locations, including the Long Branch Arsenal in Ontario. Australia had its own Sten variant, the "Austen," short for "Australian Sten," of course.

First delivered around the summer of 1942, the Austen Mark I was a copy of the Sten Mark II with the addition of a foregrip and a folding stock modeled after that of the German MP38. In the field, however, Australian troops preferred the Thompson and the Australian-designed Owen submachine gun. A 9 mm gun like the Sten and Austen, the Owen had been authorized for production, auspiciously, two weeks before Pearl Harbor. Both the Austen and Owen remained as standard equipment in the Australian army until the 1960s.

Under the heading, perhaps, of "imitation is the sincerest form of flattery," the Sten was also produced by the *Germans*. Probably "counterfeited" is a better word, as the knock-offs were intended for clandestine operations, and many were stamped as having been made at Enfield. Several thousand were manufactured by Mauserwerke, beginning in mid-1944.

In 1945, Mauser began manufacturing a cheap gun for use by the German home guard. By this time, much of Germany's industrial capacity was in ruins and the Third Reich was grasping for simple, easily produced weapons for its last desperate defense. Loosely based on the Sten, but with a vertical magazine, it was designated as the Maschinenpistole 3008, and known as the "Volksmaschinenpistole," or "people's submachine gun."

In the postwar years, the simplicity of the Sten led to its being copied in China and many places around the developing world.

This author has fired the Sten, finding it an awkward gun to handle because of the asymmetry of having the magazine extend horizontally from the left side of the gun. For someone accustomed to the feel of a rifle stock, the flimsiness of the spindly metal stock takes some getting used to. Of course, if one had to carry a submachine gun over long distances, the weight of the Sten was obviously a welcome feature.

"I don't care for the gun personally, but the Sten was a great idea," Mike Gibbons said. "It was a piece of junk, but it was cheap to make and it worked. It was a disposable gun, but for a wartime, stop-gap gun it did its job. If I had to pick an early 9 mm submachine gun, if I couldn't have a Thompson, an MP38 or an MP40 *would* be the way to go—but I'd rather have a Thompson!"

CHAPTER 28

A Chronometer to a Dollar Watch

While many GIs agreed with Gibbons, those who in the U.S. Army wrote the checks to pay for submachine guns—like their British counterparts who adopted the Sten—still saw the Thompson submachine gun in terms of the complexity of production. For Russell Maguire, the U.S. Army Ordnance Department was like a fickle lover. Almost from the first moment that the army started placing substantial orders for the Thompson, they went looking for another submachine gun with which to augment, or even to supersede, it. Some say that it was age, given that the basic Thompson design dated back to 1921, but none of the services were in much of a hurry to replace their M1911 automatic pistol, whose design predated that of the Thompson by a decade. At the very least, the army thought that a submachine gun from a second source would provide a backup option in case anything went wrong on the Savage production line.

When they were still focusing on a supplementary submachine gun, the U.S. Army had investigated and rejected the Reising gun that the U.S. Navy and Marine Corps briefly adopted just before the war. Based on the marines' experience with it on Guadalcanal, that was a good call.

In the spring of 1942, around the time that the design parameters of the M1 Thompson were firmed up, the Ordnance Department was simultaneously evaluating a weapon designed by gun designer George Hyde, who worked at the Inland Guide Lamp Manufacturing Division of General Motors, which had originated in Anderson, Indiana, in 1906, as the Guide Motor Lamp Company, and which was acquired by General Motors in 1929.

The Inland Division was already producing huge numbers of M1 carbines, as well as one of the more unique, and certainly lesser known, secret weapons of World War II. This was the "Liberator," a five-inch, one-pound, single-shot derringer that was designed to be dropped behind enemy lines to partisans and guerrillas. The project was so secret that the little pistol was not even called a gun—it was referred to in official documents as the FP-45 "Flare Projector." Someone had a sense of humor.

The documentation even referred to the trigger as the "yoke," to disguise the true nature of the little weapon. The "45" in the designation stood for its being chambered for .45 caliber ACP ammunition that was interchangeable with that of the M1911 pistol or either the Thompson or M3 submachine guns.

The idea behind the FP-45 was that someone could use the gun to kill an enemy soldier and steal his gun. With a single shot and an effective range of only a couple of dozen feet, this it about all that it could be used for. About a million Liberators were made, but apparently most were not used. Most of those that were actually distributed went to guerrillas in the Philippines and behind the lines in China.

Hyde's new submachine gun, like the Thompson, had a wooden stock and was chambered for .45 caliber ACP rounds. At nine pounds, it was slightly lighter than the Thompson, and it was somewhat simpler in its design. Though the Inland Division was no stranger to simple weapons, plans were put into motion for M2 production to be contracted out to the Marlin Firearms Company in North Haven, Connecticut, rather than to a General Motors plant, because of Marlin's experience.

With the new Thompson variant having been officially designated as Submachine Gun, Model 1 (M1), the Hyde-Inland gun received the army designation as submachine gun, Model 2, or M2.

When Maguire and the Auto-Ordnance team saw the U.S. Army testing Hyde's gun, they, too, jumped on the bandwagon of a simpler, all-new submachine gun. If the army was looking at other guns, then one of them ought to be an Auto-Ordnance gun!

The result was the Auto-Ordnance T2, designed by William Hammond of the Machinery Sales Company of Los Angeles. Compared to the Thompson, it was an ugly gun that looked rather like a log with a grip and magazine shoved into the bottom and a short muzzle protruding from one end. It was lighter than the M2, but only barely. The T2 was an open-bolt gun of which both 9 mm and .45 ACP variants were built in prototype form. The T2 was evaluated in September 1942 at the Aberdeen Proving Ground, and after an embarrassing number of mechanical malfunctions, it was deemed inferior to the M2.

By this time, however, even before the M2 or the simplified M1A1 Thompson were ready for production, the Ordnance Department decided that the Thompson would not just be supplemented, but replaced entirely by a new and different gun.

It was the same urgency for faster production and greater numbers that led the Ordnance Department to demand the simplifications that led first to the M1 Thompson and soon thereafter to the M1A1. It was the same sort of desire for a bare-bones submachine gun that led to Reginald Shepherd and Harold Turpin at Enfield being tasked with coming up with a submachine gun that was at the opposite end of the complexity scale from the Thompson.

Could this new gun be the M2?

The answer was no. In the manufacturing process, Marlin determined that the M2 was not sufficiently simpler than the Thompson to make the production go any faster. The forged steel receiver still required a great deal of handwork to finish. After just a couple of hundred were built for evaluation purposes, the Ordnance Department decided to pull the plug on the entire M2 project.

If not the M2, could this new gun be another existing submachine gun?

The U.S. Army had evaluated the Sten and Austen, and had seen what was possible with stamped, rather than machined parts. The army had even taken a close look at captured German MP40s.

None of these options was considered acceptable, and George Hyde was sent back to the drawing board in October 1942.

In record time—even considering wartime urgency—Hyde came up with an all-new design. This was the gun that became the U.S. Army's submachine gun, Model 3 (M3).

Ready for evaluation in November, the M3 was approved for mass production before Christmas 1942. Rather than turning to Marlin as it had with the M2 project, General Motors decided that the M3 would be built by the Inland Division. Indeed, Frederick Sampson, the chief engineer at Inland, influenced the design from a production point of view, helping Hyde create something that was not just a simple and effective weapon, but one that maximized fast and easy manufacturing.

Like the later mark Sten guns, the M3 had a simple metal stock and made use of stamped rather than machined parts. Like the MP40, which it resembled more than the Sten, the stock was a folding stock. There was nothing extraneous in the M3 design. It was all business, and this served to keep the weight down to eight pounds. Like the Thompson, it was chambered to fire .45 caliber ACP ammunition and to accommodate a thirty-round magazine. It operated on the simple blowback principle, and was designed for fully automatic firing only. As with the M1A1 Thompson, the firing pin was incorporated in the bolt.

The overall appearance of the M3 was very similar to a caulking gun, with which most home owners are familiar, or to a mechanic's grease gun. This earned the M3 its enduring nickname, "grease gun."

As 1943 began, the grease gun had been officially anointed as the U.S. Army's new standard submachine gun. However, the year would be half over before all the bugs were worked out of the manufacturing process and M3s could start flowing from the factory to the front lines.

When the grease gun was officially unveiled, *Time* reported it on June 19, 1943, under the heading "Cheap Firepower," and described it for the readers. "If an imaginative ten-year-old set out to make a toy gun for himself by hooking two pieces of gas pipe together, he might wind up with something looking remarkably like the U.S. Army's newest war tool, the M3 submachine gun, unveiled last week. . . . A stark, crude, unlovely shooting iron, the M3 is nevertheless rugged, light and easy to mass produce. It coughs out a clipful of .45-caliber pistol slugs, can be fired with fair accuracy at short range (as with any submachine gun, the closer the better). Of all-metal construction, the M3 weighs less than nine pounds, compared to twelve for the famous Thompson 'tommy-gun,' a standard Army weapon whose relationship to the humble M3 is approximately that of a chronometer to a dollar watch."

In this author's opinion, this assessment is accurate. The grease gun has the feel of a cheaper, inferior product. The overall sense is one of impermanence. Though lighter than the Thompson, it is no easier to handle. The flimsiness of the stock, like that of the MP40 or the Sten, is also a letdown for someone used to the rifle stock of a Thompson.

The biggest drawback to the M3, however, is a shooter's natural tendency to use the magazine as a foregrip. It is, after all, positioned in exactly the place where one naturally grabs to stabilize the gun. Indeed, we often see World War II photographs of GIs doing this. The first time I fired a grease gun at a firing range, I was cautioned not to succumb to this ergonomic temptation—because it might jiggle the magazine enough to cause the gun to jam!

Guide Lamp went on to build most of the 605,664 M3s that were manufactured. Most were essentially identical, but late in the production run the design was tweaked a bit and an "Alteration 1" variant made its appearance. As the M3 "officially" superseded the Thompson, the M3 was itself succeeded by the similar M3A1, introduced in December 1944 with a redesigned cocking mechanism, a larger ejection port, and a loading mechanism.

According to the U.S. Army Matériel Command publication *History of*

Submachine Guns, 1921 Through 1945, there were 15,469 M3A1s built in 1945, to bring the overall total of grease guns made during World War II to 621,133. Of this total, a small number, about 25,000, were cleverly designed with a conversion kit that included a bolt and barrel, as well as a magazine adapter, so that they could be converted to fire 9 mm parabellum ammo from a Sten gun clip. Another thousand were designed with a sound suppressor for use by operatives of the Office of Strategic Services on clandestine missions behind enemy lines.

As a practical matter, the grease gun never came near fully replacing the tommy gun during World War II. When the war ended on each of the various battlefronts, there were many M3s in the hands of GIs on those fronts, especially in Europe, but the tommy gun was still the ubiquitous American submachine gun.

CHAPTER 29

Kicking Down the Doors of the Reich

No battle looms larger in the American perspective of World War II in Europe than the Operation Overlord invasion of Normandy on June 6, 1944. Movies such as *The Longest Day* (1962) and *Saving Private Ryan* (1998) have made this so, first by retelling the story, and next by securing for themselves an enduring place in the collective American memory of World War II. Of course, the Thompson submachine gun plays a pivotal and prominent role in both films—just as it had in the real 1944 battle—helping to assure the Thompson's place in the collective memory of the twentieth century.

Overlord was the long-awaited moment when the Anglo-American Allies finally brought the war to the Germans in northern Europe. June 6 was merely one of a myriad of D-days that occurred throughout World War II, because the term was shorthand for the date of any planned operation. It was used in communications to avoid blabbing the real date. However, for most laymen, June 6 was *the* D-day. In terms of the scale of this immense operation, it probably was.

Operation Overlord involved putting more than 150,000 Allied troops ashore in France on the first day, then growing that force to well over a million within six weeks. It is possible that more Thompson submachine guns were fired in anger on June 6 in one stretch of the Normandy coast than in any other single place on any other day in history.

The first tommy guns to see action that day arrived from the sky. Before the troops came in from the sea at dawn, three divisions of paratroopers came in during the night. It was planned that the British 6th and the American 82nd and 101st Airborne Divisions would drop neatly behind German lines in the predawn darkness. As a nighttime airborne assault on a scale never before attempted, that it did not go exactly as planned is a given. That it was not a complete disaster is astounding.

One of the first glorious moments for the Thompson submachine gun in the Allied campaign for northern Europe came in the hands of Staff Sergeant Harrison C. Summers. Born in Catawba, West Virginia, he had grown up in coal country and had worked the mines before going into the service and becoming one of the "Screaming Eagles" of the 101st Airborne. In the darkness of the night before D-day, he had dropped into Normandy with the 1st Battalion of the 502nd Parachute Infantry Regiment, commanded by Lieutenant Colonel Patrick Cassidy.

As was the case with many airborne units that night, the men of Cassidy's battalion came down far and wide, but he was able to assemble a workable number of men, including a few from other units who landed in the 1st Battalion landing zone. They then set about to secure various objectives, including crossroads in and near the towns of Saint-Germain-de-Varreville, Saint-Martin, and Mésières.

With most of the objectives secured, Cassidy ordered Summers to take fifteen men and clear some stone buildings on the east side of Mésières that were thought to contain the German unit who staffed the coastal battery at Saint-Martin. Armed with his Thompson submachine gun, Summers led the attack, but wound up mainly clearing the buildings single-handedly.

According to Gordon Harrison, writing in *United States Army in World War II: The European Theater of Operations: Cross-Channel Attack*, published by the U.S. Army Center of Military History, "Summers rushed the buildings one by one, kicked in the doors, and sprayed the interiors with his Tommy Gun. On occasion he had the assistance of another man, but it was his drive and initiative that kept the attack going. When the last building was cleared in the afternoon, about 150 Germans had been killed or captured."

In the building that Summers had assaulted on his own, an estimated thirty German bodies were observed after he had it secured. As Stephen Ambrose later wrote in *D-day June 6, 1944: The Climactic Battle of World War II*, "Summers is a legend with American paratroopers . . . [he is] the Sergeant York of World War II. His story has too much John Wayne/Hollywood in it to be believed, except that more than 10 men saw and reported his exploits."

Summers received a field promotion to lieutenant for those exploits, and was later awarded the Distinguished Service Cross. He was recommended several times for the Medal of Honor, which he certainly deserved, but never received. He continued to serve with the 101st Airborne through France and into Belgium, survived the war, and lived until 1983.

In the aftermath of the Normandy invasion, the Germans failed to push the Allies back into the English Channel, but they did manage to keep them contained within a relatively short distance of the initial landing site for weeks. The breakout from Normandy finally came on July 25, 1944, with Operation Cobra. For the next sixty days, the Allied armies moved faster and farther than any army in any major war in the history of Western Europe.

Paris was liberated on August 25, and within weeks the Allies were so close to the German border that some optimistic commentators were predicting that the war might be over by Christmas. Of course, this was not to be. It was optimism pushed to the absurd. On Christmas, the Allied armies would be experiencing the coldest, bleakest moments of the Battle of the Bulge.

By early September, American troops had been fighting in Europe for more than three months. Except for the swift gains of August, they had been experiencing some of the toughest fighting of the war, and it was certainly on a much larger scale than on most other fronts.

In mid-September, as the Allies closed in on the Reich, and optimism was blossoming at home, the 80th Infantry Division was involved in the battle for bridgeheads across the Moselle River in eastern France. The division had initially captured the Dieulouard bridgehead on September 12, but the site was by no means secure, and it remained bitterly contested over the ensuing days. There was still a heavily fortified enemy position overlooking the bridgehead that was manned by roughly two hundred Germans with automatic weapons. Easy Company of the division's 319th Infantry Regiment was assigned the mission of taking down this German strongpoint.

Spearheading the company's effort on September 14 was a rifle platoon led by First Lieutenant Edgar Lloyd of Blytheville, Arkansas. When Lloyd's platoon had worked its way to a point about fifty yards off the enemy strongpoint, they came under heavy machine gun and rifle fire, which quickly resulted in a large number of casualties. The men immediately took cover and it seemed as though the assault had ground to a halt. Catching his breath, Lloyd jumped up. He told his men to follow him and rushed the Germans, squeezing off short bursts with his Thompson submachine gun as he went.

Lloyd and his team dodged withering enemy fire, managing to reach the German strongpoint after what probably seemed like an eternity. The lieutenant himself jumped into the first machine-gun nest, slugged the gunner with his fist, dropped a grenade, and jumped out before it exploded.

Still urging the platoon along, Lloyd dashed from one machine-gun nest to the next. He would pin down the German gunners with his Thompson until he was within grenade-throwing distance. He personally destroyed five machine guns as he led the platoon in overrunning the German positions. For what his award citation described as "audacious determination and courageous devotion to duty," Lloyd received the Medal of Honor.

Lloyd survived that day, but was killed in action two months later at Pompey, at the confluence of the Moselle and Meurthe Rivers, still in France and not far from where the 80th Infantry Division had been in September.

Three days after Lloyd's Medal of Honor action, and farther to the south, the 30th Infantry Regiment of the 3rd Infantry Division was advancing north, through the Vosges Mountains toward the Meurthe River. The steep and densely forested terrain of the Vosges was like the jungles of New Guinea—except that in the northern latitude's oncoming winter, it was dark and bone-chilling cold.

Suddenly, the 30th's Company L ran into a brutal German small-arms attack. Sergeant Harold Messerschmidt of Chester, Pennsylvania, took charge of his squad as they dug in along a forty-yard perimeter. In the reports of the battle, he is recalled as moving "fearlessly and calmly from man to man . . . encouraging each to hold against the overwhelming assault of a fanatical foe surging up the hillside."

This "overwhelming assault" reached the Company L line, and Messerschmidt was slammed by a hit from a German machine gun. He went down, badly injured, but he got to his feet in time to return fire with his Thompson submachine gun just as the enemy swarmed over the GIs. The fusillade of .45 caliber ACP rounds claimed five of the Germans, and the sergeant from Pennsylvania managed to wound quite a few others before he burned through his last magazine.

By this time, the situation was hopeless. It was down to hand-to-hand fighting, every American in the squad had been hit, and Messerschmidt was out of ammo. He turned, saw a German about to kill a wounded GI, and slammed the enemy with the butt of his Thompson as hard as he could. As that German went down, the angry American went after another with his high-tech club, bludgeoning one and then another.

Sadly, a German bullet ended his life before American reinforcements arrived on the bloody scene. Harold Messerschmidt had earned a posthumous Medal of Honor.

Also deep in the darkness of the Vosges were the nisei GIs of the 442nd Regimental Combat Team, who had distinguished themselves in Italy. They had now been attached to the 36th Infantry Division for the big Seventh Army offensive at the personal request of General Sandy Patch, the commander of the Seventh. On the evening of November 7, Company G was dug in along a steep and heavily wooded hillside near La Houssière, about five miles southeast of Biffontaine. For three days, the GIs had been trading small-arms fire with German troops that held the crest of the ridge.

Breaking the stalemate fell to Private First Class Joe Nishimoto of Fresno, California. He led his squad toward the enemy lines, crawling forward through a heavily mined and booby-trapped killing field.

When he was close enough, Nishimoto tossed a single hand grenade, blowing up a German machine-gun nest. Without pausing to admire one strongpoint down, he circled behind another with his Thompson submachine gun and opened fire at point-blank range. One gunner died quickly. The other wished he had. Putting another magazine into his tommy gun, Nishimoto charged after yet more Germans, who ran like rabbits. The psychology of being chased by someone with one of those American "gangster guns" is a curious thing to ponder, but one doesn't take time for pondering on a battlefield, especially when the *other guy* has the Thompson.

That night, for the first time since the nisei men had reached the Vosges, the rain turned to snow. As if there was any doubt after weeks of freezing rain, winter had at last come to the European battlefront.

Joe Nishimoto survived that night, but was killed in action a week later. His posthumous Distinguished Service Cross was later reviewed and upgraded to the Medal of Honor.

In the meantime, only two weeks after Harold Messerschmidt gave his life for this cause, the U.S. Army had crossed into Germany in strength. The first major city on German soil to be besieged was Aachen, the coronation site of Charlemagne, and a city of great symbolic value to the Third Reich. The 30th Infantry Division, which had gone ashore in Normandy on June 6 and fought its way across northern Europe, joined the 1st Infantry Division in the encirclement of Aachen in mid-October.

On November 16, the day after Joe Nishimoto died down in the Vosges, the 30th moved to eliminate an enemy northeast of Aachen.

On that day, at Würselen, a little more than four miles northeast of the center of Aachen, King Company of the division's 119th Infantry Regiment was spearheading the assault when they came under machine-gun attack. As the gunners pinned the GIs down in an open field about the length of a football field from a line of buildings at the edge of town, artillery began to rain down. The soldiers knew that if they remained in place they were vulnerable to deadly artillery fire, but if they stood to run forward, the machine guns would get at them.

The only solution was to eliminate one of the two threats. At last, one man decided to take on the challenge. Staff Sergeant Freeman Horner of Mount Carmel, in north-central Pennsylvania, stood up and opened fire on the German machine-gun nest with his Thompson submachine gun. It was

Specialist Jerry Santucci of the Bronx demonstrates a common practice used by GIs in the field. Taping two Thompson magazines together means that the second one is ready for use immediately, thus avoiding the necessity of digging into your ammunition pouch. He is seen here on November 18, 1944, during the Allied offensive across northern Europe. (*Courtesy of the U.S. Army via the National Archives*)

at the limits of the effective range of the Thompson, but the .45 caliber ACP rounds popping and pocking around them gave the gunners pause.

Also not effective that day was fire from the German heavy machine gun that had been peppering King Company. As Horner ran, the Germans fired but kept missing him. He closed the distance as rapidly as he could under the heavy load of extra ammo and grenades that he was carrying. Just as he took cover from one enemy machine gun, another that he hadn't seen opened fire. It also missed him, but barely.

Horner calmly turned, aimed, and unleashed a burst from his Thompson. Two German gunners went down.

Two of the machine-gun nests remained active, but they still could not hit Freeman Horner as he zigged and zagged across the last fifty yards of the open field. Throughout the Battle of Aachen, German troops had been especially tenacious, knowing that they were fighting on their own ground, but amazingly, these gunners, failing to hit this Yank with the tommy gun, turned and ran.

Reaching the head of the stairs into the cellar in which the enemy had taken refuge, Horner chucked in a couple of grenades. The grenades reduced the number of Germans within, and Horner called for the survivors to surrender. Even if there was a language barrier, the Germans got the idea. Rather than facing the wrath of the GI and his "gangster gun," they came out with hands held high. For his amazing action that day, Horner received a Medal of Honor. Later rising to the rank of major in the U.S. Army, Horner lived to the ripe old age of eighty-three.

A little over a month later, after having finally captured ground within Germany, the 30th Infantry Division found itself in the precarious predicament of doing damage control in Belgium. Since July, the Germans had been retreating, but Hitler had decided that the best defense of the Reich was a good offense. Some later called it a desperate offensive, but at the time the Allies were forced to take it very seriously.

On December 16, 1944, the Germans launched Operation Wacht am Rhein (Watch on the Rhine), a powerful offensive involving half a million troops in four field armies, including the Fifth Panzer Army and the Sixth SS Panzer Army. The plan was to crash through the mountainous and lightly defended Ardennes region, recapture Brussels and the huge port of Antwerp from the Allies, halt the Allied advance from the west, and force a stalemate.

The German armies broke through the Allied lines and within days captured a huge section of territory which looked, on battle maps, like a "bulge"; hence the campaign came to be known as the Battle of the Bulge.

On December 17 the 30th Infantry Division was redeployed to shore up the collapsing American line in the Malmédy and Stavelot area of the Ardennes. Fighting was intense, and it would be weeks before the Americans fully reversed the German tide.

On December 23, the division's 120th Infantry Regiment was at a place called Petit Coo, near Stavelot. The regiment's Company I was being slammed by tank and artillery fire, as well as being hammered by German small arms and heavy machine guns in a house two hundred yards from their position. It was an infantryman's nightmare, but there were a lot of those during that cold and snowy Yuletide in the Ardennes.

Staff Sergeant Paul Bolden was one of those in the nightmare, but he was ready to do something about it. Knowing that they could do nothing about the artillery threat, he and another man decided on their own that at least

Demonstrating the competition's gear, PFC Robert Leigh of the 83rd Infantry Division is seen here on December 16, 1944, with a collection of captured German small arms. Front and center is one of his three MP40 submachine guns.
(Courtesy of the U.S. Army via the National Archives)

they could try to do something about the machine guns. Inside the enemy strongpoint, the troops were from the elite SS, the Schutzstaffel, and not the sort to be trifled with. Nevertheless, the two GIs braved the heavy fire, crawling through the deep snow, and managed to get to within a few feet of the enemy. The farther they went, the madder Bolden was at the enemy who were raking the American positions.

With his partner delivering covering fire, Bolden tossed a fragmentation grenade into the building, following it immediately with a white phosphorus grenade.

Bolden might have left it at that, but he knew he had to finish the job and get the Nazis off the backs of Company I.

He kicked in the door and came face to face with thirty-five surviving SS troopers, still a bit disoriented and some injured from the dual blasts.

It was now the Thompson submachine gun's turn.

The SS beheld the man with the tommy gun and heard its roar. He killed twenty as they struggled to return fire. Though Bolden was hit in the shoulder, still he kept shooting. Then he was hit in the chest and in the stomach, and his buddy across the street was hit and killed.

Bolden stepped out of the building, badly injured and dripping wet with sweat and blood. He replaced the magazine in his Thompson and reentered the scene of the carnage, where fifteen SS troopers remained.

The odds were stacked against him, but the Thompson spoke and every last German died.

The badly injured GI survived the war and was awarded the Medal of Honor for that deadly day in the Ardennes.

While the 30th Infantry Division was battling the Germans in the Bulge, the 3rd Infantry Division was in the vicinity of Colmar, in Alsace, about forty miles southwest of Strasbourg—dealing with another German "bulge," that was known as the Colmar Pocket. In short, the pocket was a concentration of German forces west of the Rhine created when Allied forces reached the Rhine to the north and the south of Colmar. Defeating the heavily entrenched enemy in the pocket would hold the attention of the 3rd Division and other Allied units until February 1945.

On December 27, the 15th Regiment of the 3rd Infantry Division was battling its way through the heavily fortified town of Sigolsheim, near Colmar. Its Company L was engaged in some very nasty house-to-house street fighting, with mortar and machine-gun rounds popping and booming all around.

Lieutenant Eli Whiteley, a young Texan from Georgetown, was leading his patrol against a particular building that the enemy was using as a machine-gun emplacement when he was hit. A badly injured arm and shoulder only served to make Whiteley all the more determined. Distances were not great in the narrow, twisting streets. He just ran forward, crashed his way into the building, and cut loose with his Thompson submachine gun.

The two Germans at this location died a violent death, and Whiteley moved on to the next building, tossing a couple of grenades with his good arm as he went.

Again he ignored the flying 7.92 mm rounds buzzing around him like lethal bugs, and again he kicked in the door. Again, two Germans died, but eleven more surrendered.

Rejoined by the rest of the platoon, Whiteley continued to lead the men forward. One by one, they assaulted and took out German strongpoints. Firing his tommy gun with one arm as his left arm dangled, bloody and useless, Whiteley led by example.

Encountering particularly stubborn resistance from a large stone building, the GIs blew out the wall with a bazooka. Without a pause, Whiteley led his men through the gaping hole into a mass of Germans.

They gawked as the one-armed American raised his Thompson and killed five of their comrades. Another dozen just gave up.

Moving on to the next building, Whiteley took a bad shrapnel hit from an exploding shell. Despite being injured, this time in his eye, the Texan pressed on, cooking through another magazine in his Thompson as he went.

Eventually, his own men forced their lieutenant to a halt, constraining him and compelling him to allow himself to be evacuated to an aid station. By this time, however, the job was done. Company L's sector of Sigolsheim had been secured. Whiteley survived the war and was awarded the Medal of Honor. A plaque commemorating the deeds made possible by his Thompson submachine gun that day now hangs at Texas A&M University.

About seventy-five miles north of Colmar, the 44th Infantry Division was spending the coldest days of the coldest winter Europe had seen in years battling the Germans in valleys that drain into the Saar River, an area that was then part of Germany, but which had alternated between French and German rule for decades. Having reached the Rhine at Strasbourg in late November, the division spent Christmas east of Saargemund—known in French as Sarreguemines—preventing the Germans from counterattacking across the Blies River, a tributary of the Saar.

Men from Company I of the Division's 71st Infantry Regiment spent New Year's Eve creeping though the cold darkness in an effort to head off a feared incursion by the enemy's 17th Panzer Grenadier Division. One of the squad leaders in the company that night was Sergeant Charles MacGillivary. Born at Charlottetown on Canada's Prince Edward Island, he moved to the

United States and had joined the merchant marine as a teenager. After Pearl Harbor, he enlisted in the U.S. Army in Boston.

MacGillivary discovered the Germans, well camouflaged in the snow and darkness, digging in on the American left flank, but just as he reported this information by radio, the Germans opened fire.

Explaining to the officers that he had seen the German positions, he volunteered to personally outflank one of them. Sneaking through the deep snow and dense forest, he got within three feet of a machine-gun nest and killed two of the enemy. Other Germans, perhaps thinking that the lone sergeant was part of a sizable force, turned tail.

MacGillivary was not through. Later, in the early afternoon of New Year's Day, as Company I advanced though the forest near Woelfling, they came under fire from a half dozen German heavy machine guns and a company of German troops. Again the transplanted Canadian offered to go out alone, and again he was able to get within a short distance of an enemy machine gun. Destroying it with a hand grenade, he attacked another German machine-gun position with a Thompson submachine gun.

As the second machine-gun crew tried to turn their weapon to shoot at him, MacGillivary charged, leaping into their position and hosing them with his Thompson. Racing through the trees, he attacked a third machine-gun nest. He destroyed it, but was severely wounded in the process.

As he told a reporter from *The Boston Globe* in 1995 and as reported in the *New York Times* on June 30, 2000, "I looked down and my right arm wasn't there. When you get hit by a machine gun, it's like somebody put a hot poker in you. I stuck the stump of my arm into the snow, but the warm blood melted the snow. I figured I was dying. When they rescued me, my arm had a cake of bloody ice frozen around it, sealing the wound. If it had been summer, I'd [have been] dead."

For his heroism on that first day of 1945, Charles MacGillivary was awarded the Medal of Honor by President Harry Truman personally. While many Canadians such as Smokey Smith went home with the Victoria Cross, MacGillivary was unique. As *Time* magazine pointed out on September 3, 1945, "modest Sergeant MacGillivary became the only native Canadian in World War II to get a Congressional Medal of Honor. Then he headed for Boston. There he aimed to marry Esther Manning (who has agreed) and to find a job which he can handle with his new artificial arm."

He did find a job, and had a long career with the United States Customs Service. He died in 2000 and is buried at Arlington National Cemetery.

* * *

The 82nd Airborne Division, which had landed at Normandy on the night before June 6, 1944, also had gone on to participate in the massive Operation Market Garden airborne operations in the Netherlands during September. In December the division had been pressed into service for ground operations in the Battle of the Bulge. By the end of January 1945 the division was still in action in Belgium, and beginning on January 21 its 508th Parachute Infantry Regiment had replaced elements of the 2nd Infantry Division.

A week later, on January 29, a blizzard was lashing the mountains and forests of the Ardennes region. Charlie Company of the 508th had slogged nearly fifteen miles through the deep snowdrifts only to come under attack from German guns. When the company's executive officer was hit, First Sergeant Leonard Funk immediately took over. A native of Braddock Township in the mountains of Pennsylvania, he was in familiar terrain and used to getting things done with the resources at hand. Among the resources in his hand that day was a Thompson submachine gun.

Funk put together a makeshift combat squad from headquarters personnel, combined them with the company's 3rd Platoon, and organized a counterattack.

The Germans were firing from the relative security of about fifteen houses in the small town of Holzheim, but Funk knew that these positions must be taken down. Under his leadership, the de facto unit succeeded in doing this, capturing thirty prisoners, amazingly with no casualties.

Systematically working their way through the rest of the village, the Americans attacked fifteen houses, cleared them, and took thirty prisoners without suffering a casualty. Funk and his men had managed to increase their catch to eighty prisoners.

Posting four men to guard the captives, Funk and his small band continued to look for more Germans. Unfortunately, the Germans found the prisoners. A large enemy contingent arrived on the scene, outflanked the Charlie Company men, freed the German prisoners, and made prisoners of the GIs who had been guarding them—when Sergeant Leonard Funk suddenly came around a corner.

Confronting a superior enemy force, logic dictated, Funk probably should surrender as well. The German officer in charge certainly agreed with such a course of action as he pointed a Maschinenpistole at Funk and ordered him to do so. However, the man from Pennsylvania chose for himself.

He slowly began to remove his tommy gun strap from his shoulder, making a motion toward dropping it to the ground.

Instead, he raised it, pointed it at the German officer, and cut loose. As this man went down, Funk kept going, turning the stream of .45-caliber rounds onto another German and then another. He shouted for other GIs to grab weapons and start shooting. In the ensuing gun battle, twenty-one Germans were killed, and the remainder of this superior German force wound up as prisoners for the duration of the war. Leonard Funk was awarded the Medal of Honor.

The 36th Infantry Division had been on the front in Italy until August 1944, when it was reassigned for the Allied assault on southern France. Like the 3rd and 44th Infantry Divisions, it had been in action in the Colmar Pocket, and in the early weeks of 1945, it was fighting in Alsace, along the Rhine north of Strasbourg. During the second week of February, two GIs from the division's 142nd Infantry Regiment earned the Medal of Honor in heroic actions that were made possible by the Thompson submachine gun.

On February 11, word came that a platoon from the 142nd's Easy Company was surrounded by the Germans at Oberhoffen. Leading the rescue mission would be Sergeant Edward Dahlgren, of Perham, Maine, now with the company's third platoon. As Dahlgren led his men through the streets, he spotted a German patrol in an adjacent open space. They had not seen the GIs. The sergeant sneaked into a barn where a window overlooked the field through which the Germans were passing.

The range and position were tailor-made for the Thompson submachine gun. Taking the Germans by surprise, Dahlgren killed six and wounded a number of others with the volley from his Thompson.

Continuing the mission, the third platoon men at last made contact with the surrounded GIs. Up the street, however, was a building from which the Germans continued to fire at the Yanks with rifles and machine guns.

Dahlgren took it upon himself to deal with this problem. He carefully approached the building until he was close enough to dash in and toss a grenade. As soon as it exploded, he kicked in the door and ripped into the place with his Thompson. As Dahlgren's Medal of Honor citation reports, "This aggressive attack so rattled the Germans that all eight men who held the strongpoint immediately surrendered."

The man from Maine continued toward the next German strongpoint on the street, where he destroyed a machine-gun and its gunners with rifle grenades. However, he then came under machine-gun fire from yet another German position in a nearby barn. Dahlgren responded to this threat as he had with the first building. He tossed in a grenade and followed up with his tommy gun, firing on the run.

Having waited for the rest of the platoon to catch up, he attacked another building where he cornered a number of Germans in a cellar. A couple of grenades and probably another burst from the Thompson convinced the survivors to give it up.

The next batch of Germans that the patrol came across as they moved carefully through the Oberhoffen streets was hiding, not shooting. The third platoon and their previously surrounded comrades were now the hunters, rather than the hunted.

Again, the Americans attacked, and again the enemy retreated to a cellar. Several bursts down the stairway from Ed Dahlgren's Thompson convinced sixteen Germans that being prisoners of war was the best of the two choices they had that day.

Later that same night, a squad from the 142nd's Able Company was still in the thick of the street fighting inside Oberhoffen. Leading this squad was Sergeant Emile Deleau Jr., of Lansing, Ohio.

As was the case with Dahlgren and the Easy Company men a few hours before, it was a dangerous matter of taking down what seemed to be an endless series of German strongpoints. Unfortunately, the approach to every one of these was covered by the guns from another, so the poor GIs were constantly in the deadly sights of someone. Of course, the sights are only as deadly as the ability of the gunner, whose shooting was often not as accurate as it might have been, especially at night.

How accurate *was* the enemy fire? It was a reasonably good bet that *most* shots would go wild. It just took someone who was brave enough—or man enough—to take the bet.

Deleau had gotten close enough to one building that he was able to silence an enemy machine gun with a couple of grenades. Of course, this only brought him under fire from another. It was close enough that he just ran toward it and kicked down the door.

There are times when only a tommy gun will do, and this was one of those times. Ten Germans who survived became Able Company's prisoners.

The GIs waited here until dawn, then moved out. Soon, machine-gun fire slowed their progress, and Sergeant Deleau again took action. Dodging small-arms fire as he continued to bet against the skill of the gunners, he crossed an open patch and reached the rear of the building where two heavy machine guns were located. One disintegrated in a cloud of grenade shrapnel, and Deleau stepped back from the building a moment to get a better angle from which to pitch a grenade at the second machine gun.

It was here that Emile Deleau's winning streak ran out. His Medal of Honor would be posthumous.

A month later, the 36th Infantry Division was still in Alsace, with its 141st Infantry Regiment engaged at Haguenau, not far up the road from Oberhoffen, where the 142nd had seen intense action. Tech Sergeant Morris Crain, from Bandana, Kentucky, was a platoon leader with the regiment's Easy Company.

On March 13, it was not street fighting that occupied the men of Easy Company, but the fight to enlarge a bridgehead across the Moder River. More than just another tributary of the Rhine, the Moder formed a natural barrier to the Allied advance, and the Germans had reenforced it as a major defensive line. Getting across it was a necessary step in the effort to get Allied armies into Hitler's Reich. Once established, the precarious Allied bridgehead had to be secured and protected.

Easy Company's small part in the grand scheme was to take and hold a road junction that the Germans would fight hard to retake.

In taking the junction, Crain's platoon had killed ten Germans and captured a dozen, but the hard part was protecting it against a counterattack. Sighting their artillery on the known coordinates of the junction, the enemy brought down a hard rain of 88 mm shells, as well as mortar rounds.

Through it all, Sergeant Crain was optimistic. He encouraged the men, reassuring them with the rationale that it couldn't get much worse. Unfortunately, when the shells stopped falling, the Germans sent in tanks and infantry.

The brunt of the German attack was directed at a house where five GIs were trapped. Dodging tank and small-arms fire, Crain ran to their aid, finding them engaged in a firefight with German infantry that had gotten into the adjoining room. Meanwhile a tank was moving in behind to grip the Yanks in a deadly vise.

Crain ordered the men to run for it as he took on the German infantry with his Thompson. As the men escaped, they saw Crain kill at least three of the enemy as he sprayed them with a shower of .45 caliber ACP slugs.

The tank destroyed that building, but the Moder bridgehead survived. Crain was posthumously awarded the Medal of Honor.

* * *

The Germans fought hard to combat the Allied waves crashing against their borders, but they could not stem the tide. As March continued, the Allied troops entering the Third Reich became not just a trickle, but a flood.

The 45th "Thunderbird" Infantry Division, like many others, had come up from southern France. They battled their way through Saargemund, Germany, and once again it became—as it had before 1940—Sarreguemines, France. The Thunderbirds crossed Germany's prewar boundaries and the Division's 180th Infantry Regiment was inside the Reich near Niederwurzbach on March 18, 1945.

Lieutenant Jack Treadwell was born in Ashland, Alabama, and was in Snyder, Oklahoma, when he joined the U.S. Army. Now he was commanding the 180th's Fox Company, and his men were in tough shape. The GIs had seen some bad fighting in recent weeks, but they were no longer fighting machine-gun nests in buildings and infantry on hilltops. They were now up against the fixed bunker defenses of Germany's Siegfried Line. Built at great expense before the war, this line of steel-reinforced concrete was said to be impregnable.

Treadwell looked up the hill.

Fox Company was at the bottom.

Pillboxes filled with machine guns were at the crest.

There was nothing in between but a barren hillside. Artillery was falling.

Impregnable? It was sure made to look that way.

An eight-man squad went out to attack one machine gun.

None came back.

Jack Treadwell decided to go see for himself.

He loaded up some hand grenades, and he took his Thompson submachine gun.

Soon, he took fire from the enemy machine gunners, spraying the steep slope as this lone GI officer advanced. A majority of bullets fired in wartime, especially at longer ranges, miss. All of those fired at Treadwell missed.

As he closed on the nearest bunker, he edged out of their line of fire, closed in, and tossed a grenade. A split second later, his Thompson's muzzle poked through the gun slit inside. The sudden sight of the gangster gun was bad, but its voice was worse. One gunner died, and four gave up.

Jack Treadwell got his four prisoners back to American lines and went out again.

The crew of a second bunker faced the wrath of the gangster gun and wilted. This time the young officer from Oklahoma numbered a German officer among his captives. He turned out to be the commander of all the defenses on this ridge. No more.

Tommy gun in hand, Treadwell dodged machine-gun and sniper fire again and again. A third pillbox felt his wrath, yet none of the bullets fired in his direction seemed to find their mark.

A fourth bunker surrendered, and then a fifth and a sixth.

Impregnable? It now seemed that the Siegfried Line was anything but.

If a lone lieutenant could do this, what could a whole company do? Fox Company was now in action, and the Siegfried Line—or at least this part of it—was collapsing. Awarded a Medal of Honor for his actions that day, Treadwell survived the war and retired from the army as a full colonel.

As the Siegfried Line crumbled, the Allies swept deep into Germany. By the first week of April, the 100th "Century" Infantry Division had, like others we've seen, battled its way through the Vosges Mountains and across Alsace into the Reich. The division crossed the Rhine on the last day of March and followed the 10th Armored Division east across the Neckar River, securing a bridgehead there. By the first week in April, the Century men were closing in on Heilbronn, with the great industrial city of Stuttgart in their sights.

On April 7, the Century Division's 398th Infantry Regiment was at Untergriesheim, then a village north of Bad Friedrichshall, and now a part of that town. Private First Class Mike Colalillo, who grew up in the toughest part of Duluth, Minnesota, was with the regiment's Charlie Company as they came under mortar and machine-gun fire on the streets of Untergriesheim.

As we see so often in situations such as this, when men are pinned down by enemy fire, it takes one man standing up and shouting, "Let's Go!"

This man was Mike Colalillo, and others of Charlie Company followed. In the torrent of gunfire, he had his gun shot out of his hand, and he looked around for another.

There was an American Sherman tank on the street supporting Charlie Company, but its crew was buttoned up inside. Seeing the unused .50 caliber machine gun atop its turret, Colalillo jumped up and grabbed it, pouring fire into the nearest German machine-gun nest.

The fire directed at the young Minnesotan went astray, but he did not miss. At least ten Germans were killed or wounded as he blasted away from the Sherman's turret.

As the tank lumbered through Untergriesheim, he continued firing at the German machine-gun emplacements. He had the advantage of firing from an elevated angle. *They* should have had the advantage of firing at a totally exposed soldier, but they continued to miss.

Colalillo didn't—at least until the .50 caliber machine gun on the tank jammed.

"I told the guy in the tank that the machine gun had jammed," Colalillo told Al Zdon in an undated interview on the Minnesota American Legion Web site.

"Here, take our Thompson," the tanker told the infantryman.

"He gave me some ammo, and told me to be careful getting off the tank," Colalillo recalled. Then the hatch slammed shut.

There is a finite number of 75 mm rounds that a Sherman tank can carry. Eventually, it had to withdraw.

There is a finite number of rounds in a thirty-round clip, and eventually, the PFC from Duluth had to withdraw. The last two Americans off the battlefield that day were Mike Colalillo and the wounded soldier he carried to safety for the length of several football fields.

As he explained in his interview with Al Zdon, "I heard a voice say, 'Mike, Mike, I'm hit.' So I helped him back to our lines. We could hear other guys crying out there, but they wouldn't let us go get them. They thought maybe they were Germans trying to trick us into going out. But in the morning we did go out and picked up two guys. They were still alive."

For what the War Department called his "intrepidity and inspiring courage," Colalillo took home the Medal of Honor.

A month later, Adolf Hitler was dead, Germany had surrendered, and the Third Reich was a thing of the past.

On December 3, 1944, in the Sunday magazine section of *The New York Times*, war correspondent Drew Middleton wrote a piece entitled "The Man Who Will Win the War."

Within five months, his story came true.

"He is the foot soldier," Middleton wrote. "With his stubble beard, bloodshot eyes; he knows the price of victory. Miles of mud, days of rain and snow and cold, hours of savage fighting across ruined towns, slow, costly advances in the face of the strongest defense system in western Europe—that is the pattern for the present battle in the west, a battle which began in November and may continue in all its great and somber scope until midwinter."

Middleton had traveled with the troops and he had seen the mud and the bloodshot eyes. He had also seen, and often mentioned, the Thompson submachine gun as such an important part of the infantry identity. Even after the M3s arrived, the Thompson remained as a part of that savage fighting across ruined towns, and the slow, costly advances that ultimately overwhelmed those strongest of defenses.

According to Richard W. Stewart in his Center of Military History study of the U.S. Army in World War II, between the end of 1942 and May 7, 1945, "more than a million Americans would fight in lands bordering the Mediterranean Sea and close to four million on the European continent, exclusive of Italy, in the largest commitment to battle the U.S. Army had ever made."

From the enormous campaign of campaigns that defeated Hitler, there were five million stories, and perhaps nearly a million of these involved the Thompson submachine gun. These retold here are merely a handful of representative accounts highlighting some of the bravest of American heros, especially those awarded the Medal of Honor, and those whose use of the Thompson was integral to their Medal of Honor action.

CHAPTER 30

War Movies

The image of the Thompson submachine gun as a "gangster gun," so firmly entrenched in pop culture, is grounded in the facts of the 1920s and 1930s. Without Hollywood, however that image would not have been given its immortality. Since the 1930s, people who never came close to a real tommy gun have seen it on the screen inside theaters and prominently portrayed on the posters and lobby cards outside. When Churchill picked up a tommy gun, commentators from London to Berlin immediately used the term "gangster," and the public knew exactly what that meant, but soon this would change.

This image of the gangster gun, while accurate up to a point, is contradicted quite dramatically by stories such as those in the immediately preceding chapters. On a chronological scale, the gangster gun image was largely accurate only until 1940. During World War II the image of the Thompson submachine gun and Hollywood's depiction of it did a one eighty. Though the gangster image was—and remains—memorable, the Hollywood of the 1940s rounded out that image by putting tommy guns into the hands of the good guys.

Naturally, war movies began dominating screens early in 1942, and the image of a group of good guys in battle always seemed to include at least one good guy with a Thompson. These films reformed the image in the 1940s, and they remain embedded in the cultural heritage of that period.

Australian-born director John Farrow directed two pictures in 1942 that featured the gun. *Wake Island*, for Paramount, was a heroic depiction of the failed American defense of that island early in the year; it starred Brian Donlevy and William Bendix.

The other film, *Commandos Strike at Dawn*, was an Oscar-nominated story, also of a failed battlefront, focusing on Norwegian fisherman who escaped to Britain and returned with a group of commandos. Based on a story by C. S. Forester, who penned the Horatio Hornblower novels, the film starred greats such as Lillian Gish and Cedric Hardwicke, as well as Paul Muni, who had first handled a Thompson while playing a gangster. The poster for the film depicted a Commando brandishing an M1921 Thompson in one hand.

The Thompson also figured in another gloomy depiction of occupied Norway, *Edge of Darkness* (1943), released by Warner Brothers. Directed by Lewis Milestone, whose previous credits included *All Quiet on the Western Front*, the film's A-list cast included Errol Flynn, Ann Sheridan, and Walter Huston. Also in 1943, Twentieth Century–Fox included the Thompson in the film adaptation of *Guadalcanal Diary*, the classic account of that campaign by war correspondent Richard Tregaskis.

Making such war movies as the war raged on is a testament to the hardworking people who toiled behind the scenes in Hollywood. Getting the necessary guns was one of the challenges. Stembridge Gun Rentals, which functioned as the Gun Room at Paramount, had its arsenal of machine guns and submachine guns commandeered at the start of the war. They gradually got their guns back, but still had to improvise. Both good guys and bad guys in Westerns could use Colt .45s. In gangster pictures, a tommy gun was the only automatic weapon required. However, in war movies, it was different.

"In the early months of the war, we turned our standard machine guns into all sorts of weapons," recalled Stembridge's Fritz Dickie. "We found a photo of the German Schmeisser [MP40], the famous burp gun, in an English magazine. A Thompson and a tin jacket was our 'Schmeisser.' Such fakes were necessary at first since the industry was turning [out] so many war pictures. . . . The nations weren't selling any samples of their new weapons before the war, so we were caught short. Eventually we were permitted to purchase captured enemy equipment and allied armament which was unserviceable for combat but would do for picture purposes."

James S. Stembridge died in 1942, so the business was taken over by Dickie, as well as by Stembridge's nephew, Ed Stembridge, who had served for a time as an ordnance officer in the Pacific. In addition to supporting Hollywood feature films, Stembridge also supplied guns for training films. After the war was over, when the U.S. Army demobilized and began disposing of war surplus matériel, Stembridge was able to pick up enough to weapons to stock a small army, and at scrap-metal prices. Until the 1980s, Stembridge had in excess of ten thousand guns in their armory, but the settlement of the family estate forced the sale of most, many of them considered historic, because of their association with certain stars. A large number of these were purchased by magazine publisher Robert Petersen for his personal collection, and they, in turn, were sold by his estate after he died in 2007. This is not to say that the inventory today at Stembridge Gun Rentals is by any means insubstantial. During a visit in 2008, I noted twenty-two Thompsons neatly stacked in their vault.

One of the most realistic World War II movies released during the war was William "Wild Bill" Wellman's *The Story of GI Joe* (1945). The concept was a film based on the relationship that had been formed between regular GIs on the Italian front and famed war correspondent Ernie Pyle, who told their story for the folks on the home front. Burgess Meredith narrates the film as Ernie Pyle, and big-screen tough guy Robert Mitchum earned his only Oscar nomination as Lieutenant (later Captain) Bill Walker, the archetypical combat leader. Throughout the film, and prominently on the posters and advertising, Mitchum is seen carrying a Thompson submachine gun.

Real GIs were also featured as extras in *The Story of GI Joe,* as in many other films that were released during and immediately after the war. Notable among such pictures was Republic's *Sands of Iwo Jima* (1950). John Wayne got an Oscar nomination, but also included in the cast were three of the marines who had actually raised the flag on Mount Suribachi—John Bradley, Rene Gagnon, and Ira Hayes. Bradley's son James later wrote the book *Flags of Our Fathers,* which was the basis for Clint Eastwood's 2006 film of the same name about the bloody Iwo Jima campaign.

When discussing real World War II infantrymen who later played infantrymen in postwar films, talk always turns to Audie Leon Murphy. Both John Wayne and Robert Mitchum played a very *realistic* GI, but Audie Murphy was the *real* deal. The young Texan with the boyish grin joined the U.S. Army a few days after turning seventeen by lying about his age, earned the Medal of Honor while serving in France with Baker Company of the 3rd Infantry Division's 15th Regiment, and emerged after twenty-seven months of service as the most decorated American combat soldier of all time. (Captain Matt Urban of the 9th Infantry Division is now recognized as having exceeded Murphy in number of medals, but he did not receive his Medal of Honor until 1980, nine years after Murphy's death.)

Having earned two Silver Stars, Murphy earned his Medal of Honor and a battlefield promotion to lieutenant before he turned twenty-one. When he came home and was featured on the cover of *Life* magazine on July 16, 1945, millions saw his smiling face that week. Among them was Hollywood legend James Cagney, who invited him to Tinsel Town for a screen test. He began his acting career in Westerns and the occasional war movie. In 1949, his "autobiography," *To Hell and Back*, ghostwritten by his writer friend David "Spec" McClure, became a national bestseller. The film adaptation finally reached the screen in 1955. Initially, Murphy had declined to play himself in the film, but was finally talked into it. The film became the biggest grossing film made by Universal Studios until the release of *Jaws* twenty years later.

The original poster, and much of the advertising for the film, depicts Audie Murphy carrying or shooting a Thompson submachine gun—just as he had in combat in Italy and France. Cradling his Thompson, the handsome young man in front of the camera became, for Americans of the first postwar decade, the emblematic American hero.

Behind the camera, Murphy, like many returning GIs, suffered from the nightmares then called battle fatigue and now termed post-traumatic stress disorder. He was haunted by the demons of having seen and endured things that no nineteen- or twenty-year-old kid should have to bear—over and over and over for the entirety of those two years of his young life. He was tortured by prescription drug abuse even as he tortured those around him. He left a failed first marriage on the pile of his other personal failures.

If he had gone to one figurative hell and back in uniform in 1944–1945, he went to another within the tortured confines of his own mind over the ensuing decades. Whether he was back permanently from that private hell by the time he lost his life in a plane crash in 1971, we'll never know.

Yet this is not the way we remember him. We remember him as that emblematic hero who symbolized an American triumph back in that era when the Greatest Generation was mostly still in their thirties.

We remember him as he was and will always be in his biopic, a smiling, baby-faced kid. At age thirty, he still looked barely in his twenties. We see him solemnly posing for that famous Hollywood publicity photograph in a World War II uniform, holding his M1A1 Thompson, the lasting image of the GI foot soldier of whom Drew Middleton and Ernie Pyle wrote with such reverence and respect.

This was the image that thrilled those of us growing up in the 1950s and 1960s, when we idolized those heros who had triumphed so absolutely in that biggest of all wars.

CHAPTER 31

Blood, Sweat, Tears, and Steel

The smiling Audie Murphy of the 1945 *Life* cover and the image of total victory made possible by regular guys like him was a fitting end to a war into which America had so totally thrown itself. Yet battlefield victories and the heros that won them were only one part of a complex mechanism of victory.

The victories that were exuberantly celebrated across the United States and the world on VE Day and VJ Day were made possible by the blood, sweat, and tears of the victorious Allied troops. However, the blood, sweat, and tears spilled would not have been enough, had they not been supported by steel. Working long hours to back the soldiers with equipment were men and women at home, from captains of industry to "Rosie the Riveter," from Seattle to Pascagoula, from Oakland to Bridgeport, who shed their own sweat and tears—and occasionally blood. They, too, achieved results that boggle the mind.

As he looked out his office window on that spring morning in 1945 when the radio announced Hitler was dead, Russell Maguire could take satisfaction in knowing that he, and the Rosies and Rosses who assembled the Auto-Ordnance submachine guns, had shouldered a big part of that load of getting the steel into the hands of the American GI.

It was a monumental undertaking that should never be forgotten. Take a few examples that put things into perspective. During 1942, the first full year of the United States involvement in World War II, the American aircraft industry built 47,836 military aircraft. Two years later, at its peak, the industry built 96,318. First quarter deliveries to the U.S. Army Air Forces (USAAF after 1941) increased from 1,105 in 1941, to 5,537 in 1942, to 9,693 in 1943, and to 14,822 in 1944. According to the Civil Aeronautic Administration *Statistical Handbook*, America's aircraft factories produced 324,750 aircraft between 1939 and 1945, including 304,139 military aircraft. No aircraft industry at any other time in history, before or since, has ever matched this feat.

Alan Gropman, writing in *Mobilizing U.S. Industry in World War II*, tells that, in 1940, "the United States produced 309 tanks, versus 1,400 in Britain and 1,450 in Germany. In 1943, however, the United States manufactured 29,500 tanks, more in one year than Germany produced in the entire war from 1939 to 1945. In all, the United States manufactured 88,430 tanks during World War II versus 24,800 in Britain and 24,050 in Germany."

The miracle extended to ships as well. As Gropman further points out, in 1941 "the United States completed 1,906 ships, and in 1944, 40,265. . . . In the last half of 1943, the United States was completing 160 merchant ships per month, and in December that year 208 merchant ships were completed, for a total dead-weight tonnage of 2,044,239 tons."

He also reminds us that during World War II, American naval firepower increased tenfold, as industry produced 49 cruisers, 368 destroyers, and 8 battleships that exceeded 35,000 tons or more. This is not to mention nearly 100 aircraft carriers, including 17 capable of carrying in excess of 100 aircraft.

The whole story of the immense industrial mobilization in the United States during World War II is filled with superlatives. The part played in this by Auto-Ordnance is a small but important part.

The shipping records of Auto-Ordnance, submitted to the Springfield Ordnance District and preserved in the National Archives, detail the total number of Thompson submachine guns shipped to the United States government by Auto-Ordnance and Savage from April 1940 through February 1944 as 1,497,334. According to the U.S. Army publication *History of Submachine Guns, 1921 Through 1945* this total included 562,511 M1928A1s, 285,480 M1s, and 539,143 M1A1s.

In the month of January 1943, as the U.S. Army formally decided that the M3 would replace the Thompson submachine gun, Auto-Ordnance delivered 61,071 guns, the second highest monthly total to date, although the peak of deliveries had yet to be reached. The shipping records show that Auto-Ordnance reached this apogee of 70,000 monthly in February and March. Why these numbers are rounded off, unlike other monthly totals, has no explanation, but even if they were rounded up, they are certainly the peak months in Thompson production history.

The annual total for 1943 stood at 567,173 Thompsons, while General Motors delivered just 85,100 M3s. In 1944, the tables were turned. There were 343,372 grease guns delivered, but only 4,091 Thompsons, all of them in February. In 1945, 177,192 M3s and 15,469 M3A1s were stamped out. There were no Thompsons, and there would be no more.

How many tommy guns were made? The exact number will probably never be known because Auto-Ordnance records, such as still exist, are incomplete. *History of Submachine Guns, 1921 Through 1945* lists the total of all Thompsons ever built at around 1.75 million, of which 71.4 percent were manufactured by Savage Arms in Utica. This approximate total includes the Ordnance Department tally of 1.497 million, plus around 40 M1919s, plus the 15,000 units manufactured in 1921, plus the 107,500 that Britain ordered in 1940. The remaining 130,000 would have included guns accounted for by British and French purchase orders that were filled after the last of the original 15,000 were shipped, but before Lend-Lease.

As Russell Maguire looked out his office window, he gazed toward the tracks of the New York, New Haven & Hartford, and he realized that the train of America's greatest-ever industrial expansion had pulled out of the station.

For Maguire, it had left the station more than a year before Hitler died. Once there had been a frantic urgency to get the submachine guns off the line by the hundreds, then thousands, then tens of thousands. Now the factory beneath his feet at Bridgeport lay silent.

PART FIVE

Living Legend

CHAPTER 32

Swords into Consumer Products

Soviet soldiers searching the bodies of dead German troops on the Eastern Front in late 1942 were puzzled when among the goodies that they pilfered were some "little colored packets that looked like hotel soap." What they had actually found, according to the January 11, 1943, issue of *Time* magazine, were rations, freeze-dried, of the sort Americans have long since taken for granted, but which in 1943 were "tablet foods so long the favorite of popular science prophets."

The article went on to point out that "the revolution in foodstuffs" had also reached Connecticut, for—surprise—the "first commercial producer of dehydrated compressed foods in the United States" was none other than the Auto-Ordnance Corporation. The industry was then in its infancy (although Nestlé had been freeze-drying coffee since the 1930s).

The point of this little fable is not so much the origin of instant coffee, but that, as the submachine-gun train left Russell Maguire's platform, he began looking to the "popular science prophets" to answer the question "What next?"

By the time World War II ended, the market for military hardware had virtually evaporated. The production miracle that produced so much had in fact produced far too much. Orders were canceled. Aircraft manufacturers that had been delivering fleets of the most sophisticated equipment in the world looked at mountains of canceled orders and put their engineers to work on refrigerators and other kitchen appliances. So many boots, belts, backpacks, and canteens had been manufactured that it would keep war surplus stores in business for the next quarter century.

When he flirted with freeze-dried vegetables early in 1943, Maguire's own factory still employed three thousand gunmakers, and was still building submachine guns at capacity. However, even before the Ordnance Department officially wed itself to the M3, the writing had been on the wall.

Behind the huge numbers, in production and dollars, World War II had not been exactly days of wine and roses for the captains of America's arms industries. The pressure cooker environment that made those numbers possible took their toll. Boeing's president, Phil Johnson, for example, suffered a cerebral hemorrhage on the factory floor in September 1944 and died.

For Russell Maguire, death did not come calling during the war years, but process servers did. Auto-Ordnance Corporation was sued several times, and so was Thompson Automatic Arms, even though it had been consolidated with Auto-Ordnance in October 1941.

Ida Blish, the widow of Commodore John Bell Blish, who had invented the unnecessary lock, brought suit in the Delaware Supreme Court. Suing on behalf of herself and other stockholders, she complained that Maguire's own Maguire & Company had been illegally issued around 140,000 shares of Thompson Automatic Arms stock in 1939, including shares that were authorized to be issued to Marcellus Thompson and Thomas Kane—but instead were diverted to Maguire. The suit was dismissed on March 13, 1942, and four days later, the history of Thompson Automatic Arms officially ended as this nonfunctioning entity formally withdrew from doing business in the state of Connecticut. Of course, by now, the Blish lock was no longer being installed in the Thompson submachine guns that were being manufactured.

Richard Cutts Jr., the son in the father and son team that created the Cutts compensator, sued for royalties. Like the Blish lock, the Cutts compensator was no longer being installed in the Thompsons rolling out of the factories. Unfortunately for Cutts, his agreement with Auto-Ordnance had included a royalty ceiling, which he had signed, never imagining the wartime volume of guns that would be produced before the component was discontinued. Now he wanted to renegotiate. Unfortunately for Maguire, Cutts had inside knowledge of Auto-Ordnance from having worked there. An out-of-court settlement was reached.

As for Marcellus's widow, Evelyn, her share of the company, both inherited from Marcellus and the hundred shares issued to her personally, amounted to just over 12 percent of the authorized capital stock when originally issued by Thompson Automatic Arms in 1939. Though valuable during the war years, it verged on worthless as the company shriveled after 1944. Evelyn later remarried to Robert Barryhill Adams and moved to North Carolina. It was here, at the Cary Rehabilitation and Nursing Center in the Raleigh-Durham suburb of Cary, that she died on January 29, 2006, at the age of ninety-nine. There is no evidence that she played any role in the company, or had any dealings with Russell Maguire after Marcellus died in 1939.

* * *

The estate of Thomas Fortune Ryan had also seen the wartime success of Auto-Ordnance and filed suit against the Guaranty Trust Company, the executor of the estate, for cutting deals at "inadequate" prices. To underscore the almost comic nature of such after-the-fact pouting, *The New York Times* ran their piece about the suit in the April 26, 1945, "Amusements" section rather than on the business pages. Said the paper: "Heirs of the Thomas Fortune Ryan estate yesterday accused the Guaranty Trust Company, executor of their grandfather's estate, of selling coal lands and munitions stocks [read Auto-Ordnance] belonging to the estate at prices 'grossly inadequate and far below actual value.'"

The United States government also sent a process server knocking on Russell Maguire's door. In the footnotes behind the glorious story of America's wartime production miracle are the less glorious tales of perceived "excess profits," and truly dark tales of waste, fraud, and mismanagement.

The notion that the government might be paying more than it should in a time of national emergency was investigated both by the military services and by Congress during the war. The Senate formed its Special Committee to Investigate the National Defense Program. Chairing the committee was an obscure Missouri senator named Harry S Truman. The Truman committee was a great success, saving an estimated $15 billion. They found far more waste than fraud, but there was so much of both that Under Secretary of War Robert Patterson asked President Roosevelt to halt the committee's work on the grounds that it hurt wartime morale. Instead, Roosevelt offered Truman a slot on the ticket in 1944, and he was elected vice president. The rest, as they say, is history.

In 1943, the government had looked at what it was paying Auto-Ordnance for Thompson submachine guns. With mass production creating immense economies of scale, the government asked for a better price. They went to court, and this time Maguire lost. In a second defeat, the General Motors M3 became the U.S. Army's standard submachine gun.

According to Springfield Ordnance District records, the last batch of Thompson submachine guns was delivered by Auto-Ordnance Corporation during February 1944. By the end of March, Russell Maguire had filed papers with the state of Connecticut formally changing the name of the company to Maguire Industries. This entity would contain within it a gunmaking subsidiary that would be known as the "Auto-Ordnance Division." Nether Maguire Industries nor this familiar-sounding division would ever build a gun of any kind, but they did make radios.

* * *

Maguire, who would reinsert his first initial and become J. Russell Maguire after the war, had looked into many things to do with himself and his factory. In addition to dabbling in dehydrated corn and peas, he tried for a comeback on Wall Street in 1945. However, the Securities and Exchange Commission had a long memory, and he was sternly reminded of his prewar "flagrant violations" of the law. He would have to turn to Main Street for his next caper. On April 10, 1945, *The New York Times* business section reported tersely, "The application of Russell Maguire to register a new company, Maguire, Inc., as a broker-dealer firm was denied today by the Securities and Exchange Commission, which in 1941 found two broker-dealer firms under Mr. Maguire's control guilty of manipulating the market."

The SEC ruled out his return to old haunts, but there were plenty of options open to the old wheeler-dealer. Maguire assigned Eugene Daniel Powers, a thirty-three-year-old attorney who had served as executive vice president of Auto-Ordnance through World War II, to the task of converting Auto-Ordnance from swords to plowshares—or in this case from tommy guns to table radios. It was decided that the fastest way to accomplish this task was to find and acquire a firm that was already making consumer products. Powers did some searching and located the Thordarson Electric Manufacturing Company in Chicago.

The company had been started by Iceland-born Chester H. Thordarson, who amassed more than a hundred patents, influenced Edison, and founded a successful electrical products company. He was also famous for having designed and built a 500,000-volt transformer—then the world's largest—for the 1904 St. Louis World's Fair. Thordarson had passed away in January 1945, having sold his interest in his own company to Burgess Battery. It was from Burgess that Powers acquired Thordarson Electric on behalf of Maguire. In the meantime, Gene Powers also located and acquired the Meissner Manufacturing Company of Mt. Carmel on the Wabash River in downstate Illinois, makers of radio transformers. The two were then merged as the Thordarson Meissner Company, an entity that still exists in the twenty-first century. The merged company is still located at Mt. Carmel.

Now long forgotten, the Maguire Model 500 series offered actually quite sophisticated little table radios. They were based on an experimental concept developed by radio pioneer Sarkes Tarzian, a veteran employee of both Atwater Kent and RCA. In 1945, Tarzian not only made radios, but started a high-frequency AM broadcast radio station in New York City.

According to Andrew Mitz in a July 2004 article in *Radio Age* magazine, the motivation behind Tarzian's plan, dubbed Hi-FAM, may have been to develop a way to "permit the proliferation of local AM radio stations without the expense of transmitting or decoding FM." As Mitz explains, the Maguire 500 was "a marbleized plastic radio with a round dial on the left, speaker on the right, and the tuning control above the volume control on the extreme right front."

Functionally, it was roughly 90 percent the same as the Sarkes Tarzian set. Today, Model 500s are rare, but can still be found.

Maguire also found time to pursue an interest in black gold, having invested some of his tommy gun profits in oil land in Texas and the Plains.

The postwar American economy was growing. From the late 1940s through the 1950s, the robust United States economy far overshadowed that of any other nation. Undamaged by warfare, the United States had greatly expanded its industrial capacity and had invested greatly in new technology.

With record high prosperity and record low unemployment, Americans became consumers. After the privation and shortages of nearly two decades of depression and war, Americans went on a shopping spree. As they bought new homes and new cars, the economy boomed. More Americans bought new kitchen appliances and other consumer goods than at any time before.

J. Russell Maguire benefited from this. They bought his radios, but they also were buying record numbers of cars to commute from the growing suburban sprawl and to take those family car trips that were becoming essential to American life. Cars needed gasoline, gasoline came from oil, and Maguire was in the oil business.

In the midst of this greatly expanding consumer economy, Maguire was a millionaire—at a time when being a millionaire *really* meant something.

CHAPTER 33

A Million Tommy Guns

As J. Russell Maguire stopped making submachine guns and amassed his millions in oil, there were still a million tommy guns—more or less—in the world. Some, like George MacDonald Fraser's, lay in the muck at the bottom of a river. Some lay at the bottom of the Atlantic, still carefully packed in Cosmoline, sent into the depths by the torpedoes of German U-boats. Others lay jammed or broken beyond repair in scrap heaps from the Philippines to the Pas de Calais. Still others, however, remained in workable condition, and many of these remained in use.

They came home in the duffel bags of returning GIs as souvenirs of battles fought and won. They were tossed into basements or laid away carefully in attics. Some were shared proudly with friends or sons. Others were discovered many decades later by astonished granddaughters.

These Thompson submachine guns, casually handled in the field overseas, came home to a nation at peace, and a nation under the rule of law—including the National Firearms Act of 1934. Passed to criminalize gangsters of the Capone archetype and not war heroes, the act nevertheless banned anyone without the proper licensing from owning machine guns, defined as "any firearm which can fire more than one cartridge per trigger pull." This classification clearly included the Thompson.

Somehow, though, making criminals of returning GIs seemed like a bad idea. Eventually, Congress addressed the issue by creating a "war trophy class" of firearms. This made such guns legal if they were deactivated under the supervision of an investigator of the Alcohol and Tobacco Tax Division—later the Bureau of Alcohol, Tobacco and Firearms (ATF) and now the Bureau of Alcohol, Tobacco, Firearms and Explosives (BATFE).

In the beginning, deactivated war trophies were considered to be "unserviceable firearms" requiring paperwork each time they were transferred, so in 1955 the Internal Revenue Code was amended again. Now, the "harmless

When he was actually firing his M1928, this FBI special agent would not be
holding the fore grip this way. *(Courtesy of the FBI)*

ordnance curios" were redefined as Deactivated War Trophies, or "DEWAT"
guns.

Of course, not all the Thompson submachine guns in civilian hands in
the United States were deactivated after World War II. Some were used by
law enforcement agencies, and others remained in the possession of individuals who had proper licensing for such guns. Meanwhile, a number of
the tommy guns that came home from the war wound up in the hands of the
same sorts of nefarious characters who had made them famous in the Roaring Twenties.

It was déjà vu all over again. *The New York Times* of December 16, 1945,
reported, "Armed thugs continued their depredations in the city yesterday,
with holdup men in Brooklyn using a submachine gun, the hallmark of
crime in the twenties after the first World War."

Two years later, on June 15, 1947, the paper reported, "As youngsters at
play scurried for safety in crowded tenement-lined West Forty-seventh Street
between Tenth and Eleventh Avenues, a man wearing dark glasses and gripping a submachine gun leaped from a black sedan and shot to death
31-year-old Vincent Wice, a milk-wagon driver and former soldier."

* * *

As with the G-men and Untouchables of a generation earlier, lawmen also took to "tommy" in the years after World War II. It is from Texas that one of the more colorful, albeit grisly, tommy gun stories of the era comes. Bee County lies about midway between Corpus Christi and San Antonio, where for nearly a decade the peace was kept by Sheriff Robert Vail Ennis.

"I am hellbent to keep Beeville cleaned up so a lady can go up the street day or night," Ennis insisted. "I never take but one shot."

As *Time* magazine reported on November 24, 1947, "Sheriff Ennis has killed seven people with his .44 Colt revolver and his .45 submachine gun—not all, however, with one shot."

The sheriff killed his first man in 1943 when he shot "his way out of a tight place while making an arrest. He was tried for murder, and acquitted."

Controversy still surrounds the day in July 1945 when Ennis added three more to his tally. He went to the home of Felix Rodriguez to retrieve the man's two grandchildren on behalf of their mother, Felix's former daughter-in-law, Jesusa. After the divorce, Felix's son Geronimo had partial custody of the kids and it was his turn to share them with his ex. He didn't and the sheriff was sent.

Felix may or may not have pulled his shotgun, but Ennis pulled his Thompson. As he lay dying in his daughters' arms, Felix's brothers Domingo and Antonio, came running. Vail Ennis turned with his tommy gun and killed them both. The sheriff was acquitted on two counts of murder, and the third case never went to trial. Such was Texas justice.

In August 1947, the Wild West came east to Jersey City when the long arm of the law intervened to protect the peace from the threat of a trio of bovine rampagers. According to *The New York Times* on August 28, "Three quick, accurate bursts from a submachine gun fired by Police Lieutenant Fred Small from atop a baggage truck in the Exchange Place Terminal of the Pennsylvania Railroad cut down three runaway steers today in view of a terror stricken crowd of 500 who thronged the station during the noon hour period."

One is left to wonder whether it might not have been less messy to just get a Texas cowboy to round up the critters.

South of the border, the staccato rattle of a tommy gun burst had serenaded Mexico City streets since the 1920s, and with increasing numbers of surplus Thompsons on the market, there was little wonder that the song would continue into the 1940s. On February 10, 1947, *Time* reported that "Cinemactor Jorge Valez and his wife (by civil law marriage), Margarita Richardi de Avila Camacho, missed the plane that was to whisk them (via Manhattan) to Rome for a Catholic Church wedding. Señora Valez is the widow of Maximino Avila Camacho, fabulously wealthy brother of Mexico's wartime president. As the car with its police escort left for the airport, another car drew abreast, poured in a fusillade of 22 Tommy Gun slugs."

Six months later, the August 4 issue of the "weekly newsmagazine" carried a story about modern pirates cruising the Mediterranean with Thompsons. "The buccaneers were gone from the Caribbean; the corsairs of Barbary had long since walked the plank; but the Jolly Roger had not been furled for good," said a writer who was obviously enjoying his work that day. "From a hidden cove on the southern coast of France, five sea dogs had swooped out in a high-powered motor launch. Armed with submachine guns and dressed as customs men, they boarded an unsuspecting Italian freighter, locked the crew in the hold and sailed away to their pirate lair with two and a half tons of U.S. cigarets—in 20th Century Europe, a treasure as fabulous as Captain Kidd's."

On February 11, 1946, *Time* correspondent John Scott reported from Soviet-occupied Poland under the touching poetic headline "The Peasant & the Tommy Gun." He wrote of a "ruddy-faced, wide-eyed girl named Stenia, with a Tommy gun slung across her back. . . . Past her flowed a bustling [Warsaw] traffic of carts, bicycles, [United Nations Relief and Rehabilitation Administration] trucks, Red Army vehicles and pedestrians. Stenia was 23, but she had lived a lifetime of terror. She was a left-winger, a militiawoman, a veteran of the resistance and of Gestapo torture. The Nazis had knocked out two of her front teeth; now, when she smiled, she showed shiny, stainless-steel replacements."

Whether the actual gun that Stenia had slung over her shoulder was a Thompson submachine gun or PPSh-41 is not known. If the latter, Scott's choosing to call it a tommy gun only serves to underscore the ubiquity of the Thompson as a cultural icon, and as a symbol for all submachine guns.

CHAPTER 34

Where's My Tommy Gun?

Harry Truman won the presidential election of 1948. This was despite numerous polls that predicted he would be defeated by Thomas E. Dewey, and the famous *Chicago Tribune* headline that announced that he *had been*.

Harry Truman had saved his presidency, but he was told that the house in which he lived was on the verge of collapse. It was in 1948 that they condemned the White House. First lived in by John Adams in 1800 before it was actually completed, the old brick and sandstone Executive Mansion had been burned out by the British, rebuilt, repaired, added to, and abused for nearly a century and a half. Its aging wood frame could barely support various additions that had been made through the years, including a fourth-story attic during the Coolidge administration, and a second-floor balcony over the south portico after Truman came to office. These and, frankly, poor maintenance had taken their toll.

Truman had assured his second term in the White House, but most of it would not actually be spent *in* the White House. While it was gutted and reinforced with steel, the president moved across the street to the Blair House, the 1824 structure that had been acquired in 1942 as the official executive branch guest house.

It was at Blair House that Truman was living in June 1950 as the army of Communist North Korea flooded across the 38th Parallel into South Korea and started the Korean War. It was in Blair House that Truman lay down for a nap early on the afternoon on November 1. Perhaps his thoughts turned to the successful American invasion at Inchon six weeks earlier that had turned the tide in the Korean War, and to his famous meeting with General Douglas MacArthur two weeks earlier at Wake Island. He was probably thinking of the midterm elections a week later and the fate of the Democrats' slim majority in Congress.

Truman may also have been thinking of the unrest among the nationalist minority in Puerto Rico, upset because their fellow Puerto Ricans had just overwhelmingly voted for a commonwealth relationship with the United States.

Certainly the latter was on the minds of nationalists Griselio Torresola and Oscar Collazo that day. They were so upset at seeing their cause abandoned by a majority of Puerto Ricans that they decided to get some handguns and kill Harry Truman.

As the pair converged on Blair House from opposite directions, three White House policemen were on duty in the front of the residence. Leslie Coffelt, a uniformed officer, was seated in the doorway, Donald Birdzall was on the sidewalk, and plainclothes officer Joseph Downs had just walked back inside after chatting with Coffelt. Accounts say that they were feeling bored. Nothing ever happened.

Suddenly the monotony was broken.

Collazo opened fire with a Walther P-38 automatic pistol, hitting Birdzall in the leg. Torresola pulled out his own German pistol and put three 9 mm rounds into Coffelt. Hearing the shots, Downs returned to the front of the building, where Torresola hit him with three rounds. Downs retreated into the building, slamming the door and sealing off access to the building.

By this time Collazo was exchanging fire with several officers. Seeing that Birdzall was aiming at Collazo, Torresola fired, hitting Birdzall in the knee. Moments later, the badly injured Coffelt got off a shot at Torresola, hitting him in the head and killing him instantly.

Across the street in the White House, Robert Nixon, a correspondent with the International News Service and a member of the White House press corps, was waiting to accompany the president to a ceremony at Arlington National Cemetery that afternoon. A veteran reporter, Nixon had covered the evacuation from Dunkirk in 1940 and had just been with Truman on the Wake Island trip.

The phone at Nixon's desk rang. It was his office calling to check on a report that shooting was going on in front of Blair House. Nixon should check it out.

The reporter dashed first to the office where the president's press secretary was hanging out with James J. Rowley, the chief of the White House Secret Service detail. According to Nixon's recollection, contained in the transcript of an interview conducted in 1970 by Jerry Hess, which is now in the collection of the Truman Presidential Library and Museum, neither man had a clue about the shooting. It took a reporter to break the story to them.

Secret Service weapons instruction under way at the range at the National Arboretum in Washington, D.C., circa late 1940s or early 1950s. *(Courtesy of the Secret Service)*

"Charlie, somebody's trying to kill Truman. Do you know anything about it?" Nixon asked.

"Where is my *tommy gun?*" Rowley shouted, jumping up and racing out of the room.

In Rowley's own recollection of that day, contained in the transcript of an interview conducted in 1988 by Niel Johnson, and now in the collection of the Truman Library, it was his own assistant, Henry Nicholson, not Nixon, who informed him of the shooting. "His expression was enough to tell me, don't ask questions, to go, and I went. We ran up West Executive Avenue, and I said, 'What the hell's the matter?'"

As the men reached Pennsylvania Avenue, it was all over. The actual shoot-out is estimated to have lasted little more than half a minute.

"About that moment, President Truman came to a front window," Nixon recalled. "He had been taking his usual after lunch nap and was awakened by the shots and commotion. He came to the window in his BVDs [underwear], long handles. He looked out and then went on away. So, I knew he was all right."

Uniformed and plainclothes Secret Service agents aim their Thompson submachine guns from the firing line. *(Courtesy of the Secret Service)*

Leslie Coffelt died of his wounds several hours later, but the other two officers would recover. Torresola was dead at the scene, and Collazo was given the death penalty for his part in the affair. However, Truman himself commuted the sentence to life in prison. In 1979, seven years after Truman's death, President Jimmy Carter ordered Collazo released from prison.

Jim Rowley continued his long career with the Service. Having been photographed wielding a tommy gun as part of the Secret Service detail guarding President Franklin Roosevelt as he met with General Dwight Eisenhower at the Casablanca Conference in 1943, Rowley guarded Eisenhower as president, and was promoted to director of the Secret Service in 1962. He was in this position when John F. Kennedy was assassinated on November 22, 1963.

He never found his tommy gun that day in 1950, and in later years he insisted repeatedly that he never uttered the famous line, although Robert Nixon emphatically insisted that he *did*. Charlie Ross, the other man in the room that day, died of a heart attack just thirty-four days after the assassination attempt and could not be asked.

"He was excited and didn't know what he was saying," Nixon contends. "He was a little embarrassed, I'm sure, by this. But he insisted to me later that he never . . . said anything like that."

Nevertheless, the line remains part of the enduring lore of the Thompson.

In his March 22, 2004, article "Triggering Memories," *Washington Post* staff writer Stephen Hunter uses the phrase to begin his overview of the National Firearms Museum in Fairfax, Virginia. The gun is, of course, a featured part of the museum.

"There's nothing more dazzling to the eye and the imagination," Hunter writes, "than a room decorated in a style called 'Early Thompson.'"

Best of all, Hunter puts it all in perspective when he observes that "Rowley's cry reflects almost a half-century's worth of loyalty by American police and military men toward Brig. Gen. John Taliaferro Thompson's baby when things got shaky and high quantities of firepower were necessary."

CHAPTER 35

The Idea That Would Not Die

Had Jim Rowley asked for his tommy gun just a few years later, the answer would have been that there were no more in the active federal arsenal.

The United States government cleaned house during the 1950s. The military services had officially embraced the M3 grease gun during World War II, and federal law enforcement agencies began dumping theirs soon after. Though they scrapped most of their Thompson arsenal, the FBI did continue to use one for the dramatic conclusion of the public tour of their Washington headquarters. Up into the 1970s, the live firing of a tommy gun provided a sensational climax, and a reminder of the Bureau's "golden age" back in the era of Dillinger et al.

According to Secret Service archivist Michael Sampson, the Thompson was still in use in that agency up through the mid-1960s, but pistols remained the firearm of choice for Secret Service agents. Numerous state and local police agencies used Thompson submachine guns through the 1960s, but even here the phase-out was ongoing.

Parenthetically, and surprisingly, Thompsons can still occasionally be found in police arsenals. For example, an April 30, 2008, article in the *Watertown Daily Times* penned by staff writer David Shampine told how Jefferson County, New York, sheriff John P. Burns had finally parted with the department's last Thompson submachine gun. As he took delivery of seventeen Bushmaster carbines, Sheriff Burns handed over a single Thompson in trade. "Better known as a 'Tommy gun,' the antique has an appraised value of $30,000," Shampine explained. "The new weaponry [all 17 guns combined] has about the same value."

Had John Taliaferro Thompson knocked on the door of the U.S. Army Ordnance Department in 1951 as he had in 1921, the reaction would have been no less frosty. When World War II came to a close, the pendulum of ordnance theory swung away from submachine guns in general. Though the grease gun was used by American troops in the Korean War and still found thereafter in the occasional unit, especially the National Guard, the U.S. Army and Marine Corps both officially phased out the submachine gun as a standard infantry weapon.

Just as Thompson's brainchild had been a hard sell after the First World War, submachine guns in general were considered obsolescent as military weapons after the Second. They would be supplanted by the apparently more versatile assault rifle.

Technically, an assault rifle shoots an intermediate cartridge that has longer range than the pistol-caliber cartridge of a submachine gun, but is less powerful and has less range than the cartridge fired by a main battle rifle, such as the M1 Garand or the Lee-Enfield of World War II. An assault rifle is like a submachine gun in that it is capable of fully automatic fire, but it differs from most submachine guns in that it is capable of selective fire.

A prime example of a widely used post–World War II assault rifle is Mikhail Kalashnikov's AK-47, which equipped Soviet and other Warsaw Pact troops in the 1950s. It is still widely used by armies and guerrilla bands in more than one hundred countries around the world.

Vladimir Fedorov's Avtomat, generally recognized as the first assault rifle, was developed during World War I but saw little action, and that was mainly in the Russian civil war of the early 1920s. The first assault rifle widely used in combat was the German StG-44 Sturmgewehr of World War II. Originally designated as the Maschinenpistole 43 (and later 44), this family of guns was renamed by Adolf Hitler himself as the "Sturmgewehr," meaning a rifle for assaulting the enemy. The English translation is "assault rifle."

An ordnance concept that emerged after World War II, embraced by armed forces around the world, was for a single standardized infantry weapon to satisfy several infantry weapon requirements. This led, of course, to the assault rifle's being viewed by the bureaucrats as a single replacement for many weapons—not just the infantry's main battle rifle, but also the carbine and the submachine gun.

The idea looked good on paper. Standardization would simplify the logistics of supplying both guns and ammo to the troops. Theoretically, an assault rifle is capable of being used as either a Garand or a Thompson; it might have been used by a World War II GI although it is inferior to the former in long-range accuracy and inferior to the latter in short-range firepower.

After World War II, just as the Soviets and other Warsaw Pact armies gravitated toward the AK-47, so, too, did European gunmakers and NATO

An FBI special agent opens the gun vault to examine an M1928 Thompson
submachine gun. *(Courtesy of the National Archives)*

armies move in the direction of the assault rifle as an all-purpose infantry
weapon. Such was the case in the U.S. Army as well, where the U.S. Army
Ordnance Department, specifically Colonel René Studler, the chief of small
arms research and development, moved toward that single-weapon type
that could replace many.

The result was the M14, a select-fire automatic rifle whose lineage went
back to the M1 Garand. Developed at the Springfield Armory and adopted
in 1957, the M14 fired 7.62 mm NATO standard ammunition—which superseded the .30-'06 round for American military weapons—from a twenty-
round box magazine.

The Ordnance Department had come to the conclusion that the typical
rifle cartridges with which both world wars were fought were heavier and
more powerful than necessary, and developments in powder technology
now made an effective lighter cartridge possible. This lighter cartridge
would still theoretically be accurate at longer ranges, while its lightness
would help make the gun more controllable on full auto at closer range.

With all this in mind, the M14 was a concept that was intended to replace four separate infantry weapons, the M1 Garand service rifle, the M1 carbine, the M3 grease gun, and the Browning automatic rifle. For logisticians, it delivered as promised, but as a weapon it was an adequate replacement only as a main battle rifle replacement for the M1. Indeed, it was exceptional in this regard.

"The idea of replacing submachine guns, the M1 carbine, and the Garand, putting it all into the M14 was a bogus concept," firearms consultant Idan Greenberg told me. "It was not even really believed by anyone in the Ordnance Department who had any knowledge of combat. It was done out of politics . . . it was about allocation of resources. . . . This notion that there is one weapon system that is right for all situations is the heart of the problem, but government logistics people loved the idea of an all-inclusive system." As it was, the M14 remained only briefly as the standard American infantry rifle. Though the M14 was downgraded to "limited standard" relatively quickly, the all-inclusive assault rifle idea that lay behind its adoption was one whose time had come. The assault rifle was here to stay.

The M14 was gradually superseded in the mid-1960s by the M16 assault rifle, the military variant of the ArmaLite AR-15 that was designed by Eugene Stoner. The gun was designed to fire the 5.56 mm cartridge, similar to the civilian .223 caliber round. In an interesting twist, it was Colt that developed and manufactured the military M16, just as it had been contracted to produce John Taliaferro Thompson's original M1921 tommy gun.

The M16 family of military assault rifles achieved the goal set for the M14, or at least most of it. Except for the preposterous notion that an assault rifle could be a replacement for the BAR, the M16 succeeded in becoming an adequate substitute for rifles, carbines, and submachine guns. As an infantry weapon, certainly its weight, less than ten pounds, made it popular with the troops who remembered heavier shoulder-fired weapons. It was first widely used in the Vietnam War and it has been used by United States forces in every war they've fought since. Indeed, the M16 family of assault rifles, including the M4 carbine, remains standard with the United States armed forces in the twenty-first century. Meanwhile, a semiautomatic version of the AR-15 is today manufactured by Bushmaster Firearms International of Windham, Maine.

As Greenberg points out, the U.S. Army had finally achieved the true assault rifle purpose with the M16. However, as a jack-of-all-trades, the M16 was a master of none. As we have noted, the M14 had excelled as a replacement for the M1 Garand—unfortunately at a time when that was not what the U.S. Army sought.

Still, the M14 would have its day.

"For jungle combat the M16 was a better idea than the M14," Greenberg observes. "However, the troops have found out in Afghanistan that the M16 is less desirable for that kind of environment. That's why the army has been digging M14s out of mothballs and reissuing them as a marksman's rifle. Same with Iraq. Once the troops get out of the cities, M16s suck. You want to shoot something where you can see the bullet hit so that if you miss, you can adjust your point of aim. With a .223 caliber round [fired by an M16], you can't see it hit past two hundred yards."

Meanwhile, as all of this was going on during the late 1950s and early 1960s, the submachine-gun concept had never really gone away.

After World War I, Thompson, Eickhoff, and Payne brought forth a military weapon that was ahead of its time, and almost no traditional army wanted it—at least not for nearly two decades. After World War II, another man brought forth a brainchild that was, like the Thompson, destined to be the signature submachine gun of its era. Like John Taliaferro Thompson, he was the submachine-gun maverick of his day.

There has always been room for gunsmiths who think outside the bureaucrat's cubicle. Born in Germany in 1923, Gotthard Glass was part of the Jewish exodus that left the country after Hitler came to power. Relocating to Kibbutz Yagur in the British Mandate of Palestine, he changed his name to Uziel Gal. Eventually he became a gunsmith. In the meantime, though, he joined the Haganah, becoming one of many in Palestine, both Arab and Jew, who actively opposed one another as well as the British. He spent three years in jail on weapons charges, but was pardoned and released in 1946. When the state of Israel was declared in 1948, he joined the Israel Defense Forces (IDF) and fought in Israel's 1948 War of Independence.

After World War II, a large number of Thompson submachine guns had found their way to British Palestine and into the hands of Arabs and Jews who fought one another and the British. Some of these tommy guns were probably stolen from British stocks, while others were among the tons of surplus arms that were scrounged in postwar Europe and sent south. Reports of the fighting that was taking place during the period leading up to the declaration of the state of Israel frequently mention the Thompson.

"Uzi" Gal had ample opportunity to both observe and to use the Thompson throughout this period. Moreover, he had ample opportunity to experience the value of a submachine gun in small-unit actions taking place in real-world combat. For him the submachine gun was not an ordnance concept, it was the difference between living and dying.

On his own initiative, he designed a lightweight, easily manufactured 9 mm submachine gun, which, like the M1A1 Thompson, had a six-hundred-round-per-minute rate of fire. As with the earlier Sten and M3, the new submachine gun was made primarily of stamped sheet metal for simplicity of manufacture and maintenance. Gal submitted the gun to the IDF, which accepted it and ordered it into production. Against his wishes, the gun was named after him. The Uzi was born.

In the Arab-Israeli War of 1956, the Uzi submachine gun proved itself to be an extraordinary weapon. During the Six-Day War of 1967, it became a legend. As Idan Greenberg, who has consulted for the Israeli government, put it, the Uzi "did the job of the World War II submachine guns, but it was shorter and handier. It was very ergonomic and very controllable."

The Uzi was adopted not only by the IDF, but by military and police entities in Europe, and around the world. Through the years, millions of Uzi submachine guns have been manufactured by Israel Weapons Industries (formerly Israel Military Industries), as well as by many international arms makers, including Fabrique Nationale de Herstal in Belgium, Lyttleton Engineering Works in South Africa, and China North Industries (Norinco).

American law enforcement agencies such as the Secret Service that had dumped their tommy guns came to realize the need for the close-range firepower of a submachine gun and also cast their lot with the Uzi. Though the Secret Service did issue assault rifles to its agents, the photographs from March 30, 1981, the day when John Hinckley opened fire on President Ronald W. Reagan, show the Secret Service detail bringing out Uzis, not M16s.

The submachine gun had not gone away.

According to Idan Greenberg, the submachine gun of choice in the twenty-first century, as it has been since the last quarter of the twentieth, is the MP5, manufactured by Heckler & Koch GmbH of Oberndorf am Neckar in Germany. Designed in the 1960s by Helmut Baureuter, Manfred Guhring, Tilo Moller, and Georg Seidl, the MP5 was first adopted by the German Federal Police, as well as Bundeswehr Special Forces. It is now used by the armed forces, and law enforcement agencies, in more than three dozen countries. It can be said that Heckler & Koch dominates the global market for submachine guns, especially for those larger than 9 mm. In 1999, the company added the lighter UMP (Universale Maschinenpistole or Universal Submachine Gun) to its product line.

From the 1920s, when Captain John Stege famously told the *Chicago Tribune* that he needed tommy guns for his department, to that day in 1950 when Jim Rowley instinctively reached for his tommy gun, the attributes of the submachine gun concept have been seen as desirable at both the local and federal level.

Idan Greenberg points out, "Law enforcement agencies prefer submachine guns for their full auto controllability and accuracy at close ranges, as well as their reduced noise and penetration, particularly in an urban environment."

A somewhat different perspective on the future of the submachine gun in police work was shared with me by Seth Nadel, a retired senior special agent with three decades of service in the United States Customs Service— who also happens to be a Thompson collector. Like Greenberg, he acknowledges the role played by submachine guns in the military and law enforcement, but he sees the future of the weapon in law enforcement as being in decline.

"With the advent of the 5.56 mm round, subguns are falling out of favor in law enforcement," Nadel told me. "Anything that can be done with a subgun can be done with a 5.56 carbine—or my favorite, the Steyr AUG. The carbine can reach out beyond the useful range of a subgun."

Among the factors that he sees as affecting the change are the influx of former servicemen and women already trained on the M16 and M4, the fact that the Uzi and MP5 are of decades-old design, and that the penetrating power of higher-velocity assault-rifle ammunition is desirable.

Nadel adds that another important consideration with civilian police agencies is the liability issue.

"Unless the officer is very well trained with the subgun, he or she is, in effect, firing a shotgun when they fire a burst from an MP5 or Uzi," he says, likening the spray from a submachine gun on full auto to a shower of birdshot. "No administrator wants that kind of liability. . . . Neither gun offers the precision of an M4, even if they are all fired semiautomatically."

He sees the adoption of the midrange rifle cartridge in small carbines as potentially signaling the end of submachine-gun development.

"The subgun is not yet dead, but it may soon join the list of guns that have passed into history, like police revolvers, derringers, and police lever-action rifles."

Greenberg, on the other hand, remains a firm believer in the tactical utility of the submachine gun in situations for which it was designed. He even has a high regard for the longer-range capability of the MP5.

"The HK5 is closed-bolt, so you can put it on semiautomatic and hit a man-sized target at two hundred yards," he said. "You can't do that with an Uzi and it's very difficult with a Thompson. . . . [However] if I was going into combat with a submachine gun, it would be an M1A1 Thompson. To this day, for house-to-house fighting, I don't think that there was anything ever invented that is any better."

In the meantime, what about the submachine gun in combat situations?

Has the United States military establishment completely parted company with the submachine-gun idea and fully embraced the assault-rifle paradigm?

Yes and no.

As a general-issue infantry weapon, the answer would be yes. However, just as U.S. Army Ranger Battalions and the Marine Raiders of World War II adopted the Thompson for their work, the submachine gun lives on in today's equivalent of those units. The Rangers still use them, as does the Delta Force. Marine Corps Force Reconnaissance Companies carry submachine guns, notably MP5s, as do Marine Security Force Battalions and Navy SEALs.

"Specialist units use them when they need a quiet full-auto weapon," Greenberg told me. "With special ammo firing a subsonic bullet a [sound] suppressed submachine gun is inaudible or unrecognizable as a firearm shooting. This is particularly true with a closed-bolt submachine gun like the MP5. And since it is one of the few closed-bolt submachine guns, it is accurate as a firearm up to two hundred yards, which open-bolt guns cannot be. Assault rifles all fire supersonic bullets and cannot be as effectively suppressed as a submachine gun. I'm kind of a purist. If I want to hit things at longer range, I'm going to have something like an M14. If I want massive firepower and short-range accuracy, I'm going to have a submachine gun."

I spoke recently with Jason Dietsch, who carries both M4s and submachine guns in his work for Immigration and Customs Enforcement in the Department of Homeland Security. He has used the MP5 and UMP, as well as the Belgian-made Fabrique Nationale P90, but in his private life, he is the owner of an M1928A1 Thompson that was previously owned by the Fort Collins, Colorado, Police Department.

"I got it because of the history," he told me.

As much as he enjoys his Thompson, he prefers the newer, lighter guns for going out on the street on a daily basis. Like Seth Nadel and most people who use shoulder-fired weapons for law enforcement, he sees the M4 carbine as "more of an all-around weapon."

Dietsch is swift to add, however, that as a collector, he looks at it differently. "I was a big P90 fan and I like the MP5, but when you talk to the other side of me, when it comes to firing guns and collecting them, if you put all these guns in front of me, I'd grab the Thompson."

When I prodded him about whether he might ever *want* to take his Thompson to work, he spoke of the intimidation factor.

"People know the Thompson," he said thoughtfully. "If someone were to see law enforcement walking around with a tommy gun, it might scare them a lot more than an M4 or P90. They know what that gun did, how bad it was. That impression alone is enough to get someone uneasy . . . just seeing it. If a bunch of us were going out [in response to a potential trouble situation] and some of the guys were taking P90s, and another grabbed the M4, I might say, 'Y'know what? You guys have all that, I'm gonna grab the tommy gun.' If one person has it and [the bad guys] see that, we might not have to shoot anything."

As the popularity and perceived practicality of submachine guns ebb and flow, both the tommy gun and the Uzi will still remain household names. They are as well known to people who have only heard the name or seen them in the movies as they are to people who have carried and used them. The Thompson especially is widely recognized visually. Its distinctive appearance is part of popular culture. As Dietsch put it, "People know what that gun did, how bad it was."

CHAPTER 36

No Room for Thompsons?

Just as the submachine-gun concept did not fade away after World War II, neither did the Thompson submachine gun itself. It was phased out as a frontline weapon by the armed forces of the United States and other countries for whom it served so well, but it drifted back into many of the same shadows that it had occupied during the two decades before the war.

As noted, just as Thompsons had been sneaked into Ireland in 1921 and 1922 to fight British troops, a quarter century later they were being smuggled into Britain's Palestine Mandate for exactly the same purpose. And though the names never became well known, like those of Capone or Dillinger, a search of many a newspaper morgue will turn up crispy, yellowed accounts of desperados wielding Thompsons in bank heists through the 1950s and 1960s. The world's armies turned up their noses at the Thompson in the late 1940s as they had in the late 1920s, but heads of state in gangster-style dictatorships in Latin America treasured Thompsons in the hands of their enforcers.

We have heard the stories of the pre–World War II Chinese warlords who favored the Thompson and even made knock-offs, and we know of shipments of U.S. Army M1A1s to Chinese troops battling the Japanese. What became of these guns? Many a GI who fought in Korea between 1950 and 1953 has recalled seeing large numbers of Communist Chinese troops armed with Thompsons that were left over from World War II.

In an account published in the November 12, 2000, issue of *The Salisbury Post*, of Rowan County, North Carolina, Colonel John Gray told of battling Thompson-armed Chinese troops in 1950. During the bitter battles of the Chosin (Changjin) Reservoir that took place between November 27 and December 6, Gray was with the 3rd Battalion of the 31st Regimental Combat Team. The 31st was assigned to protect the eastern flank of the 1st Marine Division, which was making an assault along the north side of the reservoir.

Lieutenant James Arnold of the U.S. Army (third from right) teaches Nationalist
Chinese officers the nuances of the M1A1 Thompson. This is an indication
of how a lot of Thompsons wound up in China after the war.
(Courtesy of the U.S. Army via the National Archives)

A former marine, and a veteran of five campaigns in the Pacific Theater during World War II, Gray joined the U.S. Army as an officer in 1949.

One night, Gray's outfit was the object of a particularly fierce enemy assault. It had devolved into hand-to-hand combat and he was injured. "Struggling to regain my bearings, I instinctively brought my M1 rifle to bear, firing at point blank range at the assaulting Chinese," he recalls. "I continued to shoot, trying to drop the enemy before they could take advantage of my wounded condition in personal hand-to-hand combat. As I raised my rifle to shoot the last Chinese in front of me, another Chinese to my right, whom I had not seen, fired his Thompson Submachine Gun (yes, they were using Thompson Submachine Guns). His burst caught my rifle in the receiver and small of the stock. It also wounded me in the right hand."

Eventually, he was able to draw his M1911 pistol with his left hand just as three enemy soldiers—one with a bayoneted rifle, the others with Thompsons—almost fell over him.

"It was easy to imagine myself being run through by the cold steel bayonet of the one soldier as I repeatedly, with my left hand, fired the full clip into the three bunched Chinese above me," he recalled. "What a relief it was to see the tremendous shock action of the .45 slugs knock them backward and down."

Of course, the .45 caliber rounds in the Thompsons could have easily turned the tables on Gray, but he was lucky.

Though Thompson submachine guns had not been standard issue for American troops for years, there were still a number of them floating around. It is certain that an ordnance man would bristle at the suggestion, but somehow they were still there.

Just as there are many accounts from the Korean War of Thompson-armed enemies, there is no shortage of anecdotal evidence that the venerable tommy gun had not yet disappeared.

For example, Captain John Labadini, a Captain's Career Course small-group instructor at the U.S. Army Air Defense Artillery School at Fort Bliss, Texas, tells the story of Captain James McClymont, commander of D Battery, 15th Antiaircraft Artillery. McClymont earned a Silver Star while carrying a Thompson in the Chosin Reservoir campaign. The battery's self-propelled guns had been assigned to support the 31st Regimental Combat Team, but by November 29 they had run out of fuel or ammunition and were under fire. Facing up to this situation, McClymont personally led a group of GIs in an infantry assault on the enemy gun positions in the nearby hills.

As Labadini writes in an October 13, 2000, posting on The Air Defense Artillery School Web site, "Charging up the slope of Hill 1221 Captain McClymont blazed away with his Thompson Submachine Gun, taking out several Chinese positions, until he made it safely past the crest of the hill. He then led his group to the Marine positions at Hagaru-Ri."

They were among the few members of the 31st RCT to make it to safety.

A dozen years after the truce signed at Panmunjom suspended but did not end the Korean War, American troops were going into combat in Vietnam. By now, the standard-issue infantry weapon for the American services was the ubiquitous M16 assault rifle. The Thompson submachine gun was long gone—or was it?

As in Korea, there are numerous anecdotal accounts of the enemy using Thompsons. While both the North Vietnam People's Army and the Viet Cong (National Front for the Liberation of South Vietnam) were adequately equipped with AK-47s made in China or the Soviet Union, many other weapon types were also reported to have been encountered by American troops.

Dr. Fred Allison, the chief of the Marine Corps Oral History Branch, shared the transcripts of several accounts from the Oral History Branch files of Viet Cong using the Thompson submachine gun. In one such transcript, General Leslie Brown, a marine aviator who commanded Marine Air Group 12 in Vietnam, tells of encountering them one night in the spring of 1965 when the Viet Cong got inside the wire at Danang.

"The sappers were in and they were throwing dynamite [into] the tail-pipes of the [Douglas] A-4s [Skyhawk attack bombers] and rattling around with a Thompson Submachine Gun puncturing the fuel cells," Brown recalled. "Jet fuel [was] literally awash . . . on the taxiway. . . . All of [the Viet Cong] that were in our group area, we killed them all. We didn't lose a Marine. We lost three airplanes."

In clearing the Viet Cong dead, Brown's marines would certainly have recognized whether or not the enemy had been equipped with Thompsons as well as AK-47s.

Another oral history report, dated to January 1967, comes from Sergeant James Paul. He was leading a squad in the third platoon, H Company, of the 2nd Battalion, 4th Marines, as they came under enemy fire while encircling a village in Quang Nam Province.

"I noticed a puff of white smoke that [appeared to come] from right in the water approximately 25 to 30 meters in front of us . . . behind a small sandbar," Paul told Captain Robert Ross. "I took myself and two men, and before wading out to this sandbar we fired approximately 15 to 20 rounds into it. When we got around to the sandbar, we found one VC laying face down. . . . We proceeded down, the three of us, to check out the sandbar for possible other bodies laying in the water or around the water, and also for weapons that they might have left behind. We found two carbines laying in the shallow water, approximately six inches deep. We pulled those in and there was a Thompson Submachine Gun laying beside the dead VC."

Private First Class Freddy Tice, a rifleman in the platoon led by Sergeant Paul, reported another incident in which a Viet Cong arms cache was found. The patrol was taking sniper fire while sweeping an island, but they spotted the enemy and gave chase.

"We started running after them firing," Tice reported. "We got all the way to the end of the island, and they were out in the river swimming to the other side. We started firing, shooting some well-aimed shots. . . . I guess we fired about eight [M16] magazines at them. By the time we were done with that, the last guys were too far out of range to hit. We started back across the island again . . . and we started looking over the area for what we could find. We recovered two Russian rifles, 7.62s, and a .45 caliber Thompson."

Where the Viet Cong Thompsons came from is open to conjecture. It is known that some were actually scratch built by the Viet Cong or North Vietnamese. Others may well have been among the M1A1s sent to China during World War II, which showed up in Vietnam as they had on the other side in Korea. They also might have been part of the matériel that was used by American and British Empire forces in Burma during World War II.

As in Korea, American soldiers serving in Vietnam also got their hands on Thompson submachine guns. Where they came from is also a mystery, but it always seems that given enough time and ingenuity, almost anything can be scrounged during wartime.

I recently spoke with Mike DelVillar, who had been an E-3 in the U.S. Army in Southeast Asia in 1971. He ended his overseas service with the 1st Cavalry Division, but spent most of his tour with the motor transport pools of various units. His job was hauling general provisions and ammo back and forth between Pleiku and Danang. There was a constant probability that the convoys would be attacked in Viet Cong ambushes.

"We didn't get hit every time, but it only takes once or twice," he told me as he described the problem of a handful of men with small arms riding in truck cabs as the sole protection for a convoy, a problem that is still familiar to American troops. "Those poor guys in Iraq. . . . [The Army still] sends convoys out unsupported . . . without armored vehicles along or some infantry handy."

Sometimes he drove, but for much of the time, he rode shotgun, not literally with a shotgun, nor even with an M16, but with a tommy gun.

"The M16s were the weapon of choice, but they were a little bit clumsy to get out the window when you were being shot at," he told me, leading into the tale of how he got his first Thompson. It was given to him by a Ranger who was being rotated home and could not take it with him.

"Where he got it, I don't know. I didn't ask him." DelVillar smiled. "It worked very well. Saved my butt more than once."

Though his Thompson probably saved his life, it also served to run Mike DelVillar afoul of the U.S. Army's bureaucracy.

"This 'shake and bake' lieutenant comes up and informs me that I'm carrying a nonissue weapon and to turn it over immediately," he tells of the day that a greenhorn officer first spotted the Thompson. One might imagine that the lieutenant saw a prized souvenir in the Thompson, but this was not stated. "I told him it's not going to happen. He said, 'You *will* hand it over.' I handed it to him muzzle first and got brought up on charges."

This was when he was transferred to the 1st Air Cavalry Division. In retrospect, having a soldier carry his weapon of choice ought to be a charge that gets laughed out of the court-martial as a matter of course, but that's just an opinion.

In any case, Mike DelVillar had become a convert to the Thompson submachine gun.

"They refer to the guns as antiquated and obsolete, blah blah blah," he told me with a chuckle. "If I ever had to go into a firefight again, I'd take [a Thompson]. It's just that simple. I'd take one over an M16 any day."

He knows of what he speaks. Still a truck driver to this day, Mike Del-Villar may never again be in a firefight, but once again, he owns and shoots a tommy gun. It is one that he bought many years after coming back from Danang. Shortly after our conversation, he was shooting it on a gun range.

Before he ever went overseas, he already was a fan of the tommy gun. "When I was a kid, I was fascinated with the Thompson," he said. "I don't know why. I just thought they were really cool."

I was wondering what his mother would have thought about her kid with a Thompson. I know what mine would have thought. Then, suddenly, Mike DelVillar was telling me about his mother, Mary Gladys Porter.

"My mother was originally from Janesville, Wisconsin, not that far from Chicago," he explained. "I used to have a picture of my mother and Al Capone standing next to a car. Guess what was laying on the fender?"

What are the odds of the mother of a man who once shot Viet Cong with a Thompson of unknown origin having been photographed with Capone and an M1921?

"It's definitely my mother and him," he said. "It's a weird story, but it's true. I wish I still had that picture."

So do I.

CHAPTER 37

Where's My Company?

More than a year before Jim Rowley was asking after his Thompson when the assassins targeted Harry Truman, J. Russell Maguire had sold the company. Technically, he had sold the assets of the Auto-Ordnance Division of Maguire Industries. They were sold to, of all things, a toy company. Based in Westerville, Ohio, the Kilgore Manufacturing Company, which also had a division that made flare guns, had been making toy guns since the 1920s. They had also introduced a line of ten-cent cast-iron automobiles with real rubber tires in 1932 and the first injection-molded cellulose acetate plastic cars five years later. Today the Kilgore "Warrior" cast-iron cap gun, circa 1926, can fetch more than $100.

In the 1940s, Kilgore's cap guns and squirt guns sold for a dollar or so, but they had sold enough of them to be able to give Russell Maguire a third of a million for the Auto-Ordnance assets in 1949. In 1944, when Auto-Ordnance was still a corporation, its annual report noted a $14.8 million profit. Five years later, Maguire sold the whole company for less than pennies on the dollar of the wartime value.

Exactly why Kilgore, maker of toy guns, wanted the Auto-Ordnance assets, formerly maker of real guns, is unclear. Maybe it was the Thompson's colorful image, or maybe there was a profit motive. But there *was* a scheme to sell Thompson submachine gun blueprints to some shady characters in Egypt, which was still smarting from Israel's defeat of its army the year before.

Apparently the Egyptians involved in this caper did not follow through on promises made, and the deal vanished like a desert mirage. Kilgore was left with a worthless paper company on its hands. At this point, in stepped none other that Frederic Willis, the cousin of Winston Churchill who had been a vice president at Auto-Ordnance on the eve of World War II. He had left the company during the war to join another company, General Bill Donovan's OSS, the elite espionage unit that was made up of bright young men with good pedigrees who were looking for some adventure as international men of mystery. The OSS is, of course, considered to be the predecessor to *the* "company," the Central Intelligence Agency.

After the war, young Fred had put his days as a spook behind him and had become a wheeler and dealer on Wall Street. As such, Willis put together a syndicate that bought the Auto-Ordnance property and promptly flipped it. The buyer this time was George Numrich, a surplus gun dealer based in Mamaroneck, New York, just about twenty miles south on the Boston Post Road (U.S. Highway 1) from Greenwich, where Russell Maguire lived.

As Numrich discovered, the Auto-Ordnance assets consisted merely of a truckload or so of crates. Neither Kilgore nor Willis had bothered to look inside. It is probable that neither Kilgore nor Willis had even laid eyes on the crates.

Numrich did open them.

Good news and bad news awaited him. The good news was that the crates did contain immense quantities of random parts for Thompson submachine guns. Among these parts and tools were quite a few complete Thompson submachine guns. How many there were is not known for sure. Bill Helmer writes that there were eighty-six, but I have heard higher estimates. Thompson collector Tracie Hill, who now owns some of these guns, told me there were fewer, between thirty and forty. Among the guns was a presentation gun once owned by Oscar Payne, as well as early Colt-made weapons, BSA-made tommy guns, some T2 submachine guns, and at least one Autorifle. Instead of "parting out" the guns, Numrich preserved them intact and registered them with the ATF.

"You have to give them credit," Hill said. "When they opened the crates, they saved an awful lot of history. If they would have done a strictly parts transaction, all that history would have been lost."

However, bad news awaited Kilgore and Willis, who had sold operable machine guns *without* registering them. Reportedly, the feds cut them some slack with the fines and penalties, but not much.

When the dust settled, Numrich had his crates and Kilgore went back to making both cap guns and water guns. It was the 1950s, the golden age of Western movies and television, and sales of toy guns were brisk.

Russell Maguire, meanwhile, turned to other pursuits with his millions made from guns, oil, and radios. Soon he would travel full circle to the circumstances of that sticky summer of 1939 when he had relieved the family of Thomas Fortune Ryan of that "worthless" submachine-gun company.

In the summer of 1952, Maguire found himself across the table from

Tom Ryan's grandson, Clendenin John Ryan Jr. Described by *Time* on March 21, 1949, as "pink and tubby," Ryan was a multimillionaire investor who had, among other things, once battled Sosthenes Behn over control of the International Telephone & Telegraph Corporation. A 1928 Princeton grad, he was a former secretary to New York's mayor Fiorello LaGuardia and a former husband (one of six) to Austrian countess, and serial bride, Marie-Anne-Paula-Ferdinandine Wurmbrand-Stuppach, better known as Etti Plesch.

In 1950, Clen Ryan had bought *The American Mercury*, a magazine founded in 1924 by H. L. Mencken. It was a successful and trendy publication in whose pages appeared pieces by a who's who of writers, including F. Scott Fitzgerald, William Faulkner, Langston Hughes, Sinclair Lewis, Eugene O'Neill, and Carl Sandburg. After Mencken's departure in 1933, the publication became a rudderless ship, owned for a time by Lawrence Spivak, who later created the *Meet the Press* radio program, which migrated to television in 1947 and is still seen on NBC.

At the time Ryan took over the magazine, the editor was an Alabama-born navy veteran, William Bradford Huie. An occasional contributor to the magazine for many years, Huie is also remembered as the author of such works as the 1959 novel *The Americanization of Emily* and the reportage of *The Execution of Private Slovik* (1954). The plan of Ryan and Huie was to make it *the* journal of the conservative intellectual movement, a goal at which they failed, although one of their staffers, William F. Buckley, left to found the magazine that succeeded, the *National Review*.

In 1952 it was Russell Maguire's turn to buy the magazine.

He stepped into the breech of the growing rift between Ryan and Huie and bought out the heir to the family from whom he had once plucked Auto-Ordnance. Just as high on Maguire's agenda as snatching more Ryan assets was Maguire's growing interest in ultraconservative media. Whereas men such as Buckley were correctly labeled conservative, Maguire was now running with a crowd that was so far to the right that the adjective "fascist" was not whispered, but stated openly.

In reporting Maguire's crawling into bed with Bill Huie, the December 8, 1952, issue of *Time* commented, "Recently Maguire put up money to help distribute *Iron Curtain over America*, by Southern Methodist University Professor John Beaty, a book that the oldest Methodist Church periodical in the U.S., *Zion's Herald*, calls the 'most extensive piece of racist propaganda in the history of the anti-Semitic movement in America.'"

A week later, Huie resigned, citing "irreconcilable policy differences." By 1955 most of the editorial staff was gone, and in 1961 Maguire sold the publication, which then dwindled away to nothing under the ownership of a succession of fringe groups.

John Russell Maguire died on November 10, 1966, at the age of sixty-nine, having outlived the Thompsons by more than a quarter of a century. He left behind the legacy of having owned Auto-Ordnance at the moments of its greatest glory.

As successful in the business of oil and electronics as he was unsuccessful as a publisher, Russell Maguire also left behind a substantial corporate legacy. In 1961, the year he left the publishing business, Maguire Industries was renamed Components Corporation of America (CCA). It still exists as a holding company, and as of 2008 nearly all of CCA's stock is owned by Cary Maguire, Russell's son, through his Las Vegas-based Maguire Resources Company.

Significantly, CCA's own literature still notes that "the Company traces its history back to 1916"—this being the year that John Taliaferro Thompson and Thomas Fortune Ryan founded Auto-Ordnance.

When I finally tracked CCA down at its present headquarters in Dallas, Texas, the first person with whom I spoke had never heard of Auto-Ordnance Corporation, but she referred me to her colleague, Nancy Weldon, the corporate tax and accounting manager at CCA. She knew the whole story of Auto-Ordnance and CCA. Indeed, Ms. Weldon knew more than I had ever seen published in any account of Auto-Ordnance.

I learned that between 1977 and 1979, the company acquired Staco Energy Products of Dayton, Ohio, and Stacoswitch, Inc. (d.b.a. Staco Systems) of Costa Mesa, California—both makers of electrical products such as industrial switches and transformers. In 1991, CCA acquired Para Systems of Carrollton, Texas, makers of Minuteman power technology products. In 1993, CCA sold the long-held Thordarson-Meissner (later Thordarson-Meisner with one s) to a man named John Golko, who filed for Chapter 7 bankruptcy in March 2001.

Among the documents that Ms. Weldon gave me was a dozen-page corporate history written in 1968 by Eugene Daniel Powers, the Auto-Ordnance executive vice president whom Russell Maguire had once tasked with converting Auto-Ordnance from tommy guns to radios after World War II. As Nancy Weldon told me, in granting me permission to quote from this CCA document, "I don't believe any of this information is confidential. Mr. Powers died several years ago and I don't think he would have minded even if he was still with us . . . he was a fine person and very proud of 'his' company."

This document paints a detailed picture of the company as it existed shortly after the demise of Russell Maguire in 1966. At that time, CCA had 1,600 shareholders, with the National Radio Company of Melrose, Massachusetts, owning 33 percent of the nearly half million shares, and 25 percent owned by Russell's son, Cary Maguire. Sales for fiscal year 1967 had been $5.4 million, with after-tax profits of $314,000. Of the sales, 63 percent came from Thordarson-Meissner, 24 percent from a half dozen other electronics companies, and the balance from petroleum and chemicals.

Today, Components Corporation of America, the successor to Maguire Industries, which was once Auto-Ordnance Corporation, and which traces its history "back to 1916," is "actively seeking additional acquisitions."

What then happened to Auto-Ordnance as a corporate entity?

In 1968, Gene Powers clearly considered CCA to be the corporate successor to Auto-Ordnance. In his opening paragraph, Powers writes that "Components Corporation of America, was incorporated under the laws of the state of New York in 1916, for the purpose of manufacturing military small arms, notably the Thompson sub-machine ('Tommy') gun."

From this we can deduce that the crates that Russell Maguire sold to Kilgore, that Kilgore sold to Willis, and that Willis sold to Numrich, were assumed by Maguire to contain only Auto-Ordnance guns and gun parts, and not the name of the Auto-Ordnance Corporation.

As for Auto-Ordnance as a *brand*, Nancy Weldon of CCA believes that when Auto-Ordnance as a brand name ceased to be used by the parent corporation, it fell into the public domain. As she told me, "I would assume it became available to anyone who wanted to use it."

On June 14, 1974, George Numrich did exactly that.

CHAPTER 38

Not Fade Away

The postwar decades were a good time to be in the surplus gun and gun parts business. As the United States armed forces upgraded and upgraded again, there were a lot of firearms on the market, and the demand for parts was high. George Numrich was a player in this lucrative trade, buying and selling and rubbing shoulders with all the major players: Colt, Harrington & Richardson, High Standard, and Savage. During this period, Numrich Arms grew into the largest supplier in the United States of replacement parts for older and antique guns of all types.

When George Numrich took possession of the crates that were the assets of the once-proud legacy of John Taliaferro Thompson and Thomas Fortune Ryan, they were just a small footnote within his larger operation. Customers included law enforcement agencies that continued to use Thompsons, as well as the movie industry. Collectors with live and deactivated war-trophy Thompsons also came shopping for odds and ends such as sights, stocks, and compensators. By the end of the 1960s, however, most lawmen had traded their Thompsons for newer guns, and the need for the Thompson parts in the Auto-Ordnance crates tapered off.

Through the years, the notion of resuming production of the Thompson submachine gun came up from time to time at Numrich, but it never went anywhere. During the 1950s and 1960s, however, there were quite a few toy and display Thompsons made. Several companies in the United States, and as far away as Japan, produced very detailed replicas, but the last newly manufactured Thompson had gone out the door in February 1944, and that was that—for three decades.

On June 14, 1974, the Numrich Arms Corporation officially reregistered a new company by the old name, "Auto-Ordnance," as a corporation in New York State. As design engineer Doug Richardson points out, the post-1974 Auto-Ordnance Corporation "had no connection with nor was it a successor in interest to the original Auto-Ordnance Corporation of Thompson, Ryan, Maguire, and 'tommy gun' fame." It is Richardson's contention that Auto-Ordnance ceased to exist as a corporate brand name in 1944 when Russell Maguire renamed it as Maguire Industries—and gave the new entity an Auto-Ordnance *Division*. Of course, as Nancy Weldon suggests, the brand name then became available to anyone.

George Numrich revived the name thirty years later because he had been convinced that he should revive the tommy gun itself. The man who convinced him ranks second only to Numrich himself in importance among the individuals to have been associated with the tommy gun in the second half of the twentieth century.

His name was Ira Trast.

"George Numrich was my mentor," Trast told me four decades later. "He's the man who taught me everything I knew. He was a total, superb businessman. He was an individual who was really good at what he was doing."

Trast started working for George Numrich as his controller at Numrich Arms in 1966, and several years later he convinced Numrich that it was time to bring back the Thompson. In the mid-1970s, shortly after Numrich reconstituted Auto-Ordnance, Ira Trast became its president. In 1986, as George Numrich stepped aside, he became president of Numrich Arms.

For their new Thompsons, Numrich and Trast went back to a semiautomatic variant, based roughly on the concept that Marcellus and his father had once tried to market as the Model of 1927. The Numrich 1970s-era semiauto gun would be designated as the M1927A1.

"The idea to make the M1927A1 was mine, but George was the one who designed it," Ira Trast explained to me. "He was pretty good at that. . . . The design of the M1927A1 was done by George Numrich with the assistance of some very knowledgeable employees with machine skills."

ATF approval for the semiauto gun came in March 1975, and the M1927A1 soon went into production at a new facility that Trast acquired in West Hurley, located in the Catskills a couple of hours north of New York City. As Trast told me, Numrich Arms and the new Auto-Ordnance were located near one another but maintained separate facilities.

With the exception of the receiver and other internal parts, Trast was able to utilize many of the components that were still packed in the crates that George Numrich had bought back in 1951. "We could use the outside parts like the Lyman sights or the Cutts compensators or the detachable stocks," he recalled. "But the internal parts of the M1927 had absolutely nothing to do with the full automatic. When we started making the semiauto M1927, we couldn't use most of those parts. . . . [but] we were also making full automatics for anyone with the proper licenses."

Since Numrich still had a good inventory, the new Auto-Ordnance used as many original parts as possible, but certain parts had to be made new.

"The barrel, frame, and receiver were manufactured from scratch for both the full and semi," Ira Trast said. "As time went on and our parts inventory dwindled, we then manufactured everything, which included butt plates, vertical grips, Lyman sights, etc. This also holds true for the [M1928] full and M1 full. There were only 1,000 of the original 100-round [Type C] drums, so we manufactured another 1,000. As for the 50-round [Type XL] drums, we made as many as we could sell. There were no original parts for either drum, so we had to start those from scratch. Fortunately, we had the original tooling from the 1920s and 1930s, plus all the drawings for everything, so our only problem was finding a machine shop that still had old machines that could take this old tooling."

Trast has no production records for the M1927A1 semiauto Thompsons manufactured in the 1970s and 1980s, but he recalls, "In our best years we did about 5,000 per year, and I do remember some years were approximately 2,000 pieces . . . it was a very active market. . . . We came out with a bunch of different models to keep the manufacturing going."

These models included a deluxe M1927A1, with a vertical foregrip and a Cutts compensator, as well as the standard M1927A1, with a horizontal foregrip and no compensator. The M1927A3 was a scaled down .22 caliber carbine version that looked like the M1927A1, but smaller. Also produced was the M1927A5 "pistol," which had no buttstock and which resembled the old M1919 prototype guns. Trast and Numrich developed a line of box magazines, and a thirty-nine-round variation on the Type XL drum magazine.

Unfortunately, the mixing and matching of parts at the West Hurley plant during those years led to a gun that is generally considered inferior by many collectors and shooters. Indeed, the majority of the owners of "West Hurley guns" with whom I have spoken said that their weapons required at least some degree of overhaul.

"West Hurley Thompsons don't work reliably," firearms advisor Idan Greenberg told me, echoing the comments I've heard from many others. "You have to stuff them full of World War II production parts, tweak the receivers, and do milling on them to get them to function. They're awful. I have a friend who has a West Hurley Thompson that works, but it shoots at a much slower cycle rate. You can just feel all those parts grinding in there. They're just horribly manufactured guns."

Author and Thompson collector Tracie Hill told me that he considers the full-auto West Hurley guns to be "a good case of lousy American craftsmanship."

Meanwhile, artifacts of the early days of Thompson production other than what was in the crates have also been objects of interest. If Ira Trast and George Numrich were lucky enough to find some blueprints—or a microfiche of blueprints—in those crates, anyone hoping to find a parallel set in government files was long ago disappointed. Such was the case when Doug Richardson went in search of them in the 1980s.

"The United States government has apparently lost every drawing they had," he said cynically in our conversation. "The official government position was that those drawings *didn't exist* and if they did, they would be top secret. I don't know how a drawing from 1921 can be *top secret* in the 1980s!"

Richardson had asked nicely, and had figured that he was getting the runaround, so he proceeded to do a little sleuthing.

"I traced the movement of all the U.S. Army drawings for the Thompson gun, and I found the shipping records of the shipments of the drawings that the U.S. government claimed didn't exist," he said with a conspiratorial wink. "I had people at the arsenals watching for me. They helped me out and found the boxes [of documents] that officially did not exist. Now they couldn't deny they had them because they were right there. They decided that they would sell [copies] to me, so I paid the U.S. government to reproduce every drawing they had—probably 400 pages. I got beautiful Xerox copies of every drawing. That got me a big part of it. I found other drawings in the National Archives. I found drawings in estates. Except for a few drawings done for the original Colt, I have nearly all of the original drawings back to 1919."

As Trast was building new Thompsons from a mix of vintage and newly manufactured parts, Doug Richardson was making—and he continues to make—the tools that Thompson collectors use to work on their vintage guns.

George Numrich passed away in 1991, and in 1997 Ira Trast retired after more than a decade at the helm of both the new Auto-Ordnance and Numrich Arms Corporation, which was by now called Gun Parts Corporation. As he told me, he plans to write his memoirs of his many years in the arms industry.

In 1999, Gun Parts Corporation sold the new Auto-Ordnance Corporation to Kahr Arms, a handgun manufacturer headquartered in Blauvelt, New York, with a factory in Worcester, Massachusetts. Once again, the production line opened, and yet another generation of new tommy guns found its way into the market.

Kahr is best known for its line of compact 9 mm, .40 caliber, and .45 ACP steel and polymer automatic pistols. It was founded in 1995 by then twenty-five-year-old, Korean-born gun designer Kook Jin "Justin" Moon, the son of the authoritarian Sun Myung Moon, founder of the controversial Unification Church. Kahr Arms, in turn, is a subsidiary of Saeilo Manufacturing Industries, a machine tool and engineering firm controlled by the elder Moon.

An extremely wealthy anticommunist—he owns *The Washington Times*—Sun Myung Moon is a longtime supporter of conservative political candidates and conservative media in the United States. He is revered by his Unification Church followers as a "True Parent," a form of messiah, and is reviled by his detractors as the theocratic proprietor both of a mind-control cult and a shadowy network of what are perceived by some to be questionable business enterprises. Indeed, he once did an eighteen-month stretch in federal prison for filing false tax returns. When his son started a business manufacturing handguns, the conspiracy theorists had a field day.

Justin Moon rarely talks to the media, but when he does, he prefers to talk more about Kahr Arms than the Unification Church. However, for an article published in the November-December 2001 issue of *American Handgunner* magazine, Massad Ayoob asked him to comment on speculation that his father or his church owns Kahr.

"I currently am the majority shareholder of Kahr and operate my business to provide high quality firearms to the public and to make a profit," Moon told Ayoob. "I am a member of the Unification Church, but I do not hold any formal positions in the church."

While marketing pistols of its own design under the Kahr brand, Kahr Arms markets both .45 caliber 1911A1 pistols and semiauto .45 caliber replicas of the Thompson submachine gun under the Auto-Ordnance brand. The company sells variations on the M1927A1 line under the "Thompson 1927A1" product name, as well as a military replica designated "Thompson M1." Kahr has made full-auto Thompson 1928 and Thompson M1 variants for sale to law enforcement and for export, but they are not currently in production.

Kahr Arms has had its ups and downs, notably *not* involving the Thompson submachine gun. An up came in 1998, when the Kahr K9 pistol was approved by the New York City Police Department for officers to carry off duty and as a backup gun. The downs include the company's having been named in a wrongful death lawsuit after the 1999 murder of a man named Danny

Guzman in Worcester, home of Kahr's factory. It turned out that the murder weapon was one of more than four dozen that were smuggled out of the factory—prior to being stamped with serial numbers—by employees, including a man named Mark Cronin.

This incident was profiled by Christopher Stewart in a piece in the October 2007 issue of *Condé Nast Portfolio* magazine, for which he interviewed a number of individuals who have explored the business dealings of Sun Myung Moon. He spoke with Justin Moon himself, but got off on the wrong foot while interviewing him at a Florida gun show. Stewart picked one of Moon's guns up from the display table and wrapped his finger around the trigger.

"I know nothing about guns," Stewart conceded when he was cautioned not to put his finger on the trigger of a gun so indifferently. "They scare me."

The rest of us are more scared of an admittedly inexperienced person who puts his finger on the trigger of a gun when he doesn't know for sure whether or not it is loaded.

Later, he was taken to a gun range by Frank Harris, the director of sales and marketing for Kahr, to actually shoot a gun such as the one he had handled. Afterward, Stewart observed that "the sound and violence of the gun's action are much more dramatic than anything I'd seen on TV."

Though Stewart was not shooting one of Kahr's M1927s, the latter comment clearly underscores the often repeated maxim that most of what the general public knows about submachine guns comes from the two-dimensional experience of television or silver screen.

When I spoke to Frank Harris a few months after the article appeared, he was still fuming, claiming that Stewart had misrepresented himself to get a sensational article. He added that his boss had, as a result of the article, made himself unavailable for media interviews. This was unfortunate, because I had hoped to speak with him about his motivation for purchasing the Thompson brand from Numrich and about his views on the Thompson's place in history. I wanted to know his thoughts on the headline he uses on the cover of Kahr's Auto-Ordnance catalog. It seems to sum up the company's marketing strategy: "Own a Piece of American History."

I did discuss this with Frank Harris, who told me that Moon is a student of military history, and that in buying Auto-Ordnance, Moon felt he "wasn't just buying a few items. It was an asset purchase . . . it was buying all of the history that came before. This motivated him very strongly to make the decision."

Citing the company's advertising, such as their use of the famous photo of Winston Churchill, Harris added that "We don't have to make stuff up with this product line. We don't have to make up ads. That's history that already happened."

He told me that, about 2004, Kahr began working with members of the Thompson Collectors Association (TCA) to get feedback on features that collectors and shooters would like to see in a Thompson. TCA is a group started in 1990 by a small circle of Thompson collectors and hobbyists that has grown to a worldwide membership of more than 200. Among those at TCA whom Harris singled out as having been especially helpful was Tracie Hill, the well-known Thompson appraiser and collector, who later left TCA to found the American Thompson Association (TATA).

Hill is also noted for having perhaps the largest and most comprehensive collection of Thompson submachine guns in private hands. At a recent National Rifle Association (NRA) convention held in Louisville, Kentucky, Hill exhibited his collection in conjunction with a rare out-of-state showing of the two tommy guns from the St. Valentine's Day Massacre, which were brought down from Michigan by Lieutenant Mike Kline. Needless to say, both exhibits drew plenty of interest from attendees.

As Hill told me, Kahr first approached him at an NRA convention a few years back. He went on to say that they had struck up a relationship and the result was a tweaking of the design of the Kahr M1927s.

When I asked Hill to name some of the most significant design changes from the earlier "West Hurley" Thompsons, he singled out Kahr's changing the actuator knob from the cylindrical (World War II–style) design to the spherical ball-shape of the classic M1928. "This changed the character and the look of the gun considerably," he said.

In our conversations, both Hill and Harris mentioned the redesigned safety lever based on the original design of the M1921, and the reintroduction of the removable buttstock. Harris cited machined chamfers, where the magazine is inserted, as on the older models, another feature that goes back to the M1921. These were all features that were deemed unnecessary in World War II production and not revived during the Numrich/West Hurley period when stocks of existing parts were being used.

"Our strategy is to make everything new," Harris said. "We don't want to deal with surplus parts."

Harris told me that current production data for Kahr Arms are proprietary, although the BATF keeps track and its data are published in *Shooting Industry Magazine*. The most recent information shows Saeilo, Kahr's parent, with an annual production of 17,070 pistols and 5,833 long guns. Given the company's product line, the M1927 series would seem to comprise the lion's share of the latter production block, although the company also makes replicas of the World War II–era M1 carbine.

He said that the most popular Kahr Thompson by far is the M1927A1 Deluxe model, which most closely resembles the classic M1928 tommy gun and comes with a hundred-round drum and a thirty-round stick magazine. In second place is the TM1, which is modelled after the M1A1 of World War II. As Harris put it, the two guns appeal to completely different markets, with the TM1 going to collectors with a sense of World War II history. In 2002, Kahr added the Vector M1, a Thompson replica paintball gun, to the product portfolio.

Most of the guns in Kahr's Auto-Ordnance catalog retail for between $1,500 and $2,000, less than ten cents on the dollar for the price of a collectable original tommy gun. Tracie Hill characterizes the Kahr Thompsons as being good-looking guns for the price, describing them as good starter guns to give an interested collector a foot in the door without having to sink up to $30,000 or more into his hobby.

As for the cost and availability of vintage Thompson submachine guns, I spoke with a number of collectors, as well as David Terry, a federally licensed firearms dealer who operates Defense Consulting, Incorporated. He told me that even at five-figure prices, the market has remained constant, especially with the M1921 Colt Thompsons.

"The consensus is that fewer people can afford the Colts at the upper end and Thompsons in general sell well in today's market, even the dealer samples," he told me.

Kahr Arms also sells drum and stick magazines separately from the guns, along with a variety of Thompson accessories. These range from sweatshirts to gun cases—including a viola-shaped case that can accommodate a fully assembled tommy gun. Frank Harris told me that the case—actually manufactured by an outside vendor—is hugely popular.

"We sell a ton of them," he told me. "People absolutely love them."

Why should such a theatrically nontraditional case be so popular? What self-respecting duck hunter would show up with his shotgun packed in a saxophone case? Because the tommy gun is not just another gun. No other twentieth-century American gun has an image that goes beyond its being just a gun.

The tommy gun is not just a gun, it is an enduring artifact of American culture, with an image that has been crafted and massaged by popular culture for nearly a century. Were it not for popular culture, and what we know about the Thompson from the movies rather than from history, Kahr would not be selling violin cases by the ton, and the replica guns themselves by the thousand.

Indeed, it came as no surprise when Harris told me that sales of Kahr's replica of the World War II Thompson got a boost in the wake of the release of *Saving Private Ryan*, in 1998, about the time Kahr was doing the deal to make the acquisition from Gun Parts.

Whether from the sense of drama that is conveyed by the two-dimensional experience of movies or television, or the sense of history upon which Kahr capitalizes, the tommy gun survives. Thirty years after Russell Maguire watched the last M1A1 go out the door at Bridgeport, Ira Trast and George Numrich brought the Thompson back, and thanks to them, and to Kahr Arms, it has been in production off and on ever since.

Nearly a century after it was conceived, the Thompson submachine gun still so fires the imagination that there continues to be a demand for more replicas of them to be made, just as there is a demand made of men such as Doug Richardson to produce the tooling and equipment that is necessary to keep vintage choppers chopping.

If Jim Rowley were to ask for a tommy gun today, the Secret Service would hand him an MP5, but a Thompson would not be hard to find—for the right price.

Just as necessity was the mother of invention that brought the Thompson into the world, there is something inherent in the look, the feel, and the history of the gun that has put it on the short list of classic twentieth-century industrial artifacts that are still in production.

It is no longer necessity that keeps the Thompson alive, but desire. The Thompson is no longer the gun that you need, but the gun that shooters and collectors *want*.

John Taliaferro Thompson's brainchild has outlived the bureaucratic naysayers to become the gun that will not die. When I asked Ira Trast how he sees the importance of the Thompson as part of American history, he replied: "Just say the words 'tommy gun' to anyone, and I think that answers the question."

CHAPTER 39

Thunder on the Back Lot

Having embraced the Thompson for a few fleeting years, the U.S. Army then sought to erase it, but thanks to Hollywood, this is a battle the U.S. Army will never win.

As is indicated by sales of Kahr's violin case, and the spikes in Frank Harris's sales that parallel Hollywood film releases, the Thompson submachine gun is still, and it long has been, a movie star. As with any other movie star, the way that most people perceive machine guns is molded by what we see on television and in the movies.

Within just a few years of World War II, fiction was already superseding reality. Just as the famous 1955 publicity still of Audie Murphy from *To Hell and Back* pictures him with an M1A1 Thompson, our permanent image of the American GI often as not includes the gun. A decade after his service to his nation in the war had ended, Murphy answered the call and went *back* into the same uniform in the service of another cause. This time, he and many other American vets returned to serve the image and memory of the American soldier of that heroic period.

Of the many GIs who answered this second call, some would say they were paying tribute, others that they were perpetuating a myth. Probably, it was a bit of both. In any case, they were forming a concrete image of the World War II GI as a figure of American folklore. Thanks to videotape, DVDs, Blu-rays, and "technology yet to be invented," that image remains.

World War II movies, like those of many other genres, have come and gone in waves. The 1960s, despite or perhaps because of the Vietnam War, saw a revival of World War II films. The gun rooms at the major studios were kept busy supplying Thompsons for the host of films roughly sandwiched between two great 20th Century–Fox blockbusters, Darryl Zanuck's *The Longest Day* (1962) and *Patton* (1970) with George C. Scott in the Academy

Award–winning title role. With its star-studded cast, *The Longest Day* told the story of the 1944 Normandy invasion in a reasonably accurate way, although nitpickers point out that the GIs armed with Thompsons are carrying Garand ammo pouches.

Blockbusters aside, postwar Hollywood perpetuated the image of the military Thompson best in the 152 episodes of the television series *Combat!* Aired on the ABC network between 1962 and 1967, and repeated in recent years on cable, the series has been available on DVD since 2004. Starring Rick Jason as Lieutenant Gil Hanley and Vic Morrow as Sergeant Chip Saunders, their mythical Company K spent five years battling their way through France, reliving five months in the second half of 1944.

A widely circulated urban legend, which probably has a basis in fact, has it that both lead characters were supposed to be armed with Thompson submachine guns, but that they found the Thompson too heavy to carry. To remedy the situation, Selmur Productions gave Jason an M1 carbine, and had a lightweight, wooden replica Thompson made for Morrow. (As a sergeant, his character would almost certainly require a Thompson in order to be period correct.) Morrow *did* pick up a real Thompson when live fire was required. The Thompson he picked up, however, was an M1928A1 with a Cutts compensator. An infantry sergeant in France in 1944 would most likely have had an M1A1.

Another fictitious sergeant who *never* complained about his Thompson being too heavy was Sergeant Frank Rock. Indeed, Rock frequently had no qualms about *firing* his M1A1 with one hand, and he usually hit his target. If Vic Morrow's Sergeant Saunders kept the Thompson on American television screens for half a decade, Rock kept it on the bookshelves of boys of all ages for nearly three decades, and may have made an even more indelible mark on American pop culture than Morrow.

Sergeant Rock was a comic book character created by writer Robert Kanigher and illustrator Joe Kubert. He made his first appearance in the January 1959 issue of *GI Combat* from DC Comics. Three months later, DC relocated him to *Our Army at War*, which was renamed *Sgt. Rock* in 1977. As with the Sergeant Saunders of the *Combat!* series, Rock mainly inhabited a finite historic period between the Normandy invasion and the defeat of Germany less than a year later. Kanigher and Kubert made him a master sergeant, a platoon commander's rank, although as a practical matter he ran the whole company. The company in question is repeatedly identified as Easy Company, although his regiment is never stated. Though the comic series ended in 1988, Sergeant Rock graphic novels illustrated by Kubert have continued to appear, as have various Thompson-armed action figures.

Having grown up with Rock and Kubert, I recently had the pleasure of discussing the immortal sergeant with the artist. When I asked him whether he had intended the Thompson as an essential part of Rock's identity, as much a part of him as the stripes on his helmet or the stubble on his chin, the answer was a simple yes.

On the subject of his choice of the Thompson as Rock's signature weapon at a time by which the grease gun had been made official, Kubert's typically terse answer said it all: "The Thompson *looked* better."

It was a similar reply when I asked him why he frequently pictured Rock firing his Thompson with one hand. "It just looks more heroic."

While the Rock action figures that have been licensed through the years are properly armed with Thompsons, another action figure is notable for *not* carrying a Thompson. "Tommy Gunn," produced in England by Pedigree Toys during the 1960s, is a British infantryman who carries not a tommy gun, but a postwar British Sterling submachine gun. He was also made available in a World War II uniform, armed with a miniature Sten.

Amazingly, the obvious nickname Tommy Gunn has been used sparingly through the years. Perhaps this is because it is so conspicuously hackneyed. There was Tommy "the Machine" Gunn, the character that professional boxer Tommy Morrison played in Sylvester Stallone's *Rocky V* in 1990. Recently, adult film actor Thomas Joseph Strada has adopted the Tommy Gunn nom de guerre. He is not to be confused with an unrelated Reverend Tommy Gunn who is associated with a sideshow troupe calling itself the Freak Show Deluxe, which hires its zany actors out for private parties, trade shows, birthdays, weddings, and bar mitzvahs in Southern California. There was (and may still be) a boutique on Queen Street in Auckland, New Zealand, called Tommy Gunn.

As interest in World War II films dipped into a quarter-century hiatus in the aftermath of the Vietnam War, the career of the Thompson submachine gun in Hollywood remained undiminished. Most Hollywood prop masters and armorers will confirm that the call for Thompsons in the last quarter of the twentieth century—as it was back in the 1930s—has been for gangster pictures.

Ever since Edward G. Robinson first picked up a tommy gun on the set of *Little Caesar* (1931), back when Al Capone was still at the peak of his power,

Charles Bronson in the title role of *Machine Gun Kelly* (1958).
(Collection of the author)

the moviegoing public and the studios that love them have been infatuated with gangsters. Of course, the M1921 Thompson with its drum magazine is as essential to the image of the Roaring Twenties outlaw as his pinstriped suit or his trunk full of bootleg bourbon.

Hollywood had been cranking out gangster pictures since Bonnie Parker was just a Texas teenager. As other genres have come and gone, gangster pictures have been a perennial.

Prewar tough guy Jimmy Cagney was, to quote the poster, "Red Hot" in Raoul Walsh's *White Heat* (1949), and so, too, were the barrels of the blank-firing tommy guns. Roger Corman put Charles Bronson on screen in the title role of *Machine Gun Kelly* in 1958, but unlike the real George "Machine Gun Kelly" Barnes, Bronson's character had no qualms about living up to the nickname's most grisly potential.

During the 1960s, as *Combat!* did with the World War II image of the Thompson, it was a television series that perhaps best perpetuated the Thompson in its gangster-era incarnation. In 1957, shortly before his death, former Treasury agent Eliot Ness finally signed off on the final draft of his autobiography, coauthored by Oscar Fraley. It was, like Ness's incorruptible

Robert Stack, seen here with a genuine M1921 tommy gun, portrayed Roaring
Twenties treasury agent Eliot Ness in the 1959–1963 television series
The Untouchables. (Collection of the author)

Prohibition-era team, called *The Untouchables*. Ness would not live to see the
book made into the hugely successful television series of the same name.

The show was one of the key claims to fame for Robert Stack, who portrayed Ness in all of the 118 episodes that aired from 1959 to 1963 on ABC,
and repeatedly in syndication thereafter. *The Untouchables* was not only very

popular in the United States, but developed a strong cult following in Europe, solidifying the American gangster—and his indispensable tommy gun—as a global pop culture icon. Thanks to electronic media, the image of Robert Stack's stern visage and his tommy gun have never faded. The covers of the series DVDs, released in 2007, feature Stack, front and center, prominently brandishing an M1921 Thompson.

The popularity of *The Untouchables* also led, as is often the case in Hollywood, to talk of a feature film. This idea, as is often the case in Hollywood, was a long time coming—a quarter century. Finally, in 1987, Paramount brought it to the big screen, with Brian De Palma directing and with Kevin Costner as Ness and Robert De Niro as Capone. Once again, of course, there was a Thompson submachine gun front and center in the advertising poster, this time in the arms of Sean Connery, who was cast as one of Costner's team.

John Taliaferro Thompson, who conceived of his gun as being "on the side of law and order," would have approved of Stack and *The Untouchables* plot lines. However, he would not have been pleased with the turn that Hollywood took in the late 1960s, that of making the bad guys into heros. Such was the case in 1967, with Arthur Penn's *Bonnie and Clyde*, the bloody biopic that made Parker and Barrow into the romantic first couple of the pop culture version of 1930s gangsterdom. What might have displeased Thompson most was that Penn armed Faye Dunaway and Warren Beatty with tommy guns, rather than the BARs that Clyde Barrow favored. Perhaps Penn got the idea from director William Witney, who put a tommy gun in the arms of bouffant blond Dorothy Provine for his 1958 film, *The Bonnie Parker Story*.

The importance of Penn's film can be measured both by the volume of pressroom ink devoted to it at the time and the number of similar pictures that it "inspired." Roger Corman's *The St. Valentine's Day Massacre* (1967), with Jason Robards as Capone, appeared the same summer, with Thompsons naturally playing their key role. Corman then turned to Ma Barker and her family, with *Bloody Mama* (1970), featuring Shelley Winters in the title role. Serving as both writer and director, John Milius cast Warren Oates in the title role of *Dillinger* (1973), and the poster prominently depicts Oates holding an M1928 Thompson.

Through the years, Thompson submachine guns have cropped up in a wide array of film genres. Take for example, those strange 1950s B movies that have as their premise, some wild pseudoscientific accident—often related to nuclear testing—that results in giant, menacing creatures. In Gordon Douglas's *Them!* (1954), the prop man handed James Arness a tommy gun with which to battle giant man-eating ants. Three years later, Arness's

Warren Beatty and Faye Dunaway portrayed Bonnie Parker and Clyde Barrow as
"Romeo and Juliet in a Getaway Car" in Arthur Penn's classic 1967 film. The real
Clyde used a BAR, but Beatty was armed with a tommy gun. *(Collection of the author)*

brother, Peter Graves, is using an M1928 Thompson to fight enormous grass-
hoppers in Bert Gordon's *Beginning of the End.*

Tommy guns were also used against vampires in *The Last Man on Earth*
(1964) with Vincent Price, and to shoot at zombies in *Dawn of the Dead* (1978).
Elvis Presley is seen holding an M1921 in *Follow That Dream* (1962), and
another Thompson was on screen in *Diamonds Are Forever* (1971), Sean
Connery's last James Bond picture.

Few movies that featured tommy guns failed to prominently include that fact on their posters. Sometimes you run across these in dusty memorabilia stores or at swap meets. The eye cannot resist a double take on the poster that screams "One woman alone resisting a brutal oppression! Fighting to love and live!" In this case, the film was *Guerrilla Girl*, the release date is 1953—though the film is set in Nazi-occupied Greece—and the villain is Helmut Dantine, an Austrian-born anti-Nazi who actually had a bit part in *Casablanca*. In the title role was a woman who, like Madonna and Cher, went by a single name. However, unlike them, stardom was not to be hers. "Marianna" put down her tommy gun after this lone film and disappeared without a trace.

Part of what makes most of yesteryear's B movies so charming is the amusement that we can take from their improbability. Certainly this is true in the case of the forgettable movies that Elvis made, and those that feature characters desperately trying to use Thompsons to kill bugs or zombies. If anything is going to kill a creature that's already dead, it's a Thompson.

If we can laugh off giant bugs and zombies, one thing about midcentury films that many people find truly upsetting is period incorrectness. Vic Morrow's wooden Thompson or the appearance of a Model 1873 Springfield in a Civil War film can be distracting. Once upon a time, filmmakers were not especially attentive to the hardware they included in their films. A lever-action Winchester was seen as usable in any Western, even if it was a Model 1894 and the film was set in 1874. The same is true of films set in the 1950s, in which viewers spot modern automobiles parked in the distance.

By the 1970s, the tide of imprecision was beginning to run the other way. In my conversation with Hollywood armorer Mike Gibbons, he dated this paradigm shift to the gradual collapse of the studio system and the rise of independent production companies. When a studio controlled all aspects of a production, they would use the weapons they had in stock. Today, independent producers rely on specialty prop suppliers, such as Gibbons's firm.

"If you look back at the old films from the early days, you find that the firearms used were what was the most convenient," he said. "Today, they insist on using what is correct. The authenticity of the types of weapons used in films has come up several notches. I think it's a healthy thing."

Gibbons told me that his own first introduction to the Thompson submachine gun came when he was working for Stephen Cannell Productions on the television series *The A-Team*, which aired from 1983 to 1987. The lead actor in the series, George Peppard, was fond of the Thompson and used it occasionally in the show. "He had been in the Marine Corps and had used Thompsons a lot," Gibbons explained, while he had no experience with the gun himself at the time. "I was new at Cannell, and I went up to him and told him I'd never had these on a show before. I told him that he probably knew more about them than I did."

This apparently set a positive tone, with Gibbons allowing Peppard to assume the role of teacher in the relationship between star and prop man. The two men became friends and got along well. For Gibbons, his newly formed relationship with the gun itself was somewhat of a revelation.

"When I was a kid, a friend of my father's had been in Korea and had been issued a Thompson," he said. "I don't know the condition, but he complained that one little piece of dirt and the gun wouldn't run. When I first got into the industry, my first experience shooting them with blanks wasn't so great, so I sort of thought what he had told me was true. But once I'd rebuilt those guns and got honest-to-goodness, un-screwed-with Thompsons and took them out and shot them live, they were wonderful, just wonderful. They were exceedingly reliable and durable."

He went on to explain that one of the major problems that he had encountered with Thompsons during his early years in the industry was derived from the type of powder, since changed, that was then used in blank ammunition. It was apparently not so much of an issue with single-shot weapons, but caused serious problems when firing the types of full-auto bursts that directors and audiences love.

"The powder mix they used at the time consisted of a type of smokeless powder, a little black powder, and flash powder [metallic powder mixed with an oxidizer as used in pyrotechnics]," he said. "Because this burned so dirty as you shot the weapon, especially in a damp environment like a jungle, the chamber got rusty and the head space [within the gun] changed. This was a recipe for disaster, especially on the old [prewar] Thompsons with the floating firing pin."

One of Gibbons's most memorable experiences with the Thompson in the movies came with the 1990 incarnation of that perennial favorite character, Dick Tracy. Directed by and starring Warren Beatty, this personification of the great detective on film is still a legend among Hollywood armorers for its having used more working Thompson submachine guns than any other film in recent memory. The order came in to Stembridge Gun Rental, where Gibbons was working at the time.

"They wanted twenty-five Thompsons. . . . We hadn't used that many Thompsons on a show in many years," he explained. "We had a conversation and decided we were going to rebarrel, reblue, and reblank all the guns with the help of Joe Swanson, who loads many of the movie blanks used in Hollywood. I rebarreled and headspaced every gun that we had on the show, so that they would run. We had nineteen guns running on the show one night [at the Universal back lot] without a problem."

With that many guns on the set, it was obviously essential to have them all working flawlessly. Keeping guns operating is a perennial challenge for a movie industry armorer, just as it is in law enforcement or the military.

In Hollywood, however, there is usually an understudy, a backup gun. In my conversation with Syd Stembridge, the great-grandnephew of J. S. Stembridge, armorer to Cecil B. DeMille, he explained that it was usual to go out to a shoot with a backup Thompson. He told the story of the time he personally took tommy guns to the filming of a Michael Jackson music video. The script called for the pop star to do a complete spin, firing all fifty rounds from a drum magazine.

"The first time he fired, it jammed and broke the ejector," Stembridge recalled. "He handed the gun back to me and left the stage with his entourage. I got it fixed but we didn't have to use it because we had a backup gun, . . . [but we did have to] wait a half hour for them to decide to come back in. This time, he fired all fifty and it worked fine. In a very soft voice, he said, 'Thank you.' I said, 'Thank *you*.' "

Stembridge went on to say that the "Making Of" video that complements the music video contains a clip of him fixing the first tommy gun—with a big motion picture camera pointed at his head. At least he earned his combat pay.

Another story that Syd Stembridge shared was about the night on the set of the film *1941* (1979) that he introduced the Thompson submachine gun to Stephen Spielberg. This was back in the days when the powder mix still gave the Thompson a bad reputation throughout the film industry.

"Spielberg never thought that Thompsons were good guns for firing blanks," he told me. "John Milius, one of the writers for *1941*, had used our Thompsons on *Dillinger* in 1973, and he told Spielberg that they had worked great. I was on the stage, and Stephen was on the phone. He wanted know how the guns were working, and Milius said, 'Listen to this!' He fired fifty rounds up in the air with a Thompson. It was all right. Everybody was happy."

Spielberg later cast the Thompson in prominent roles in his two well-received turn-of-the-century depictions of World War II action. He produced and directed *Saving Private Ryan* (1998), arming lead actor Tom Hanks with an M1A1, then turned to coproducing the television miniseries *Band of Brothers*

(2001) with Hanks. In both projects, which were filmed in Europe, the weapons were wrangled by British armorer Simon Atherton, whose credits have ranged from *Black Hawk Down* (2001) to *The Bourne Ultimatum* (2007).

When I first made contact with Atherton, he was working with Russell Crowe and Ridley Scott on a period film in the United Kingdom. Atherton describes his company, Zorg Ltd., as a project management enterprise. He often gets involved in films at an early stage.

"You would approach us with your project and we would advise you on the historical accuracy of your script," he told me. "We'd guide you through what weapons you need for your project. We'd source them, and if we couldn't source them, we'd make them."

Among the many weapons that have been handmade by Zorg were the William Wallace sword in *Braveheart* (1995) and the Maximus and Proximo swords in *Gladiator* (2000). Atherton's firearms business involves sourcing and supplying weapons from muskets to M16s, as well as futuristic guns for films such *The Fifth Element* (1997)—and, of course, Thompsons. He currently owns four M1928A1s and fifteen M1A1s, all of which he acquired in England. He told me that on *Saving Private Ryan*, when Tom Hanks was issued the M1A1 with Zorg Armoury Number 13, he asked the actor whether this was a problem. Hanks said that it wasn't. Coincidentally, the same Thompson was later used by Tom's son Colin, who played Lieutenant Henry Jones in *Band of Brothers*.

As with many people who got involved in the film industry in the 1980s, Atherton's first experience with the Thompson was a disappointment for the same reasons that Mike Gibbons and others have mentioned with regard to the powder mix that was being used in blanks.

"I used to work for a prop-hire house called Baptys in London, and would occasionally be sent out with Thompsons," he explained. "I used to dread this, as they were very unreliable—not the weapon's fault, rather the poor quality blanks we had to use in them. Subsequently, when I set up on my own, one of the main priorities was to find a good source of blank ammunition—for all my guns, not just Thompsons, I should add."

This took him to Joe Swanson, who runs Motion Picture Blanks, Inc., in Arizona, and whose name comes up repeatedly in conversations with movie industry armorers as an ammunition source.

"With a good blank, our Thompsons became very reliable," Atherton continued. "The only other problem we found with them was the insistence of some actors on slamming magazines into them, which eventually made the round sit too low and the weapon not function properly."

Atherton went on to relate an interesting story about art unexpectedly imitating life on the set of *Saving Private Ryan*. In preparation for shooting the opening scene, he and Spielberg studied actual film footage of the Normandy invasion that had been shot on June 6, 1944.

"Something we noticed when we watched the real footage of the beach landings was that people were at the top of the beach cleaning their guns," he said. "We wondered why . . . We couldn't figure out why they were cleaning them within 250–300 yards of the beach until we did the film and actually had explosions going off next to the guns. As the explosion came down, all the sand and muck would land completely in the mechanism of the weapon. The identical thing happened to *us*. We were at the top of the beach and we had to clean the weapons before we could carry on. They were just fouled."

He said that this was not such a problem with the Thompson, where the ammunition is more self-contained in the magazine. With the M1 Garand magazine the cartridges are not fully enclosed, and therefore open to the potential for dust and dirt to get into the action of the gun, causing it to jam.

"As your ammo is being taken out of your pouch, if it drops on the ground it gathers dust and you feed that dust into the mechanism. The odd bits of sand and grit foul them completely."

Having used the leading man of *Saving Private Ryan* as a metaphor in my introduction to this book, I thought I should ask Atherton about working with Tom Hanks on a war movie.

"Tom was great to work with, always very professional," Simon assured me. "He always made a point of queuing up with the extras at the end of a day's shooting and returning his own weapon instead of sending some runner to do it. This then made all the other actors queue up and do the same thing, which was great. He felt he had a job of work to do and did not feel he should be treated any other way than the other guys. This was on *Saving Private Ryan*, when he also did all the boot camps to get into character and be treated the same as everyone else."

However, the armorer added that the actor had displayed a bit of cultural insensitivity during the filming of *Band of Brothers*: "We did have one small thing with him when he used our weapons and our blanks to celebrate the Fourth of July by firing a few rounds off. . . . Being true Brits, we had to protest about this, but he took the heat out of the situation by sending a large case of beer to the armory, accompanied by a note saying 'To Freedom and Independence.' We drank it all the same! He was very good to work with. It would be nice if everyone was like that!"

*   *   *

Another man active in the business is the colorful Jefferson Wagner, known to many as "Zuma Jay." He is well known in Southern California as a surfer and surf shop owner, but he actually makes his living operating guns for the movies. He also serves as a Malibu city councilman and choreographs Opposing Force training at Marine Corps Base Camp Pendleton or the Marine Corps Air Ground Combat Center at Twentynine Palms.

"The surf shop breaks even," he told me. "It's an office for the movie business. If I put guns and bombs in front of my store [in liberal Malibu], I'd be out of business. So I just keep it low-key with a surf shop out front. Nobody figures it out, but when they need me on a movie, they'll say, 'Aren't you the surf guy? What are you doing blowing up that car and shooting full auto?' I tell them that's what I do for a living."

Wagner started in the industry in 1985, handling a Thompson on the set for the first time in *Betrayed* (1988). All shooting by actors on the set involves blanked guns, but in this case, Wagner was firing live rounds with the Thompson so that the camera could film real bullet impacts rather than using squibs, the small explosive devices that simulate bullets hitting in the movies.

"In the scene, all the actors, including Deborah Winger and Tom Berenger were target practicing with their automatics," he explained. "[The director] wanted bullet hits on the targets, so we shot the Thompson rounds to simulate the [hits from the] 9 mm MAC-10s that the actors were supposedly shooting. A 9 mm doesn't make much of a hole, but a .45 is a very dramatic hole for Hollywood to be filming. The gun wranglers were actually shooting the real guns for the look. You can't let the actors shoot the real guns. They all want to, but the legal departments won't let them."

However, Wagner regularly shoots off camera with many well-recognized Hollywood actors such as Charlie Sheen, and he taught Burt Reynolds to shoot a Thompson when they were working on *Hunter's Moon* (1999). He still remembers being on a firing range in the early 1990s with future NRA president Charlton Heston and Stirling Silliphant, the Oscar-winning writer of the film *In the Heat of the Night* (1967).

"We put out a table of guns and the actors picked them up," Wagner explained, noting that Heston chose a vintage Thompson.

"He saw it on the table and said, 'I'm gonna shoot that one next.' I remember those words. I smiled and thought, 'Yep, that's the first one I would've shot, too.' Heston knew what he was doing. He knew how to control it. He knew that the muzzle burst would impact his vision. He handled it pretty well. He knew his weapons. He wasn't a phoney."

* * *

Though they have had hundreds of types of guns in their respective arsenals through the years, most motion picture armorers betray a sense of true affection in their tone of voice when discussing the Thompson submachine gun.

"It's probably the most dependable period piece on the market," Jeff Wagner told me, describing the Thompson as an "up-close, push-some-lead-around, 'kick-ass' door opener."

Wagner acquired his own first Thompson, an M1921, from writer-director John Milius, for whom Syd Stembridge had once supplied tommy guns. Hollywood is a small town.

Speaking of his own first M1921, Mike Gibbons told me, "It has a cool movie history. . . . It's been on a bunch of shows. . . . It was on *The Phantom* (1996), *Last Man Standing* (1996), one of my favorite Thompson movies, and *Road to Perdition* (2002). It was also in *Indiana Jones and the Kingdom of the Crystal Skull* (2008). It was fun for me on *Road to Perdition* because I had some input on what kinds of guns were going to be used," he said. "We knew we were going to have Thompsons because we had gangsters, but we were also trying to do some different stuff, such as the little Savage pistol that the bad guy used. You hardly ever see those in a film."

This isn't to say that the film did not present some technical problems for Gibbons and his team.

"When they came back to town [from extensive location shooting in the Midwest], they had a scene over at the Warner Brothers back lot where Tom Hanks fires a Thompson. The rain machine was on, and they stood talking for a few minutes before he fired the gun. It was late at night, so they could only use quarter loads, which is not a lot of powder. With that little bit of powder, there is not a lot of flash, and it's problematic if you get any moisture in the gun."

Gibbons could see that there was going to be a problem, so he told the production team why.

"I don't know what you guys are going to do," he told them. "You're not going to stand there in the rain for two or three minutes worth of dialogue and pick that gun up and shoot it. You're gonna have to put the gun in at the last minute or something. It won't work."

They didn't want to do it that way, but according to Gibbons, they learned the error of their ways the hard way. The gun was cocked. The bolt was open and there was rain running down the barrel. The gun didn't go off. It was jammed with wet powder.

"I was trying to put something over the [ejection] port that wouldn't be too obvious, but which would keep the water out," he explained. "Tape wouldn't work because it wouldn't get out of the way. Finally I had the idea to use sheet beeswax and it worked. It kept the water out long enough, and the first piece of brass that came out of the gun took the beeswax off and it kept running. They got a good take."

As armorers working in the industry today will tell you, getting a good take remains the important thing, but it is no longer the only thing. The emphasis on accuracy in historic films that emerged in the latter decades of the twentieth century has now evolved into an obsession for some, albeit not all, directors. Simon Atherton pointed out that while armorers tend to push for period accuracy, "You will find some directors who want to move history about."

Nevertheless, a big part of what armorers and prop wranglers like about their work is the opportunity to provide something that is believable to the viewers, many of whom are enthusiasts themselves, people who really do take note of the correct models of various hardware—from cars to guns.

"It's a lot of fun to do the research," Mike Gibbons said. "To find out what's right, get it, and put the right item on camera."

As he told me, putting the right weapon on the set usually begins with a call from the prop master. As was the case with Simon Atherton's description of the process, customers will ask the armorer to do the research and pick the gun that is correct for the historical period or, in the case of a biopic, the gun that is correct for the specific character. As Gibbons said, in some cases directors and propmasters have done their own homework, and they ask for a specific weapon.

"More often than not, if it's a big show, we end up doing a show-and-tell," Gibbons explained. "We'll take a whole bunch of guns down to the production office, or to the studio, and the director will pick what he wants."

He told of working with director Michael Mann on *Public Enemies* (2009), a gangster film starring, among others, Johnny Depp as John Dillinger. He found that Mann was not, at least as far as his hardware was concerned, one of those directors who likes to move history about.

"For *Public Enemies*, they wanted period correct for 1933–1934," he said. "Michael Mann is the best I've ever worked with. He spends a lot of time and a lot of effort training his actors to look the part, act the part, and *shoot* the part. He's directed some of the greatest shoot-outs that have ever been put on film. He's a shooter himself, and he likes to do things the right way."

Still Kicking

Doing things the right way. This was how Mike Gibbons had characterized the attention to detail demonstrated by Michael Mann in the casting of weapons for his films. It's also an appropriate metaphor for the industrial design philosophy of Thompson, Eickhoff, and Payne back in the closing days of World War I, as their submachine gun was taking shape. The result of their doing things the right way is an enduring example of fine engineering and the gunmaker's art. If that was all there was to it, their gun would still be worthy of note, and of its place in history. Of course, it is more than that. As we have seen, the Thompson submachine gun became one of the enduring cultural artifacts of the twentieth century.

What then, is its place in the twenty-first century?

For someone in my own profession, doing things the right way sometimes means getting away from the mountains of paper under and on my desk. Sometimes, you have to push yourself away from the keyboard and get out into the field to see and to touch your subject firsthand. This is what led me, along with my friend and fellow writer, Brian Sobel, to a shooting range in the Arizona desert and the annual Western Thompson Show and Shoot.

The highway that leads us here is a perfect allegory for the tommy gun. Indeed, the old U.S. highway known as Route 66 is another classic example of a cultural icon that would not die. Both were designed for a straightforward utilitarian purpose, and like many utilitarian objects, they reached a point of perceived obsolescence and were scheduled to be replaced. However, in the course of their utility, a funny thing had happened. Both took on a larger-than-life identity.

As with the Thompson, the powers that be in Washington decided, in their infinite wisdom, that Route 66, like most of America's first generation of two-lane paved highways, was obsolete. The energetic boosters of the Interstate Highway System decided that America's outmoded two-lanes would be replaced by a vast network of controlled-access four-lanes. Like the Thompson submachine gun in the 1940s, Route 66 was not only superseded, but also *decertified*. In 1943, the M1A1 was decertified as the standard-issue U.S. Army submachine gun. In 1985, the shields identifying Route 66 were officially removed from the road maps and road signs. The portions of the road itself that still existed became merely a frontage road subordinate to a parallel Interstate.

However, like the Thompson, the highway that John Steinbeck called the "Mother Road" refused to disappear. A groundswell of nostalgia and cultural affection would not let it die. In the 1990s, a quarter century after it was replaced by the Interstates, the road signs went back up and the road was reborn as *Historic* Route 66.

With unintentional irony, one of several annual events celebrating the Thompson submachine gun is held less than a quarter of a mile off Historic Route 66. Just as people with motorcycles and motor homes cruise the Mother Road to enjoy its undying allure, so too do Thompson aficionados cruise this section of Route 66 on their way to experiencing the undying allure of the tommy gun.

Don Hall started the Western Thompson Show and Shoot in 1995. A police reservist and National Guardsman, he retired to Arizona from the upper Midwest, where he had participated in the Thompson Collectors Association (TCA) Show and Shoot events that are held annually in Ohio.

"I love it out here in the wide open spaces," Hall told me.

However, he found that he missed the camaraderie of get-togethers with fellow Thompson fans, so he began wondering, "Why don't we have one out here in the West?"

The rest is history.

The Show part of the event is like any kind of collectibles show. We've all been to them. The themes range from railroadiana to sports memorabilia, from teddy bears to porcelain figurines. It's just that here we have a whole room themed with tommy guns. The Show provides an opportunity for collectors to, well, show off their collections. There are vintage Thompsons, of course, as well as magazines both of the periodical and ammunition kind. There are tables arranged with ancillary gear and a myriad of Thompson-themed artifacts—from old manuals to cigarette lighters incorporating tommy guns.

Neatly framed World War II magazine ads hang near vintage war bond posters of the kind that fetch hundreds of dollars on eBay, and several people have posters for movies, some of them for films that most of us have never even heard of. There are familiar ones for *Bonnie and Clyde* and *Machine Gun*

Modern Thompson submachine gun aficionados take aim with vintage M1928s and M1A1s in a round of competition at the Western Thompson Show and Shoot. The annual event takes place just a short distance north of Route 66. *(Photo by Bill Yenne)*

Kelly, as well as a poster for *Bowery Midnight,* a forgotten film from 1942. If anyone remembered it long enough to forget it, that would be because it starred Bela Lugosi. Imagine Bela Lugosi with a tommy gun.

It's hard to speak of the quality and complexity of the Thompson's engineering without thinking of Doug Richardson, the engineer who describes himself as "the only source of gunsmithing tools for the Thompsons in the world."

He has his table set up at the show today, so I sit down with him to examine some of the precision equipment that he has made in his tiny shop out in California.

"I've established a priority on the tools so that the guys who build the guns aren't short the tool that they need," he says, elaborating on how his business evolved. "You can do anything once. Twice, you start to wonder if it's the best way to do it. By the tenth time, you're trying to design a tool. Each of these are something that I developed for my own use, and people started wanting them."

I've spoken with Doug on the phone before about technical issues related to the Thompson, but today will be an opportunity to get a feel for the zeal that has led him to develop his considerable expertise. If they had an encyclopedia entry for "lifelong passion," beside it they would include a picture of Doug Richardson.

"I have no memory in my life that doesn't have Thompson guns in it," he says with a straight face. When he was a young man in his twenties, his mother handed him a scrapbook that he had made when he was five years old in the 1940s. He discovered that it was nothing but pictures of Thompson submachine guns clipped from magazines.

"This is sick . . . this is really *sick!*" Richardson laughs with a gleam is his eye. "My wife . . . claims that I actually *talk* to Oscar Payne. I don't believe in the supernatural, but I'll go to bed at night, and I'll have a question on Thompsons that I may have pondered for months, and I'll wake up in the morning and I'll know the answer. I start calculating the thing and I *know* what Oscar was doing."

The Shoot portion of the Show and Shoot begins at dawn on the second day. Sunrise in the desert is a beautiful thing. There are regional artists and photographers all across this part of the United States who make a decent living depicting the sun's orange and purple light cast across the mesas. Being up at sunrise, especially when the sun is at your back and Route 66 is spread out before your windshield, is one of those quintessential American road-trip moments around which poets grapple for the right words.

As Bobby Troupe invited us in the highway's signature song, today is the day to get our "kicks on Route 66." Thompson submachine guns—like the hot rods and motorcycles that are the icons of this road—are among those "extreme" toys that are the guilty pleasures of the little boys who became adults without really growing up.

At the firing range, steam wafts from hot coffee in to-go cups as those former little boys begin to gather near the firing line to unpack their gun cases. When you look a little closer, though, you realize that not all of today's shooters are *men*. American girls and women have routinely been hunters and shooters. It should be remembered that legendary sharpshooter Annie Oakley honed her skills while putting protein on the family dinner table. She was not alone. Frontier women, like women in rural America today, are used to firearms.

And so it is in today's world of those extreme sports that have been considered archetypically male. Girls, too, want to have in on the fun. As with

Joyce Moore and Carlyn Terry are just two of the many women who participate in Thompson submachine gun competitions. Why let the boys have all the fun?
(Photo by Bill Yenne)

their sisters who have been climbing behind the wheel at the NASCAR track, or who catch the biggest waves on the North Shore of Kauai, women have long since joined their boyfriends, husbands, and brothers in both serious and friendly competitions. So it is today.

Carlyn Terry is a special ed teacher working with at-risk high school students in the Elk Grove Unified School District in Sacramento County, California. Like her husband, David, who operates Defense Consulting, Incorporated, a few hours east of Sacramento in Nevada, she is a federally licensed firearms dealer. Carlyn tells me that she and David have brought six guns to the shoot today.

"We started with an inexpensive West Hurley Thompson and moved up to owning a couple of [M1921] Colts," she said, explaining how the Terrys entered the world of Thompson collecting. "We love the Thompson, and we like the people who collect them. They're charming, they're diverse, and more than happy to share their knowledge. The Thompsons are beautiful to look at and fun to shoot. As a collectible, you really can't beat it. It's an investment that we will ultimately hand down to our daughter. There are certain guns she won't part with."

Maybe I'm just buying into a cliché, but it's a bit beyond the ordinary to be chatting with a special ed teacher who is talking about handing down a Thompson submachine gun to her daughter. "We're a machine-gun family," she laughs, explaining that their daughter would have been here today, if not for her class schedule at college.

Joyce Moore, a nurse from Newport Beach, California, who works in hospital marketing, is another woman who has a reputation for turning in a good performance at the shooting range. A young woman with a warm demeanor and a good sense of humor, she has the sort of friendly smile that you appreciate in a nurse but don't expect in your stereotype of a tommy gun enthusiast. Indeed, Joyce herself never really expected to become a tommy gun enthusiast.

"My husband talked me into coming out here," Joyce says, recalling that time a few years back when she was dragged along to the Show and Shoot against her will. "There was a bunch of scraggly old guys. I took my *Vogue* and my newspapers. I sat in the car and read the whole time, with my nose up in the air. I wouldn't talk to anybody. I just thought it was stupid. Then I went to lunch with Don Hall and the guys. He's a charmer. He said you ought to try it, you're gonna love it. We got back to the range, he put the gun in my hand, I shot it, and I fell in love. I light up every time I talk about it. I love shooting it."

Joyce's husband, Moe, who has been shooting a bit longer than Joyce, but with no less enthusiasm, is in the motorcycle business. He operates Cycle Garden in Huntington Beach, where they repair, rebuild, and restore more vintage Italian Moto Guzzis than anyone else in the world.

Moe agrees when I suggest that Thompsons are like Moto Guzzis in that they are both specialized brands within their category, and that both appeal to a special brand of enthusiast. The longest continuously produced European motorcycle, the Moto Guzzi dates back to 1921, coincidentally the same year that the tommy gun first entered production. Moe adds that "for people who collect unique items, you will get a good mix of people that think out of the box . . . people who think for themselves . . . people who are not concerned with fads."

Of Joyce, Moe says that she is rarely happier than when she is talking about shooting a gun.

"I just love it," Joyce says, about to share an intimate secret. "I stuck my foot in my mouth last year. I made quite a statement . . . Shooting a gun is better than sex. No offense to my husband. It just came out. He just shook his head like there she goes again. I like it better than he does . . . shooting a gun."

Moe patiently rolls his eyes.

Walking up to the firing line, planning to observe, and perhaps get a chance to take a shot or two, I greet Bob Gollberg of Texas City, southeast of Houston, who handled the paperwork that had officially invited Brian and me here.

"You can't be here if you don't compete," he says, looking up from unpacking his gear. He hands me his M1A1 Thompson.

"It's a midproduction model with a protected rear sight," he tells me when I ask about the history of the weapon I'm about to fire. "It was a World War II 'bring-back' from the Pacific, that belonged to a marine colonel from the Houston area."

Scribbling out a check to pay for the ammo, I prepare to fire in a Thompson competition for the first time. I feel like a kid thrown off the dock and told to learn to swim. Bob opens a carton of .45 caliber ACP cartridges. He thumbs one round into an empty twenty-round magazine and tells me that's how it's done. For my participation in the shoot, I'll need to load twenty rounds each into four of these magazines, so I go to work.

Eighty ACP cartridges later, I'm ready to advance to the firing line, gun in one hand, magazines in the other.

Shooters advance to the line a half dozen at a time, taking turns until two dozen or so of us have had the chance to shoot. I've fired Thompsons at gun ranges before, but the competition is an all-new experience for me. I glance left and right, following the moves of those more practiced than I.

Precision reigns, and safety is the gospel.
Ear protection.
Eye protection.
Flags in the chambers.
The safety is on.
Nothing is left to chance.

Retired U.S. Customs agent Seth Nadel is functioning as range master for this segment of the Shoot, as he will on those in which he doesn't shoot. This morning, he is the central casting image of the stern, no-nonsense drill sergeant.

I stare downrange at my target, fifty yards away—half a football field. Impossibly far. With the sighting mechanism of an M1A1—greatly simplified from the complicated Lyman sights with which Eickhoff and Payne sent M1921s out the door—how can I possibly avoid missing the target and putting all my lead into the distant desert?

Those with experience tell me that these sights can be used out to one hundred yards, but that is the voice of experience, not that of the guy who barely knows what to do. Shredding targets at an indoor range is mere child's play compared to this.

"Alright shooters," Nadel shouts through a megaphone. "First course of fire is twenty rounds on one target. You may fire semiautomatic. You have one minute. Load and make ready."

He pauses until six shooters are lined up and aiming downrange.

"Is the line loaded and ready?" Nadel asks rhetorically. Everyone appears to be ready, but this would be an opportunity for anyone who is not to say so.

"The line is ready."

"Ready on the right."

"Ready on the left."

Even in the audiotape that I made of another six shooters in a later group, the tension is palpable—at least for me.

"Ready on the firing *line.*"

The emphasis that Seth Nadel puts on the last word underscores the finality of the moment.

"Fire."

All hell breaks loose. Even through the padded earmuffs, I hear the thunder of a hundred bullets popping almost simultaneously.

I attempt to aim and I squeeze off a short burst. At this range, and with my naive unfamiliarity with what the hell I'm doing, it is hard to tell.

I squeeze again, trying my best as I feel the Thompson rumbling in my arms.

Again and again I squeeze, and finally the hammer clicks against an empty chamber.

I lower the muzzle and glance around at others doing the same as they squint downrange at distant targets.

"Cease fire," Nadel's voice booms.

How long has passed?

How long does it take at six hundred rounds per minute if you are firing in bursts?

Six or eight seconds? Maybe ten at the most?

"Let's go score," Nadel orders.

We all extract our empty magazines, lay our weapons down on green felt blankets, and march down toward the targets, those fifty impossible yards away.

Amazingly, I have managed to put nine of my twenty shots into a target just eighteen inches wide while firing bursts from an unfamiliar weapon. Not bad for amateur work, I convince myself.

As alluded to earlier, I attribute this as much to the precision of the Thompson as to the shooter, although I look around and see people with more experience, yet somewhat poorer scores.

I think for a moment about that marine who held this very gun on some distant island or islands out there in the Pacific. Did this gun serve him as well?

I guess it must have. He came home.

The next course will find us closer to the target, but with less time, and on full auto.

"This will be twenty rounds on three targets in four seconds," Nadel announces though his bullhorn, adding with a grin, "Four seconds is a lot of time."

"Is the line loaded and ready?"

"The line is ready."

"Ready on the right."

"Ready on the left."
"Ready on the firing *line*."

All around me is the hammering of the Chicago typewriter. You don't often hear the sound of a good typist on a manual typewriter anymore. Some people have never heard it. Ditto for the Thompson, although it is much louder, even with ear protection.

This time I do less well than I had hoped, but I'll have two more opportunities.

As on the second, the third course of fire will be twenty shots on three targets in four seconds. This means that three side-by-side targets must be hit on full auto with no hits scattered in the eight-inch spaces between them.

Again, as before, I aim and squeeze.

This time, I'm slightly more comfortable with the feel of the tommy gun, and with the way it feels when it's firing.

A Thompson submachine gun on full auto, hammering .45 caliber ACP rounds just inches from your face is a powerful thing to ponder, but there is little opportunity for pondering.

Four seconds is a lot of time?

Strangely, it is.

"Let's go score."

For a third time, I lower the muzzle, glance around and extract an empty magazine.

As I lay the Thompson on the blanket, my hand brushes near the barrel and I can feel the heat that is now radiating from the steel.

I reach my trio of targets, and as before, I begin to count.

Can it be?

I count again.

All twenty bullet holes are in a target, with none in the eight-inch interval between.

Again I look around and see some disappointed shooters. I also see others who have put most of their hits into the bull's eye at the *center* of their target.

Back to the firing line for the final, full-auto burst.

"Is the line loaded and ready?"

"The line is ready."

"Ready on the right."

"Ready on the left."

"Ready on the firing *line*."

Photographer Herb Schroeder told us that she planned to photographically capture a .45 caliber ACP round emerging from the muzzle of a tommy gun. Some were doubtful, but Herb silenced the naysayers. *(Photo by Herberta Schroeder, used by permission)*

I'm clearly getting the feel for the Thompson. I'm not Sergeant Rock. I'm not even Bob Gollberg, but I've accomplished what I set out to do. I've reached the comfort level with the subject of this narrative that I had hoped to achieve. I have now both fired a Thompson submachine gun, and I have become comfortable firing one in a competition.

As I wrote in my introduction, nearly every American has heard of the tommy gun, but almost no one has actually fired one. Most have never touched one. Of course, who touches a manual typewriter these days, either?

For the fourth time, I extract my magazine, lay down the weapon, and walk toward my trio of targets.

For a second time, my count reveals what I had once perceived as impossible for an amateur of my novice standing. Again, all twenty bullet holes are in a target, with none between.

"They no longer make guns like this," Carlyn Terry observes later in the afternoon as we discuss our day of shooting. "When you're shooting, you're shooting a piece of history. You feel powerful."

That just about sums it up.

To use a tool that is a piece of history is to become, at least for a brief moment in time, *part* of that history. Remember those grade school field trips when they took you to stare at glass cases in museums, and how this contrasted so dramatically with the field trips where they let you swing an ax or build something. We easily forget the former, but the experience of the latter lingers long. So it is with objects that are so ingrained in our culture. There is something about the sense of touch that provides us with a feeling of affinity.

In Greco-Roman mythology there are the gods who personify the forces of the natural world, but also the heroes and antiheroes, heroines and antiheroines, who personify the best or worst of human nature and human ability.

So it is when we touch the Thompson submachine gun.

To hold it and to shoot it is to be one with Al Capone, but also to be one with Audie Murphy. They are two sides of a coin, an antihero and a hero. Both are men from the mythology of the twentieth century who were once real, but who have long since become allegorical. To stand in their shoes, and to wrap your finger around the trigger of their gun, is to feel, for a moment, the extremes of human nature that they represent.

Preparing for the long drive back to California, Brian and I fall into conversation with firearms consultant Idan Greenberg, who is packing up his own Thompson. Talk turns to cultural mythology and to the abstract notion of what separates the faddish from the iconic. When it comes to machines, what is it that separates the merely utilitarian from the true masterpieces of industrial design?

"There is a balance between technology and what pleases human beings," Greenberg says thoughtfully, before telling us of a masterpiece that is near and dear to his own experience. "I'm restoring an older car, a 1937 Cadillac Series 60 four-door sedan, with the original 346 cubic inch flathead V-8. I've driven it at seventy miles an hour without the throttle being close to open. When you pull up in that car, you have *arrived*. A new Cadillac? They're comfortable and they handle great and they get much better mileage than older cars, but they don't *turn heads*. They're designed by computers. When you're driving an older car, you feel better, you feel like you're in something substantial."

To drive a piece of history is to become, at least for a brief moment in time, *part* of history.

The author on the firing range.
(Photo by Brian Sobel)

There is no question that a classic Cadillac, like a Duesenberg or a mid-fifties Chevy Bel Air, is a true industrial-age masterpiece.

How, then, can we *quantify* an attribute so abstract?

Certainly it is not simply that something is the best in its class, although that certainly adds points. Inherent in Greenberg's description of his Caddie are two elements that cannot be overlooked. To achieve masterpiece status, an object of industrial design must have stood the test of time and—arguably more important—it *must* turn heads.

Fifty years from now, will people go out of their way to cruise Route 66 in 2009 Chevys as they do now in '57 Chevys?

Probably not.

They'll probably *still* be cruising in '57 Chevys!

Fifty years from now, will people come to this desert for an MP5 Show and Shoot?

Probably not.

"Every generation is remembered for the artifacts that it leaves behind," Greenberg says as he gently places his gun case in the trunk of his "other" car, a ragtop two-seater. "I was brought up as a gunsmith to believe that if it isn't milled steel from a forging—using traditional machining methods—with a walnut stock, it isn't worth bothering with. I can see plastics, carbon fibers, and aluminum alloys for some things, but are the firearms made from those materials going to turn our cranks? No, they're not! That's the fascination of the Thompson."

Sunset in the desert is a remarkable time of day when the sun's fading light reflects off the brass of those thousands of rounds of .45 caliber ACP ammo that were used today.

After a day of burning through such ammo, we hit the road, heading west from the range, west toward the Black Mountains and the setting sun.

Once again, the road is the Mother Road, and a half hour later, we make a stop at Cold Springs, pulling into one of those early twentieth-century gas stations pictured on the vintage postcards that show up in collections of Route 66 ephemera. Sipping a Route 66 "Route Beer," I glimpse a man and a woman on an eastbound Harley-Davidson, packed heavy for a long ride. They shoot past going east and quickly shrivel to a tiny speck on the distant two-lane blacktop.

The words of Idan Greenberg stay with me. Every generation is remembered for the artifacts that it leaves behind. Some will be forgotten. Some will *always* be remembered.

The two people on the bike will likely never pass through Cold Springs again. They may one day sell the Harley and buy a sensible car. Or they may come to a fork in the highways of their lives and go off in separate sensible cars with separate sensible people.

Wherever their roads lead, though, they will likely never forget that bike, and they will probably never forget this day on Route 66, with the desert sun at their backs, and what it was once like on the open road.

Nor will we, as a culture, ever forget Route 66 and the Harley-Davidson. Even for those of us who have never ridden a Harley or watched the stripes on 66 zipping past, both will always be remembered as artifacts left for future generations as part of our collective heritage—indeed as part of our cultural identity.

The tommy gun is another of those truly classic American machines that have stood the test of time, and that still turn heads. It is indeed one of those artifacts that are part of our culture, part of our heritage, and an important part of our history.

The Thompson submachine gun is an American icon, an immortal icon.

ACKNOWLEDGMENTS

First of all, my thanks go to Jake Elwell, my agent, without whom this book would not exist; to Peter Joseph, my editor, whose enthusiasm for the project fulfills the hopes and dreams that Jake and I had when we cooked it up; and to my friend and fellow author, Brian Sobel, with whom I always enjoy great conversations on topics of mutual interest, and who joined me on a fascinating road trip into the world of the tommy gun that contributed so much to this project.

Anyone who writes of the history of the Thompson submachine gun must stand on the shoulders of William J. Helmer, who did his original primary research and wrote of the Thompson half a century ago when many of the original figures from Auto-Ordnance, such as George Goll and Theodore Eickhoff, were still alive and able to be interviewed. He also had access to Thompson family scrapbooks, loaned to him by the widow of Marcellus Thompson. Mr. Helmer's essential work on the subject is the cornerstone of any research into the Thompson.

Thanks also to Bob Gollberg, who opened the door that led me to many excellent sources—and who lent me his Thompson for my first-ever competition shoot. Special thanks to Doug Richardson and Gordon Herigstad, whose commitment to the technical nuances of restoration and operation of Thompsons is legendary within the community of Thompson collectors and Thompson shooters.

In Hollywood, I spoke with Jefferson "Zuma Jay" Wagner, and with Syd Stembridge, whose family has been in the business of providing weaponry to the motion picture industry since his great uncle, the legendary James S. Stembridge, rented guns to Cecil B. DeMille in the 1920s. Across the water in the United Kingdom, I communicated with Simon Atherton, who handed a tommy gun to Tom Hanks for him to use in *Saving Private Ryan*. I also sat down with Mike Gibbons, who has served as the armorer to numerous films, and whose firm, Gibbons, Ltd., provides firearms to half a dozen television series and three to six features a year. Among his recent films that feature Thompsons are *Road to Perdition* from DreamWorks, and Michael Mann's *Public Enemies*.

From within the walls of government, I was supplied valuable information by Dr. Fred Allison, Chief of the U.S. Marine Corps Oral History Branch; Darrin Blackford of the U.S. Secret Service Office of Government and Public Affairs; John Fox, historian for the FBI; James L. Jones of the U.S. Army's Rock Island Arsenal Museum; and U.S. Secret Service Archivist Michael Sampson.

Thanks for additional pictures goes to Gina McNeely, who plumbs the depths of the National Archives on my behalf; to Herberta "Herb" Schroeder; and to Chuck Schauer for the use of the photograph of the tommy guns used in the St. Valentine's Day Massacre that he took in the Berrien County Sheriff's Office.

For essential information and enjoyable "war stories," my thanks go to Don Johnson in Brisbane, whose father, also Don Johnson, carried a Thompson with the Australian army in New Guinea; to Jason Dietsch for sharing his stories and his pictures of his visit to the Thompsons in the gun vault at the Garda headquarters in Dublin; to Joe Kubert, the creator of Sergeant Rock and a boyhood hero of mine; to Mike Hensley, who shared the contents of Theodore Eickhoff's typewritten autobiography, a document that has been in his family for over half a century; and to Nancy Weldon, who opened for me a door into the world of the companies that succeeded the Auto-Ordnance Corporation.

Two people with whom I enjoyed lengthy conversations, as well as an exchange of e-mails are Seth Nadel, a retired senior special agent with three decades of service in the United States Customs Service; and Lieutenant Mike Kline of the Berrien County, Michigan, Sheriff's Office, where, as the department's quartermaster, he is charged with the safekeeping of those two tommy guns used in the St. Valentine's Day Massacre. Occasionally he even gets to shoot them.

Finally, a special thanks goes to Idan Greenberg, whose business card calls him a "firearms advisor," but who is more than that. He has a wealth of information about a whole spectrum of worldwide firearms and is someone who speaks with great eloquence about the enduring place in history that is occupied by the Thompson submachine gun.

Thompson Submachine Guns Produced Before World War II

Predecessor prototypes resembling the Thompson submachine gun included the Persuader of 1917 and the Annihilator of 1918.

M1919   There were forty serial numbers assigned to prototype Thompson submachine guns that were handmade in or about 1919, although the exact number of prototypes was probably fewer than forty. These were the first Thompson submachine guns offered for sale.

M1921   There were 15,000 serial numbers, beginning with 41, assigned to the Thompson submachine guns produced under license by Colt in 1921 as Model of 1921 (M1921). A few of these were later modified and sold with designations including M1923 and M1927 (the semiautomatic variant). Fewer than half of the original M1921s were sold as M1921s before 1928, and most of the remaining guns sold thereafter were retrofitted with various updates, including the Cutts compensator, and redesignated as M1928 guns. Birmingham Small Arms (BSA) licensed production of the Thompson submachine gun in England in the 1920s, but fewer than a dozen guns were actually produced. Bootleg Thompson submachine guns were reportedly made in China before and after World War II and in Southeast Asia after World War II.

---

*NOTE: For more information, the definitive reference work on the initial production batch of 15,000 Thompson submachine guns, including all M1921 and M1928 guns individually described, is *Colt Thompson Serial Numbers,* the 1,200-page book written by Gordon Herigstad and published by him through GordonsThompsonAccessories.com.

Thompson Submachine Guns Produced During World War II

SOURCE: Springfield Ordnance District records held in the National Archives

1940	Monthly Total	Cumulative Total
April	201	201
May	627	828
June	2,051	2,879
July	2,784	5,663
August	5,372	11,035
September	5,607	16,642
October	7,554	24,196
November	9,678	33,874
December	9,937	43,811
Total Delivered in 1940	*43,811*	
M1928A1	*100 percent*	

1941	Monthly Total	Cumulative Total
January	9,222	53,033
February	13,068	66,101
March	18,679	84,700
April	17,145	101,925
May	21,875	123,800
June	19,548	143,348
July	22,379	165,727
August	29,946	195,673
September	25,328	221,001
October	36,601	257,602
November	34,502	292,104
December	39,056	331,160
Total Delivered in 1941	*287,349*	
M1928A1	*100 percent*	

1942	Monthly Total	Cumulative Total
January	42,248	373,408
February	44,649	418,057
March	47,140	465,197
April	53,361	518,558
May	59,293	577,851
June	55,709	633,650
July	32,627	666,187
August	49,812	715,999
September	50,342	766,341
October	62,504	828,845
November	50,965	879,810
December	46,260	926,070
Total Delivered in 1942	*594,910*	
M1928A1	*57 percent*	
M1	*42 percent*	
M1A1	*1 percent*	

1943	Monthly Total	Cumulative Total
January	61,071	987,141
February	70,000	1,057,141
March	70,000	1,127,141
April	60,943	1,188,084
May	55,000	1,243,084
June	50,837	1,293,921
July	30,000	1,323,921
August	27,006	1,350,927
September	36,568	1,387,495
October	30,696	1,418,191
November	44,000	1,462,191
December	31,052	1,493,243
Total delivered in 1943:	*567,173*	
M1928A1	*< 1 percent*	
M1	*6 percent*	
M1A1	*93 percent*	

1944	Monthly Total	Cumulative Total
January	0	1,493,243
February	4,091	1,497,334
Total delivered in 1944	*4,091*	
M1A1	*100 percent*	

Basic Specifications

M1928 Thompson Submachine Gun
SOURCE: U.S. Army Field Manual (undated, circa 1939)

Diameter of bore	0.45 in.
Length	
with stock	33.75 in.
without stock	25.25 in.
Barrel	
without Cutts compensator	10.5 in.
with Cutts compensator	12.5 in.
Weight	
without magazine	10.0 lbs.
with 20-round magazine	11.25 lbs.
with 50-round magazine	14.75 lbs.

M1928A1 Thompson Submachine Gun
SOURCE: U.S. Army Field Manual FM 23-40 (August 1940)

Diameter of bore	0.45 in.
Length	
with stock and Cutts compensator	33.69 in.
Weight	
without magazine	10.0 lbs.
with 20-round magazine, empty	11.13 lbs.
with 20-round magazine, loaded	12.06 lbs.
with 50-round magazine, empty	13.38 lbs.
with 50-round magazine, loaded	15.7 lbs.

M1 Thompson Submachine Gun
SOURCE: U.S. Army Field Manual TM 9-215 (October 1942)

Diameter of bore	0.45 in.
Length with stock, without Cutts compensator	32.0 in.
Weight	
without magazine	10.5 lbs.
with 20-round magazine, empty	10.9 lbs.
with 30-round magazine, empty	11.0 lbs.

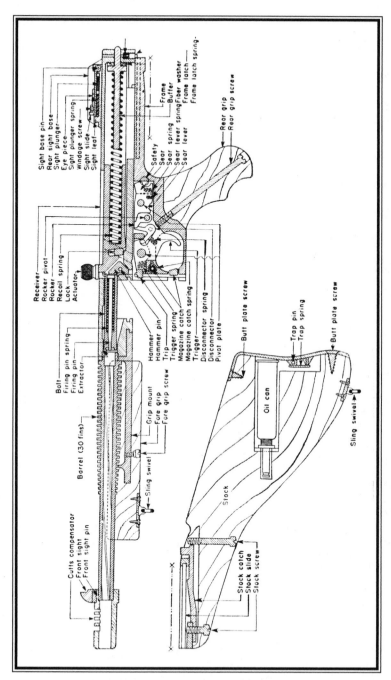

This drawing, from an official U.S. Army field manual, shows the inner workings of an M1928A1 Thompson submachine gun. *(Collection of the author)*

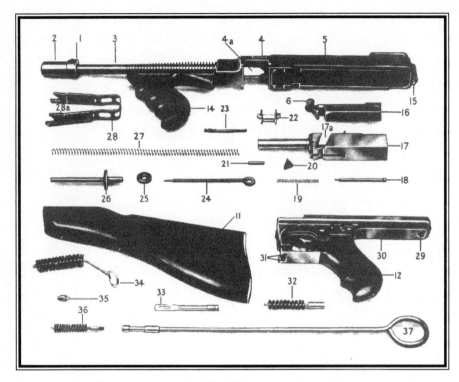

The components of the M1928 Thompson submachine gun:

1 Fore sight	23 Extractor
2 Cutts compensator	24 Recoil spring stripping tool
3 Barrel	25 Buffer fiber disc
4 Ejector	26 Buffer
4a Ejection port	27 Recoil spring
5 Body	28 Breech oiler
6 Cocking handle	28a Breech oiler felt pads
11 Butt	29 Notch in frame for butt catch
12 Pistol grip	30 Frame
14 Fore grip	31 Vertical grooves in frame for ribs
15 Stud	of box magazine
16 Actuator	32 Barrel bristle cleaning brush
17 Bolt	33 Cleaning rod brass loop,
17a Slot in bolt for H-piece	flannelette
18 Firing pin	34 Chamber cleaning bristle brush
19 Firing pin spring	35 Cleaning rod adapter
20 Hammer	36 Barrel wire cleaning brush
21 Hammer pin	37 Cleaning rod
22 H-piece	

(Collection of the author)

BIBLIOGRAPHY

Albert, David, and Sig, Mike. 2005. *Thompson Manuals, Catalogs, and Other Paper Items.* Self-published.

Ambrose, Stephen. 1994. *D-day June 6, 1944: The Climactic Battle of World War II.* Simon & Schuster.

Bannan, James F., and Hill, Tracie L. 1989. *Notes on Auto-Ordnance.* South West Publishing Co.

Barry, Tom. 1955. *Guerrilla Days in Ireland: A Personal Account of the Anglo-Irish War.* Mercier Press.

Bergreen, Laurence. 1994. *Capone: The Man and the Era.* Simon and Schuster.

Collins, Frederick L. 1943. *The FBI in Peace and War.* G. P. Putnam's Sons.

Cox, Roger A. 1982. *The Thompson Submachine Gun.* Law Enforcement Ordnance Company.

Dunlap, Roy F. 1948. *Ordnance Went Up Front.* Samworth Press.

Eickhoff, Theodore H. "The Development of the Thompson Submachine Gun." mikesmachineguns.com

Ellis, Chris. 1998. *The Thompson Submachine Gun.* Military Book Club.

Fraser, George McDonald. 1994. *Quartered Safe Out Here.* Harper Collins.

George, John. 1948. *Shots Fired in Anger.* Samworth Press.

Gillies, Midge. 2006. *Waiting for Hitler: Voices From Britain on the Brink of Invasion.* Hodder & Stoughton.

Gropman, Alan. 1996. *Mobilizing U.S. Industry in World War II.* McNair Paper Number 50.

Gudmundsson, Bruce. 1995. *Stormtroop Tactics: Innovation in the German Army, 1914–1918.* Praeger.

Harrison, Gordon A. 1951. *United States Army in World War II: The European Theater of Operations: Cross-Channel Attack.* Center of Military History, United States Army.

Helmer, William J. 1969. *The Gun That Made the Twenties Roar*. MacMillan; Gun Room Press.

Herigstad, Gordon. 1996; 5th ed. 2006. *Colt Thompson Serial Numbers*. Gordons ThompsonAccessories.com.

Hill, Tracie L. 1996. *Thompson: The American Legend*. Collector Grade Publications.

Hogg, Ian. 1977. *The Encyclopedia of Infantry Weapons of World War II*. Photobook Information Service.

Hogg, Ian V., and Weeks, John. 1989. *Military Small Arms of the 20th Century*. DBI Books Inc.

Huon, Jean. 1995. *Les pistolets-mitrailleurs Thompson*. Barnett Editions; Editions Crepin-LeBlond.

Iannamico, Frank. 2000. *American Thunder: The Military Thompson Submachine Gun*. Moose Lake Publishing.

Iannamico, Frank. 2004. *American Thunder II: The Military Thompson Submachine Gun*. Moose Lake Publishing.

Iannamico, Frank. 2004. *United States Submachine Guns*. Moose Lake Publishing.

Johnson, Don. "Men of Courage." Unpublished manuscript.

Lindsay, Patrick. 2003. *The Spirit of the Digger: Then and Now*. Pan MacMillan.

Lowenthal, Max. 1950. *The Federal Bureau of Investigation*. Greenwood Publishing Group.

Mayo, Lida. 1966. *The Ordnance Department: On Beachhead and Battlefront*. U.S. Army Center of Military History.

Miller, John, Jr. 1949. *The War in the Pacific, Guadalcanal: The First Offensive*. U.S. Army Center of Military History.

Nelson, Thomas B. 1963. *The World's Submachine Guns*, vol. 1. International Small Arms Publishers.

Olive, Ronaldo. 1996. *Guía Internacional de Submetralhadoras*. Editora Magnum Ltda.

Smith, Charles H. N.d. *A Brief History of Auto-Ordnance Company*. Auto-Ordnance/ Kahr Arms.

U.S. Army Matériel Command. 1945. *History of Submachine Guns 1921 through 1945*.

U.S. Congress, Senate (74th Congress, 2nd Session. 1936. *Report of the Special Committee on Investigation of The Munitions Industry* (The Nye Report).

Weeks, John. 1980. *World War II Small Arms*. Galahad Books.

Wilson, R. K. 1943. *Textbook of Automatic Pistols*. Small Arms Technical Publishing Company.

Periodicals referenced:

American Handgunner, 2001
Arms & The Man, 1913
Army and Navy Journal, 1921
Austin American, 1959
The Boston Globe, 1995
Chicago Daily News, 1927
Chicago Herald and Examiner, 1925
Chicago Tribune, 1926–1931
Condé Nast Portfolio, 2007
The Guardian (U.K.), 2006
Honolulu Star-Bulletin, 2000
Life, 1945
The London Gazette, 1943–1945
Marine Corps Gazette, 1927–1930
The New York Times, 1921–1945
The Orange County Register, 2006
Radio Age, 2004
The Salisbury Post, 2000
Shooting Industry Magazine, 2008
Style, 2005
Time, 1929–1952
Today, 1934
The Washington Post, 2004
Watertown Daily Times, 2008

Other Sources

Oral history interviews from the files of the U.S. Marine Corps Oral History Branch

Theodore Eickhoff manuscript (unpublished) in the collection of Mike Hensley

Don Johnson manuscript (unpublished) in the collection of his son, Don Johnson

Medal of Honor citations from the collection of the U.S. Army Center of Military History

Oral history interview from the files of the Harry S. Truman Presidential Library and Museum

INDEX

Index entries referring to illustrations and photographs are italicized.